Negotiating Globally

JB JOSSEY-BASS

Negotiating Globally

How to Negotiate Deals,
Resolve Disputes, and Make Decisions
Across Cultural Boundaries

Second Edition

Jeanne M. Brett

John Wiley & Sons, Inc.

Published by Jossey-Bass
A Wiley Imprint
989 Market Street, San Francisco, CA 94103-1741-www.josseybass.com

Jossey-Bass books and products are available through most bookstores. To contact Jossey-Bass directly call our Customer Care Department within the U.S. at 800-956-7739, outside the U.S. at 317-572-3986, or fax 317-572-4002.

Library of Congress Cataloging-in-Publication Data

Brett, Jeanne M.
  Negotiating globally: how to negotiate deals, resolve disputes, and make decisions across cultural boundaries/ Jeanne M. Brett.—2nd ed.
      p. cm.—(The Jossey-Bass business & management series) "A Wiley Imprint."
  Includes bibliographical references and index.
  ISBN 978-0-7879-8836-4 (cloth/cd)
1. Negotiation in business—Cross-cultural studies. 2. Negotiation—Cross-cultural studies. 3. Decision making — Cross-cultural studies. 4. Conflict management—Cross-cultural studies. I. Title.
  HD58.6.B74 2007
  658.4'052—dc22

                                                        2007019065

Printed in the United States of America
SECOND EDITION
HB Printing   10 9 8 7 6 5 4 3 2 1

The Jossey-Bass
Business & Management Series

Contents

CD-ROM Contents   ix

Preface   xi

Acknowledgments   xix

The Author   xxv

1.   Negotiation Basics   1

2.   Culture and Negotiation   25

3.   Culture and Integrative Deals   53

4.   Executing Negotiation Strategy   79

5.   Resolving Disputes   115

6.   Third Parties and Dispute Resolution   155

7.   Negotiating Decisions and Managing Conflict in Multicultural Teams   175

8.   Social Dilemmas   219

9.   Government At and Around the Table   245

10.   Will the World Adjust, or Must You?   279

Notes   289

Glossary   325

Index   335

How to Use the CD-ROM   349

CD-ROM Contents

Chapter One

Negotiation Planning Document

Exercise 1.1. Personal Choices in Decision Making

Chapter Two

Case 2.1. System Modification for Japan

Chapter Three

Case 3.1. A Scandinavian Scare

Chapter Four

Guide to Listening to Your Negotiation Audio Recording

Chapter Five

Case 5.1. Nichia Corporation Versus Shuji Nakamura:
The Blue LED Dispute

Chapter Six

Being Effective in Mediation When You Are the Disputant

The Mediation Process

Additional CPR Model Clauses

Chapter Seven

Exercise 7.1. Cultural Metacognition

Exercise 7.2. Identifying Effective Strategies
for Multicultural Teams

Chapter Eight

Case 8.1. OPEC Negotiations

Chapter Nine

Case 9.1. Nokia and Motorola Versus Telsim

Case 9.2. Newbridge and Chinese Negotiations Over
Shenzhen Development Bank

Case 9.3. The Checkered Negotiation History of the
Dabhol Power Project

Preface

If you must negotiate deals, resolve disputes, or make decisions in multicultural environments, this book is for you. If you have had formal training in negotiations but no training in culture, the book will extend your negotiating skills and knowledge across cultural boundaries. Be prepared to discover that old, familiar negotiation concepts, such as power and interests, take on somewhat different meaning in different cultures. If you have had no formal training in negotiations, the book will introduce you to all the fundamental concepts in negotiation and explain how the concepts apply in different cultural settings.

Although the book emphasizes negotiations in a multicultural business environment, its advice is relevant not just to managers and management students who expect to be negotiating across cultural boundaries but also to lawyers and law students, and to government officials and students of public policy who are concerned with economic development in a global environment. Global negotiations occur in multiple legal, political, social, and economic environments. International agencies and national and local government officials are frequently at the table in negotiations that cross cultural boundaries.

Negotiating Globally focuses on national culture, because nation-state boundaries are both geographical and ideological. The ideology or theory underlying a nation's social, economic, legal, and political institutions affects the way people interact. When negotiators are from the same culture, ideology is the backdrop against which deals and decisions are made and disputes are resolved.

When negotiators are from different cultures, each may rely on different assumptions about social interaction, economic interests, legal requirements, and political realities.

In today's global environment, negotiators who understand cultural differences and negotiation fundamentals have a decided advantage at the bargaining table. This book explains how culture affects negotiators' assumptions about when and how to negotiate, their interests and priorities, and their strategies: the way they go about negotiating. It explains how confrontation, motivation, influence, and information strategies shift due to culture. It provides strategic advice for negotiators whose deals, disputes, and decisions cross cultural boundaries.

Researching Multicultural Factors

Until recently, most of the knowledge about how to negotiate deals, resolve disputes, and make decisions in teams came from U.S. researchers studying U.S. negotiators negotiating with other U.S. negotiators. The evidence is overwhelming that U.S. negotiators leave money on the table when they negotiate deals, escalate disputes to the point where costs outweigh gains, make suboptimal decisions in teams, and allow their emotions to interfere with outcomes.[1] Their outcomes also often fall short of the outcomes they could have obtained if they had integrated their interests fully with those of the people across the table.

Armed with knowledge about this gap and what can be done about it, my colleagues at the Kellogg School of Management at Northwestern University and I have worked with thousands of students, managers, and executives who wanted to improve their negotiation skills. In the early 1990s our student population and their interests started to shift. Managers from all over the world began to come to our executive programs. We were invited to teach negotiation in Europe, Latin America, and Asia. Kellogg's students became decidedly international. We could not avoid dealing with the question of whether what we were teaching applied across cultures. Was the same gap present in other cultures, or was it exclusively a U.S. problem? Would the same skills close the gap in other cultures? What about negotiating across cultures? What adjustments needed to be made to take what we knew about negotiations effectively across cultures?

These questions motivated the research that underlies this book. The task was to determine how culture affects negotiation processes and outcomes in the settings of deal making, dispute resolution, and multicultural team decision making. Since 1992, I have traveled widely and worked with scholars around the world, studying how managers negotiate in different cultures and also how they negotiate across cultures. We have talked with managers from many different cultures about their strategies, collected their stories, and shared some of our own. But we have also systematically collected data on their strategies, processes, and outcomes, using the same methods that we have used with U.S. managers. These data provide a strong foundation for the insights in the book, its illustrations of cultural differences in negotiation, and the strategies it recommends.

The book is not about how to negotiate in Israel, Russia, Japan, Brazil, Thailand, Spain, India, France, Germany, Sweden, or China—all countries where managers and management students have helped us understand culture and negotiation and where we have done research. Instead, the book focuses on what we know theoretically and empirically about negotiation and how negotiation strategy needs to be modified and expanded to take cultural differences into account. Rather than advice about how to act when in Rome negotiating with a Roman, the book provides practical advice about how to manage cultural differences when they appear at the bargaining table. The book challenges negotiators to expand their repertoire of negotiation strategies, so that they are prepared to negotiate deals, resolve disputes, and make decisions regardless of the culture in which they find themselves.

The Plan of the Book

If you are already an experienced negotiator, having closed deals, resolved disputes, and even taken a negotiation course or workshop, the basics in Chapter One should be familiar. Chapter One describes the different venues for negotiation: deal making, dispute resolution, and multicultural team decision making—and introduces fundamentals of negotiation strategy. It describes how to develop a negotiation planning document and how to execute a plan with respect to choices regarding confrontation and integrative versus distributive strategy.

Chapter Two introduces culture and provides a model explaining how culture affects negotiators' interests, priorities, and strategies.

Chapter Three provides criteria for distinguishing good deals from poor ones. It explains distributive and integrative negotiations. Understanding these two types of negotiation will significantly improve your deal making, so Chapter Three offers a concrete analysis of a negotiation with integrative potential. The main ideas in the chapter are illustrated with data from Israeli, Chinese, German, Japanese, Brazilian, Indian, and U.S. negotiators. You will notice that negotiators all over the world leave about the same amount of money on the table when negotiating deals: outcomes are quite similar across cultures. However, the strategies negotiators use to make deals are cultural and distinct.

How culture affects negotiation strategy is the main theme of Chapter Four. You may already know about integrative negotiations, but do you know how to get the information you need to construct an integrative deal when the other negotiator is from a culture such as China's, where negotiators may be reluctant to answer questions directly? The chapter relies heavily on our research to describe how negotiators around the world get and use information and influence in negotiation. It also reveals the effect of such strategies on integrative and distributive outcomes.

Chapter Five moves from making deals to resolving disputes. Few books on negotiation address dealing (buying and selling) and disputing (claiming and counterclaiming) separately. But in some cultures managers negotiate directly and aggressively when making deals but do not do so when trying to resolve disputes. This makes the strategies needed to resolve disputes across cultures not quite the same as those that are needed to make deals. The chapter provides negotiators with practical advice about how to resolve conflict via direct confrontation and how to use peers, bosses, and information indirectly to confront and resolve conflict.

Chapter Six discusses what options negotiators have when dispute resolution negotiations breaks down. In the global environment, there is no culturally common or culturally neutral legal system to turn to when negotiations reach an impasse. The chapter discusses third-party conflict resolution, suggests where to find appropriate third parties, and gives advice on how to select them.

Chapter Seven focuses on multicultural teamwork, using rich examples from the experience of many multicultural team members to illustrate the challenges. It discusses task and procedural and interpersonal conflict in teams, and introduces collaboration models to manage procedural conflict. The chapter suggests how team leaders and members can make high-quality integrative decisions and manage conflict. It also argues that multicultural teams cannot be left to their own devices to make decisions and manage conflict as best they can.

Social dilemmas, the topic of Chapter Eight, are special cases of team decision making. Teams with members representing many different nations currently are struggling with dilemmas concerning global resources, including forests, fisheries, air, and water. Social dilemmas are multiparty extensions of the famous Prisoner's Dilemma. If everyone on the team acts to maximize personal gain, everyone is worse off than if everyone acts to maximize collective gain; yet acting to maximize personal gain is always better for the individual team member. The chapter describes different types of social dilemmas and how to manage them.

Chapter Nine returns to some of the cultural themes in Chapter Two, this time analyzing the role of government in global negotiations.

It looks at government's interests, including power, economic development, security, and sometimes personal enrichment. The chapter also examines the interests of foreign investors: political and economic stability, dealing with corruption, keeping employees safe, and reducing human rights abuses.

The final chapter addresses the question of whether Western negotiation strategies will soon dominate global negotiations, just as English dominates global communications. It also gives some final advice about how to adjust to the challenges of negotiating globally.

New in This Edition

The second edition of *Negotiating Globally* has benefited from the feedback I've received from those reading the first edition and using it in the classroom. Chapters One and Two have been restructured to introduce negotiation basics and cultural factors separately and in more depth. Chapter Four is all new. Readers of the first edition will see other new content and organization throughout, along with many new examples.

Chapter Seven has much new material based on our study of the challenges faced by multicultural teams. It also introduces the new idea of collaboration models to manage cultural differences in team processes. Chapter Nine has new sections, one about keeping your employees safe and negotiating with hostage takers, the other about public interests and human rights.

For this new edition, there are supplementary materials on the accompanying CD-ROM. The CD-ROM is organized by relevant chapter of the book. It contains charts and forms, additional reading, and real-world cases and problems. Information related to case and problem solutions is available on-line only to instructors who are teaching a course on negotiations. However, the CD-ROM materials should be useful to you, the reader, whether or not you are enrolled in a course. You will notice CD-ROM callouts referring to this material throughout the book.

Handling Terms

Between the language used to talk about negotiation and the language used to talk about culture, there are an awful lot of terms in this book that have specific meaning in the context of negotiation. Part of becoming a better negotiator is learning negotiation strategies. Unfortunately, all these strategies have names. Do not get annoyed by terminology. There is a glossary at the back of the book! The sooner you learn negotiation terminology, the sooner you will be able to incorporate new negotiation strategy into your own negotiations.

Negotiating globally is not easy, but it can be made easier by paying close attention to negotiation strategy and knowing how to adjust your strategy when you cross cultural boundaries.

Evanston, Illinois   Jeanne M. Brett
June 2007

To all the negotiators who shared their experiences
so that others could learn

Acknowledgments

Since the 2001 edition of *Negotiating Globally* I have had the privilege of continuing to do research with old collaborators and the opportunity to do research with some new ones. I have also been traveling and talking to managers whose experiences negotiating globally I have documented in new data and new stories in the 2007 edition.

Several new collaborations have had a major impact on the revision of *Negotiating Globally*. Chapter Four in the 2007 edition, on culture and the negotiation process, grew out of Wendi Adair's dissertation, our subsequent collaboration on the "Dancers" paper, and a new study with Wendi and Laurie Weingart on offers. In 2002, when I was still recovering from writing the first edition, Michele Gelfand persuaded me to join her in hosting a conference on culture and negotiation, the papers from which are collected in *The Handbook of Culture and Negotiation* (Stanford University Press, 2005). She particularly encouraged me to think about culture as being embedded in knowledge structures—a new idea that is introduced in the heavily revised Chapter Two. Research with Maddy Janssens on fusion collaboration processes in multicultural teams is introduced in revised Chapter Seven, which covers multicultural teams. Kristin Behfar and Mary Kern insisted I join them in a study of the challenges managers face when on multicultural teams. Am I glad I did! Although I cannot thank the managers who shared their experiences with us by name, their stories, usually told with a lot of self-insight and humor, are scattered throughout the book—from the manager who "almost had an attack" when the Koreans wanted to start over at the beginning of the agenda to the American woman given office space in a storage closet at her company's Japanese affiliate to the American manager running a call center in India telling us "I don't care if you say you're Sue from Indiana, our customer knows you're not." Most recently, Susan Crotty has been challenging me to think about pluralism in multicultural teams, but you'll have to wait for her dissertation or the next edition of *Negotiating Globally* to benefit from what we are learning about how teams manage cultural diversity.

When I wrote the acknowledgments in 2001, I said what a great privilege I had had to work in an environment in which many scholars were investigating negotiations. Although my colleagues at the time, Max Bazerman and Margaret Neale, have moved to other schools, I continue to be grateful to them for the energy they gave to the study of negotiations at Kellogg. My colleague Leigh Thompson is still at Kellogg and, joined by Keith Murnighan and Adam Galinsky, we still have an active incubator for negotiation research. Other colleagues not at Kellogg have been long-time collaborators—a sign of how much we continue to teach each other. For example, Laurie Weingart and Mara Olekalns continue to challenge my understanding of the negotiation process and make me learn new statistics! Zoe Barsness, Maddy Janssens, Anne Lytle, Catherine Tinsley, and I spent two years in the early 1990s studying the cross-cultural research in psychology and developing facility with cross-cultural research paradigms. The two chapters we published in 1995 and 1997 about how to do cross-cultural research have served us well, but more important, they continue to be in demand today—a testimony to the scholarship that resulted from this collaboration.[1] Anne Lytle's dissertation was our first comparative cross-cultural negotiation study. The study of U.S.-Japanese intercultural negotiations that I conducted with Tetsushi Okumura was our first attempt to understand cross-cultural negotiations. Catherine Tinsley's dissertation and the subsequent research done jointly with her provided many of the ideas for the chapter on dispute resolution. Research done with Maddy Janssens and Ludo Keunen enriched my understanding of multicultural teams. Studies done with Laurie Weingart and Debra Shapiro, along with research they have done without my involvement, have enriched my thinking about multicultural, multiparty, multi-issue negotiations in a global context. Kim Wade-Benzoni and Tetsushi Okumura worked with me to understand social dilemmas. More recently, my Kellogg colleague Angela Lee has been challenging me to understand fairness perceptions in social dilemmas. James Gillespie, Wendi Adair, Shirli Kopelman, Dania Dialdin, and Ashleigh Rosette have stimulated my thinking about what happens when cultures clash and were involved in collecting the U.S.-Israeli, U.S.-German, and U.S.-Hong Kong Chinese intercultural data. Wendi Adair became the expert on reciprocity in negotiations, Shirli Kopelman on social motives and social dilemmas, Dania Dialdin on distributive negotiations, and Ashleigh Rosette on virtual negotiations.

I owe an enormous intellectual debt to all of these people. I hope that they have learned as much and enjoyed as much working with me as I have with them. I am confident that they will not agree with all my conclusions and encourage the interested reader to seek out the original research papers and my colleagues' independent work.

Max Bazerman and Ann Tenbrunsel wrote the original exercise on which Cartoon was based. I am grateful to them for letting us adapt it for research and use it in this book. The dispute between U.S. and Chinese joint venture managers described in Chapter Five was inspired by an example given by Karen Jehn at the 1998 International Association of Conflict Management meeting at the University of Maryland. The rattling bicycle story was told by Jeff Palmer at the 1999 International Executive Masters Program at the Kellogg School of Management. Madame Petit's grandson shared the book and the pumpkin story with her shortly before she died.

Much of the research underlying this book was supported by the Dispute Resolution Research Center at the Kellogg School of Management, Northwestern University. I appreciate the willingness of the members of the center's research committee—Keith Murnighan,

Margaret Neale, Max Bazerman, Adam Galinsky, and Michael Roloff—to comment on and ultimately to invest in cross-cultural research.

So many people have helped in the research for and production of the book, including Northwestern undergraduate students and DRRC staff. For the first edition, students Man Ho Han and Sara Bachman managed the data sets, and Michael Teplitsky and Sara Bachman worked on the references. Linda Stine produced the tables and figures, Jason Bladen formatted the book, and Mary Kern read the proofs. Anne Lytle, Maddy Janssens, Jacques Tibau, Wendi Adair, Zoe Barsness, Judy Krutky, Julianna Gustafson, and several anonymous reviewers gave me wonderful feedback, support, and encouragement in making the final revisions. For the second edition, students Raina Dong, Martin Siow, and Brian Tam managed the data sets, and Minjee Kang formatted the book and worked on the references. Nancy McLaughlin was the book's all-around troubleshooter. Jenny McGrath produced the book for the publisher.

The staff of the Dispute Resolution and Research Center—Rachel Hamill, Margaret Dash, Linda Stine, and Jason Bladen for the first edition, Nancy McLaughlin, Nicole Lehming, and Jennifer McGrath for the second edition—have been extraordinarily gracious in supporting my getting the book written. I am sure they are looking for another project for me so that I will not be tempted to meddle in their competent and independent running of the center.

Jossey-Bass gave me a developmental editor to work with for the second edition. Although I have never met Alan Venable, I am extremely grateful for all his gentle direction, the timeliness of his feedback, and his unfailing enthusiasm for the book.

There is no way to properly thank my host professors and all the participants in the executive, M.B.A., and law programs I have had the pleasure to work with since 1981. Professor Bala Balachandrin invited me to teach in India; Dean Israel Zang, to teach in Israel; Professor Eric Langeard (deceased), to teach in France; Professor Akihiro Okumura, to teach in Japan; Professor Bing Xiang, and more recently Professor Zhixue Zhang, to teach in China; Professor Toemsakdi Krishnamra, to teach in Thailand; Professor Steve Chi, to teach in Taiwan; and Professor Lourdes Munduata, to help her teach in Spain. Dean Donald Jacobs made the negotiations course a major element of the Kellogg curriculum, and later encouraged me to extend the course cross-culturally.

I am deeply grateful to all the participants in these programs and in Kellogg's M.B.A. and Executive Masters programs for sharing their negotiation insights and experiences. I hope that what you learned from me has helped you understand as much about negotiations as what I have learned from you. I see you again from time to time at Kellogg alumni events around the world, in airports, on the lakefront, and in cards and e-mails in which you bring to my attention the odd negotiation term that catches your eye in an ad or a street sign. These brief interchanges do not do justice to my debt to you. You have made all that Kellogg has supported in the area of negotiations possible. Bob Dewar, my department chairman in 1981, encouraged me to take the risk and teach a negotiation course. My husband, Steve Goldberg, gave me the idea to do it in the first place and then negotiated with the faculty at Harvard Law School to let me use their cases, even to write the lawyers out! Seventeen students took the course that first year. It was student response in 1982 that brought the course to the attention of Dean Jacobs and caused our infamous negotiation over class size and the beginning of Kellogg's incubator for teaching new negotiations faculty. It was the student response that moved the course from an elective to a core course in the Executive Masters Program, and that encouraged those running Kellogg's far-flung joint ventures to bring their participants to Evanston for the opportunity to learn negotiations in an intercultural setting. It was the student support that justified hiring Max Bazerman and then Maggie Neale and Leigh Thompson, and Adam Galinsky. Their research, along with that of psychologists Reid Hastie and Tom Tyler, game theorists Roger Myerson and Robert Weber, and law professor Stephen Goldberg, allowed us to seek the support of the William and Flora Hewlett Foundation and develop the Dispute Resolution Research Center. Funding from the Hewlett Foundation and the Alan and Mildred Peterson Foundation has been instrumental in making Kellogg not just a major site for teaching negotiation but also a major negotiations research center. Thank you to everyone who has made Kellogg's negotiations initiative possible.

My daughters, Gillian and Amanda Goldberg; my husband, Steve Goldberg; and my gardens all learned to get along with less attention as the first edition of the book took shape. Gillian and Amanda avoided the worst of the second edition, leaving the responsibility to balance the responsibilities of the second edition with the rest of life in their father's competent hands.

—J.M.B.

The Author

Jeanne M. Brett is DeWitt W. Buchanan Jr. Distinguished Professor of Dispute Resolution and Organizations at the Kellogg School of Management, Northwestern University, where she is also the director and a founding member of the Dispute Resolution Research Center. Brett initiated Kellogg's popular Negotiation Strategies for Managers course and then extended the course to negotiating in a global environment. She conducts research and negotiation training programs at Kellogg and in executive programs around the world. She is the author of several books, including *Getting Disputes Resolved: Designing Systems to Cut the Costs of Conflict* (Jossey-Bass, 1988), written with William L. Ury and Stephen B. Goldberg, and numerous scholarly articles.

Negotiating Globally

Chapter One

Negotiation Basics

Negotiation is the process by which people with *conflicting interests* determine how they are going to allocate resources or work together in the future. Negotiators are *interdependent*, which means that what one wants affects what the other can have and vice versa. Because negotiation involves conflicting interests and interdependence it takes some skills to be an effective negotiator. One of the purposes of this book is to help you improve your negotiation skills. Another is to get you prepared to negotiate with people who do not share your cultural background, people who you cannot assume even think about the process of negotiations in the same way you do.

To get you prepared to negotiate globally we begin with the basics. If you are already an experienced negotiator, having closed deals, resolved disputes, and even taken a negotiation course or workshop, the basics in this chapter should be familiar. But if you have never negotiated in a global environment—or have and were not satisfied with the result—you need the overview of culture in Chapter Two to get up to speed. For those with a background in international business, Chapter Two will not so much be new as a new way to organize your thinking about your experiences working in an international setting. Whatever your background, the first two chapters of the book provide all the language and conceptual frameworks to get you ready for learning how to negotiate in a global setting. By the time you get to Chapter Three, which leads you through the process of analyzing a cross-cultural negotiation and preparing a strategy, and Chapter Four, which coaches you on implementing that strategy, you'll be ready to negotiate globally!

Venues for Negotiation

Negotiation is not just for making deals. People use, or should use, negotiation skills for resolving disputes and reaching decisions in teams and other multiparty environments. Let's begin by briefly visiting deals and these other venues in which negotiation occurs, before moving on to understanding what negotiators are trying to accomplish, the general nature of negotiation strategy, and how to plan for a negotiation.

Deals

It's important to distinguish between two overlapping types of deal-making negotiations: distributive and integrative.

Distributive Deals. After viewing the terra cotta warriors, my friend and I visited the Muslim market, or souk, in Xian, China. A small brass incense burner caught my eye. I asked the shopkeeper the price, came back to him with an offer for 50 percent less, he came down, I came up, he didn't move, I started to walk out, he came after me with a new price, and we ultimately split the difference between my second and his third price.

The shopkeeper and I were engaged in *distributive* deal making, which means that we were negotiating over a single issue, price, and in conflict over how much I would pay and how much he would get. In distributive negotiations, parties assume a *fixed pie* of resources and negotiate about how to cut up the pie (distribute resources) or *claim value*. In the negotiation in the souk, the shopkeeper started high, I countered low, and we made reciprocal concessions until we reached an agreement that was better than no deal to each of us.

Many people throughout the world treat negotiation as distributive deal making—start high or low, concede only enough to avoid impasse—but as you will see in this book, although every negotiation is in part a distribution of resources, distribution is only one aspect of negotiation.

Integrative Deals. When my daughters were in grade school in a small village in the south of France, the teacher asked my husband and me to plan a Halloween party. He wanted his class of thirty-two children to carve pumpkins. My job was to buy the pumpkins. I looked everywhere, finally locating a roadside stand with exactly thirty-two pumpkins. I immediately accepted the seller's price, because I had no other source of pumpkins. (It's also not customary in outdoor French food markets to negotiate prices.) But when I told the seller that I wanted to buy all her stock, she shook her head no. What to do? My alternative was poor. Offer her more money? Try sympathy, tell her why I wanted all thirty-two? Instead, I asked her why she wouldn't sell me all her pumpkins. She said if she sold all her pumpkins to me, she would have no seeds to plant the next year. "Chere Madame," said I, "if I bring you all the seeds November 1, will you sell me all your pumpkins?" She said yes, each child got a pumpkin to carve, and a picture of the children and Mme. Petit's pumpkins, as I later learned her name was, graced the front page of the local newspaper.

Mme. Petit and I were engaged in *integrative* deal making. We refocused the negotiation from distributive over the single issue of price to integrative over the multiple issues of pumpkin seeds and pumpkin rind. Mme. Petit got the seeds, which were more important to her than to me, and I got the rind, which was more important to me than to her. Integrative negotiation concerns how the negotiators *expand the pie* of resources or *create value* in negotiations. They typically do so by identifying more than one single issue, so that issues can be traded off.

There are many opportunities for integrative negotiations throughout global negotiations if negotiators have the motivation and the strategy to transform single issues into multiple issues and make trade-offs.

Conflict Management and Dispute Resolution

No culture is immune to conflict. Disputes often arise when deals do not work out quite the way parties had envisioned. People everywhere negotiate to resolve disputes. What works often depends on cultures. Following are two examples in which negotiation took a path it might not have taken had both parties been American.

Avoiding Direct Confrontation. A U.S. entrepreneur had a contract from a German buyer for bicycles that were being produced in China. When the first shipment was ready, there was a problem. The bikes rattled. Knowing that rattling bikes would not be acceptable to the German customer, the U.S. entrepreneur went to the Chinese plant, inspected the bicycles, rode a few, and asked about the rattle. "Is this rattle normal?" "Do all the bikes rattle?" "Do you think the German buyer will think there is something wrong with the bikes if they rattle?" Soon after he left, the bicycles were shipped to Germany without any rattles.

In U.S. culture the normal approach to the problem of the rattling bicycles would be to tell the manufacturer that rattling bicycles were unacceptable, and that the problem had to be fixed before shipping to Germany. In China such a direct confrontation would be extremely rude and cause much loss of face. Knowing this, the U.S. entrepreneur resolved this important point of dispute by some indirect negotiation.

Third-Party Conflict Management. When a U.S. manager in a U.S.-Chinese joint venture did not receive the information he was expecting in a report, he asked the person responsible for the report, a Chinese woman, for a meeting to discuss his needs. She politely put him off. A day later he was called into her manager's office and told that there was no problem with the report. The report had the information it always had, and the report could not be changed. From the U.S. manager's perspective, his Chinese counterpart's behavior—refusing to meet with him, getting her superior involved, stimulating a reprimand from the superior—was inappropriate. He had wanted to talk about his interests; she had turned the situation into a power play that he lost. From her perspective, she knew that she did not have the authority to change the report. So involving her superior, who had the authority to change the report, was, for her, the right approach.

As this example shows, dispute resolution negotiations are not always direct verbal interactions between principals. Sometimes a third party gets involved as a go-between, conveying information between disputants and others with interests in the outcome. Sometimes the third parties are superiors with status and authority to impose an outcome, sometimes they are peers whom both disputants respect, and sometimes they are independent professionals who are hired for the purpose of helping resolve the dispute.

Multiparty Negotiation and Team Decision Making

There are many challenges associated with being a member of a multicultural team. For example, a U.N. peacekeeping task force consisting of army officers from Russia, Germany, Turkey and the United States was charged with preparing for the exhumation of a mass grave in Bosnia. One of the U.S. members of the team described the situation, "Everyone kind of viewed the Turks as a second-class military. The Germans and the Russians didn't really hit it off too well. And we [Americans] were viewed with kind of different levels of trust or skepticism by everybody else."[1] The task force leader, a Russian major, realized that the task force had to find a way to work together. So he separated the task into four subtasks and then assigned a multicultural team of one Russian, one U.S., one Turk, and one German officer to each subtask. Each day four Russians, four Americans, four Turks, and four Germans would leave their respective camps to go to a central meeting place, split up to work in their assigned subgroups, and then at the end of the day regroup and drive back to camp. Inevitably the talk in the car on the way home was about how things had gone that day. And surprisingly,

everyone began to recognize the value of the Turks, whose experience in post-earthquake relief was more relevant to the task than
any of the other officers' experience. The small teams still had to
negotiate with each other to coordinate the execution of their different subtasks, but the multicultural structure of the small teams
transformed that negotiation from being one army's way versus another to a cooperative effort that respected expertise.

Planning and negotiation strategies, especially those based on integrative negotiations, are extremely relevant to capturing the value
of teamwork in multiparty, multicultural negotiations. Chapter Seven
focuses on using negotiation strategies in multicultural teams.

Social Dilemmas

This next example illustrates one of several types of problems
(called commons problems in economics) that psychologists call *social dilemmas*. In these interdependent situations, incentives lead individuals to take from the common pool of resources, but the more
that individuals take, the more rapidly the resource disappears. The
common interest is to cooperate to maintain the resource. But of
course the dilemma makes cooperation a negotiation challenge.

In May, 2003, 250 Canadian crab fishers from New Brunswick
went on a rampage to protest the federal government's policy transferring their crab quotas to lobstermen and an indigenous group.
They burned four fishing boats and a processing plant and threatened to boycott the two-month crab-fishing season altogether,
putting $80 million in crab exports in jeopardy.

This violent response to the reassignment of 23 percent of the
crab fishers' annual quotas needs to be understood in the context of
what the crab fishers had negotiated to manage the resource on
their own. They had succeeded not just in maintaining but in re-
plenishing the stock of crabs by self-regulating fishing and investing
more than $1.5 million of their own money in research. The gov-
ernment's action in opening up crab fishing to other groups broke
the negotiated bond within the community.[2]

This type of social dilemma is ubiquitous. All over the world, resources are threatened and require negotiations to transform takers into sharers. In Chapter Eight we'll look at a variety of types of social dilemmas and ways to use negotiation skills to generate cooperation in these innately competitive situations.

Net Value Outcomes—What Negotiators Are Trying to Accomplish

In all the different negotiation venues described in the previous section, negotiators are trying to reach a net value outcome: an agreement that is better than their alternative of no agreement. No agreement would have meant the seller in the Muslim market in Xian made no profit, I would not have a pumpkin for every child, the German buyer would likely have refused the shipment of rattling bicycles, the joint venture manager would have had no data, the military team would have failed in its mission, and the crab fishers would not have replenished their stock of crabs, just to have their quotas cut.

Looking at negotiations from the perspective of net value outcomes has four important implications. First, identifying the no-agreement alternative helps negotiators clarify what they need in order to reach an agreement. Second, identifying the other party's no-agreement alternative helps negotiators identify how much they can ask for at the negotiation table. Third, *thinking net* helps negotiators avoid satisficing—that is, accepting an outcome just a tiny bit better than the alternative. *Thinking net* helps negotiators stay motivated to find an outcome that is much better than their alternative. Fourth, *thinking net* helps negotiators recognize that they need to develop a strategy, if they are going to achieve a high net value outcome.

How can negotiators develop strategies that are capable of generating a high net value outcome for all parties? The next section introduces the fundamental building blocks of negotiation strategy. A subsequent section describes a very useful negotiating planning document that can help you assemble the blocks. The final section introduces the main strategic choices that negotiators need to make.

In the following sections, I'll be using many useful terms and concepts related to negotiation. If most of them are new to you, be easy on yourself about learning them all at once. There will be lots of repetition of terms to help you get comfortable with them. Once you are, you will find you can use them to build a negotiation strategy. In later chapters you may occasionally want to refer back to these sections, or you may find all the reminders you need in the glossary at the back of this book.

The Building Blocks of Negotiation Strategy

There are five fundamental building blocks of negotiation strategy: parties, issues, positions, power, and targets.

Parties

The first block in building a negotiation strategy is identifying the *parties* to the negotiation. Although it seems obvious that the parties must be the people sitting at the negotiation table, in fact, in some negotiations, decision makers are not at the table. A manager on a team representing a U.S. company describes negotiating a lease agreement with representatives of a Saudi Arabian company as follows: "The negotiation on the Saudi side was carried out by 'messengers.' These were often British-educated, rather high-level managers, with significant Western-culture experience who nevertheless were not making any decisions themselves but going to their respective bosses. Prior to a negotiation meeting the Saudi side always wanted a list of questions and points that we wanted to cover, and they would get back to us, preapproving some questions [presumably those for which approval came from the principals] and indicating others were not approved. We were pretty sure the information provided to the Saudi 'bosses' was being filtered by the messengers, and we couldn't always tell the spin they would put on information."[3]

In other situations the party at the negotiating table may not represent the powerful interests of those not at the table. The French branch of an international consulting firm learned this when it negotiated a contract to audit the efficiency of several ministries of a North African nation. Contract negotiations went fine, but in starting the audit the French consultants were stymied by the lack of cooperation of the ministries being audited, who had not been at the table, and who feared they would lose jobs and power as a result of the audit.

Identifying parties turns out to be a task of identifying whose *interests* are involved in the negotiation. (*"Interests"* is a negotiation term that I use throughout the book. It refers to the concerns, needs, fears, underlying desires, or people affected by the negotiation). Even though parties whose interests are important to the implementation of the negotiated agreement may not be at the table, it's important to recognize who these parties are and to understand their interests.

Issues

The second step in building a negotiation strategy is identifying what *issues* are to be negotiated. This, too, is not a trivial step. Negotiators should know what issues are important to their side of the table, but when negotiations are complex with many elements, it often takes a negotiating team to represent all the issues that need to be negotiated. Managers who are interviewed about their experiences negotiating in teams most often state that the reason for having a team is to handle the variety and complexity of the issues to be negotiated.

Negotiators may not always know all the issues that are important to the other party. This requires informational meetings with the other party, but some parties may be reluctant to share even this level of information, concerned that identifying issues that are important to them may make them vulnerable. We will talk in detail later about strategy to get information sharing going. It may be necessary to put a list of issues on the table and ask the other party, "What are we missing?"

Try to avoid negotiating over single issues. You always need multiple issues in order to negotiate integratively. In the pumpkin negotiation at the beginning of the chapter, Mme. Petit and I essentially transformed a single-issue price into multiple issues: seeds and rinds. If there appears to be only a single issue in negotiation, either transform it to multiple issues or identify other issues that can be negotiated. For example, in buying a house there is always price, but there is also closing date. If you can be flexible on closing date, the seller may be flexible on price.

Positions, Interests, and Priorities

Positions are what negotiators say they want. Your *position* is what you ask for in a negotiation. Before you can determine your positions, you need to know the issues to be negotiated.

An interest is *why* negotiators want what they want. *Interests* are the needs or concerns that underlie positions. Sometimes one or the other party has not thought hard about its interests; in this case you should ask them a few questions to get this process started. The key to uncovering interests is asking *why* and *why not*. That worked for me with Mme. Petit. However, such direct questioning might not work everywhere in the world. In some places the approach needs to be indirect: put an offer on the table, ask for a counteroffer, and infer the other party's interests from the way the counteroffer differs.

In their seminal book *Getting to Yes*, Roger Fisher and William Ury (current editions with Bruce Patton) urge negotiators to get behind positions to interests, for it is in the arena of interests that integrative agreements are found.[4] This is excellent advice, because focusing on interests will give you a more flexible goal than will positions. By my focusing on my interests (pumpkins to carve) and Mme. Petit's focusing on hers (seeds to replant), we were able to make her position (do not sell all the pumpkins) and my position (buy all the pumpkins) moot.

Furthermore, since not all your interests are of equal importance, one of your first analysis steps is to rank-order the issues on the basis of your interests. In a multi-issue negotiation, it's unrealistic to expect to get your position on every issue. Be prepared to trade off less important issues to get your interests met on issues that are more important to you.

BATNA: *Alternatives as Your Source of Power*

The acronym BATNA was coined by Fisher and Ury to represent your main source of *power* in negotiation. BATNA stands for Best Alternative To a Negotiated Agreement. It is what you are going to do if you do not reach an agreement. Your BATNA is your best option outside the current negotiation. If you are negotiating a deal, it is an alternative buyer or seller. If you are negotiating with a supplier over a poor-quality shipment, it is the next dispute resolution step in your contract—maybe mediation, arbitration, or going to court. If you are facing the failure of a multicultural team to reach agreement, your BATNA may be a decision (that no one on the team will like) made by higher-level management. If you cannot reach a cooperative agreement about resource conservation, your BATNA is a shared loss of opportunity and the likelihood of government regulation.

Your BATNA is your source of power because the better your BATNA, the more you can demand from the other party in the negotiation. My BATNA in the souk was to buy the incense burner in another shop. I'd seen several as we walked through the market. The shopkeeper knew this and must have known I had seen them elsewhere. His understanding of my BATNA is probably why he came after me when I started to walk out. My BATNA in negotiating with Mme. Petit, in contrast, was terrible. I had no other source of pumpkins! When your BATNA is poor and your negotiation has hit a temporary impasse, as mine did with Mme. Petit, you become highly motivated to create value!

BATNAs are important to markets. They are how active markets keep prices down. Maintaining BATNAs is also how antitrust regulation maintains competition.

BATNA is not the only source of power in negotiations globally. As we shall discuss in the next chapter, on culture and negotiation, status also confers power to a party. But for now let's stay with this important BATNA construct.

Fisher and Ury chose the phrase "best alternative" because in most situations there are many alternatives, and negotiating strategy depends on knowing which alternative is the best. For example, if your company wants to acquire a new technology, you might buy another company that owns patent rights to that technology, or you might license that technology, or you might develop your own competing technology. The anticipated costs and gains will be different, depending on which option you choose. Analyzing these costs and gains is an essential step in business strategy that precedes negotiation. Once the analysis is done, negotiations can proceed with the party that holds the lowest-cost, highest-gain choice. But this choice is not static. When negotiations with the low-cost, high-gain choice are not going well, negotiators may threaten or actually break off negotiations and start anew with the second-best option. How do negotiators know when to turn to the second-best option? This requires the introduction of another negotiation concept: reservation price (also called "walk away" or "bottom line"). We'll address reservation price in the next section, but before we do, we need to understand one more very tricky aspect of BATNA. This has to do with independence.

So far, we've mostly been discussing BATNA as it applies in a deal-making setting in which both parties are free to break off negotiations and turn to an alternative buyer or seller. Their BATNAs are *independent* in the sense that neither party can negatively affect the other party's BATNA. But there are venues in which parties are not free to turn to their *best* alternative, which would be to just walk away from the negotiation. If you are the defendant in a dispute you cannot just walk away, unless the other party withdraws. If you negotiate to an impasse, your BATNA is what the other party does next, for example, file a lawsuit or demonstrate outside your house. It is in this respect that BATNAs in dispute resolution are *linked*. When disputants cannot reach an agreement, disputant A may drag disputant B to disputant A's BATNA. Perhaps the most common example of this is when parties withhold payment for a poor-quality shipment. This could have happened in the rattling bicycle dispute. If parties to a dispute do not agree, each has to consider his or her BATNA as being the worst thing the *other* party can do, be it ship the rattling bicycles or withhold payment. Once my students understood that in dispute resolution BATNAs are linked, they came up with a new acronym: WATNA, or worst alternative to a negotiated agreement.

BATNAs are also linked in multicultural team decision making and in social dilemmas. In team decision making, if the team cannot reach agreement, top management usually steps in and makes the decision, and the team loses control. In social dilemmas, if people cannot reach agreement to self-regulate their use of resources, all suffer from the loss of the resource, and may also suffer from the costs of imposed government regulation.

Regardless of whether BATNAs are independent, as in most deal making, or linked, as in most other negotiation venues, BATNAs serve the important function of providing a standard for determining when negotiators should call an impasse.

BATNA and Reservation Price. A reservation price, walk away, or bottom line is the most that you are willing to give or the least that you are willing to get and still reach a negotiated agreement. To determine your reservation price (the term used in the rest of this book) you must know your BATNA, or WATNA as the case may be. Your reservation price is a just-noticeable difference from your BATNA or WATNA. I like to think of reservation price as being inside the negotiation and BATNA or WATNA as being outside the negotiation. Knowing your reservation price gives you discipline in negotiations. You know that until you have an offer that meets or exceeds your reservation price, you do not have an agreement that you can accept.

Setting a reservation price can be challenging. People seldom go into negotiations either with an absolute assessment of the cost and value of the BATNA or with certainty that the BATNA will be available at that cost. Negotiators need to consider both of these aspects of the BATNA: how sure they are of its value, and how sure they are of being able to negotiate a deal at the estimated cost. The greater the uncertainty about the BATNA, the more you should discount its value when you use it as a standard for setting a reservation price.

Here is some advice for setting BATNAs and reservation prices:

- *Understand how the deal you are planning to negotiate fits into the larger strategic picture.* What is the goal of this negotiation (for example, to enter new markets, or to gain access to new technology)? How else might that goal be met other than reaching an agreement in this negotiation?

- *Know your BATNA.* You always have a BATNA, even if it is simply staying with your current course of action.

- *If your BATNA is poor, try to improve it.* Generate a better alternative.

- *Use your BATNA to set a reservation price.* Do not change your reservation price unless you receive new, credible information that changes your BATNA. Credible information about your BATNA is not likely to come from the other party. After all, it is in that party's interest for you to think your BATNA is poor.

Targets, BATNAs, and Opening Offers

Your target in negotiation is what you think is reasonably possible to get in a negotiation. It should be optimistic, but not ridiculous! Having a target will keep you negotiating (as you should!) even after you know that you can agree because you've already received an offer that is better than your reservation price. Having targets helps negotiators increase their net gains. Setting targets is another challenge, but BATNAs can serve as a guide.

In principle you set your target as a just-noticeable difference from the other party's BATNA. But in practice it is even harder to evaluate the other party's BATNA than your own. This is because you usually lack information about the other party's BATNA, and because it is difficult to get deep enough into the other party's mind to know exactly how the other party rates his or her BATNA.

A fallback in setting a target is to find out about precedents. When buying a house you know to find out what other houses in the neighborhood sold for. You know also to find out about the particular house you are interested in: how long it has been on the market and why the sellers are selling. The value of precedents is no less in business negotiations. When you have a dispute with a supplier, you ask your lawyer how much disputes like yours normally settle for (and how long it will take), and then you evaluate this particular supplier. Is the supplier engaged in other disputes? Are you an important customer? Is reputation at stake? All this information will help you set an optimistic but realistic target.

Here is some advice for setting targets:

- Know your industry and market. What are the characteristics of recent deals like the one you will be negotiating? Get as much information about them as possible. Is there reason to think the market has changed since the most recent deal?
- Determine the other party's BATNA. The other party is not going to agree to a deal that is worse than its BATNA.
- Be optimistic and realistic.
- Don't lose sight of your target as soon as you get an offer better than your BATNA. Keep working toward the target.

Here is some advice for using targets when making an opening offer:

- When your information about the other party's BATNA is good, there is likely to be significant benefit in opening first. The opening offer can act as an anchor.[5] When you open first, the other party has to figure out how to get you off your position, not vice versa.

- When your information about the other party's BATNA is poor (and there had better be a very good reason why you have little or no reliable information about their BATNA!), there is likely to be some benefit in waiting for the other party to open. If you really do not know the market you are operating in (why are you there with so little knowledge?), the other party may surprise you by the generosity of their opening offer.

- The other party's opening will anchor you if you are not careful. Don't assume you can just reject their offer as inadequate, and don't expect the other party to unilaterally improve their offer. Smart negotiators do not negotiate with themselves! Instead, give the other party an excuse to move, reject their offer as inadequate, and make a counteroffer.

Combining Fundamentals:
The Negotiation Planning Document

The Negotiation Planning Document (shown in simple form in Exhibit 1.1 and included in MS-Word format on the CD-ROM that accompanies this book) is a useful tool for building a coherent negotiation strategy. It provides a row for every issue and a column for you and each "other" party (in this case one). You may want to add additional columns for the parties who may not be at the table but who have interests in the negotiation. The boxes defined by the intersection of row and column are further subdivided into three parts. The top part is for entering the position on the issue, the bottom is for entering the priority (shaded) and the interest(s) underlying that position. Beneath the issues are rows for entering BATNAs, reservation prices, and targets (for both you and other parties). You know the other party's target to be their perception of your BATNA.

The Negotiation Planning Document is extraordinarily useful. Completing it means that you have to identify your issues, positions,

Exhibit 1.1. Negotiation Planning Document.

Issue	Self		Other	
Example	Position		Position	
	Priority	Interests	Priority	Interests
Issue 1				
Issue 2				
Issue 3				
Issue 4				
Issue 5				
Issue 6				
Issue 7				
BATNA				
Reservation Price				
Target				

interests, priorities, BATNA, reservation price, and target. When you are representing your company in a complex negotiation, you may have to engage in internal negotiations to get agreement on the entries in the planning document. The planning document also may act as a stimulus to generate helpful information from people in your organization who are not on the negotiating team but who have knowledge relevant to the negotiation. One leader of a negotiation team told me, "In just about every internal negotiation planning we bring three or four members of the business together, and they have to hash out their different opinions with each other before they give us some direction."[6]

As a second useful point, trying to complete the planning document for the other party in the negotiation clearly identifies what you know and what you don't know about their positions, interests, and so on. Further filling in the other party's column should be the first thing you do once the negotiation begins. Doing so also has the very nice effect of directing early negotiations to the discussion of issues, interests, and priorities.

A third useful point is that the planning document keeps all the pertinent information on one page in front of negotiators. (I do not advocate long, detailed, multipage planning documents that you have to leaf through to find information that should be at your fingertips and will be with a one-page form!)

Fourth, the one-page planning document also is very useful for maintaining discipline on a negotiating team. Another negotiating-team leader told me, "Whenever my team would lose focus, we'd go back to the planning document [and] ask the question, Have we learned anything to cause us to make a change in the planning document? If the answer was yes, we'd work through how that change affected all other elements of our plan. If the answer was no, [then] the planning document helped us to stay focused."[7]

Fifth and finally, the planning document is very useful for constructing settlement offers, because it helps negotiators keep all the issues linked. There will be more about this in Chapter Three.

Strategic Choices in Negotiation

Strategic choices refers to how negotiators implement their negotiation strategies: how they act and react at the negotiation table. Don't overlook the word *react*. Negotiation is social interaction. What transpires at the negotiation table is a function of negotiators' plans, their enactment of those plans (negotiation behavior), and their response to the other's negotiation behavior.

Negotiators have two fundamental areas of strategic choice about how they will act at the table; one area relates to what we call *confrontation*, the other to what we call *social motivation*. The choices negotiators make in these areas depend on their personalities, their cultures, and characteristics of the negotiation situation and the other party. Depending on the combination of factors, some choices are more likely than others to facilitate negotiating a high net value outcome. Let's start with confrontation.

Confrontation

Negotiations vary in the degree to which parties whose interests are at stake are directly involved in the negotiation. The shorthand term for this is *confrontation*. Confrontation ranges along a continuum from direct, face-to-face negotiation between two or more principals to electronically mediated negotiation between agents to indirect confrontation via the media or a third party in which meaning must be inferred.

Parties all over the world engage in direct, face-to-face deal-making negotiations, from the night markets in China to cross-border mergers and acquisitions to small and large sales of products and services. As in the Saudi example involving messengers, principals are not always at the table. In addition, more and more frequently, face-to-face meetings are supplemented or supplanted by electronically mediated communication via e-mail, chat, telephone, or teleconference.

One leader of a negotiating team told me about negotiating a contract to buy via conference calls and chat.[8] The potential supplier was not far away geographically, so the two parties could have met face-to-face, except that the buyer's team was internationally dispersed. The product was to be used at several international sites, and those sites' needs had to be met. During negotiations the whole buyer team was linked not just by an open conference call with the sellers but also by a closed chat room. The team leader named one team member as lead negotiator and made him responsible for both monitoring the team chat and negotiating across the table. The team leader was quite certain that this electronically enhanced process had given his team a strategic advantage.

Even when negotiations are face-to-face, there is often a lot going on away from the table. Take the June 2006 Arcelor-Mittal negotiations that resulted in a steel giant with a 10 percent world market share. When Lakshmi Mittal first made an unsolicited bid for Arcelor on January 27, 2006, he was rebuffed publicly in a news conference by Arcelor's chief executive, Guy Dollé. Dollé made much of Arcelor's European cultural values, saying, "That means a lot in terms of employee relations with their employer, and sustainable development." The subtext was that Mittal's firm was not a suitable buyer for a European company, that it did not share European values but instead had enriched itself at the expense of its workers. Dollé was negotiating indirectly via the press and public opinion.[9]

There has been a lot of speculation about how confrontational a negotiating party should be[10] but not much formal research. Are face-to-face negotiations more likely to result in net value outcomes superior to those carried out via electronic media? We do know that it is more difficult to build trusting relationships negotiating via e-mail rather than face-to-face.[11] *Trust* is the willingness to put yourself at risk in the hands of another party. When negotiators trust one another, they share more information about their priorities and interests. When negotiators share more information about their priorities and interests they negotiate higher net value outcomes.

It is pretty clear that e-mail can exacerbate problems of information sharing, because of the trust problem, but e-mail may also facilitate negotiations when the medium fits with the culture. In one study we did with Hong Kong Chinese and U.S. undergraduate management students, the Hong Kong Chinese e-mail negotiators achieved higher net value outcomes than did the Hong Kong face-to-face, U.S. e-mail, and U.S. face-to-face negotiators! The e-mail medium apparently released the Chinese students' inhibitions to open aggressively and facilitated their proclivity to bundle all the issues together and make multi-issue offers.[12]

Does negotiating in public and in the press risk relationships and deals? There were several possible tactical reasons behind the Arcelor chief executive's decision to speak as he did to the press. His aim may have been to generate support for Arcelor's rebuff of Mittal. Or it may have been to offend Lakshmi Mittal personally and so discourage the takeover attempt. Or it may have been to provoke Mittal into improving the offer. If the CEO's aim was to generate support, it worked only for a short time. Mittal's opening offered such a premium over the current stock price (a strategy designed to discourage other bidders) that shareholders were interested even if current management of Arcelor was not. If the CEO's aim was to offend and discourage, it simply did not work. "Mittal in a February interview described himself as being 'really sad listening to the outburst and emotions of various people.' But he declined to trade barbs. Instead he sought to cast himself as an entrepreneur tearing down protectionist barriers so that other emerging-market companies would be spared the trouble." But an aim to make Mittal improve the offer clearly succeeded: Mittal paid €40.37 per share, nearly double what Arcelor was trading for in January when the first offer was made.[13]

Decide prior to negotiation how confrontational you will be. As we will explore in subsequent chapters, your decision will be informed by the venues of the negotiation (deal making, dispute resolution, or other) and by your knowledge of the culture of the other party.

Social Motivation and the Choice Between Distributive or Integrative Negotiation Strategy

A negotiation *strategy* is a set of behaviors that serve a specific negotiation goal. *Social motives* affect negotiation outcomes by affecting negotiators' strategies. *Social motivation* describes people's goals in contexts of social interaction.[14] Four social motives are relevant in negotiations: individualism, cooperation, competition, and altruism. Socially *individualistic* negotiators seek to maximize their own outcomes; socially *cooperative* negotiators seek to maximize their own and the other party's outcomes; *competitive* negotiators seek to maximize their own outcomes at the expense of the other party's outcomes (that is, maximize the difference between their own and others' outcomes); and *altruistic* negotiators seek to maximize others' outcomes.

The most widely used measure of social motives asks a person to make nine choices related to allocating resources (See "Personal Choices in Decision Making" and "Norms for Managers' Social Motives by Culture" on the CD-ROM.) Depending on the pattern of choices, it then characterizes the person as individualistic, cooperative, competitive, or with no dominant social motive. After using this measure with thousands of managers around the world, I can report three definitive findings about social motives and negotiations:

1. The managerial world I've studied is dominated by cooperatively motivated negotiators (53 percent) compared with individualistically motivated negotiators (37 percent). There are relatively few competitively motivated negotiators (3 percent). About 7 percent have no dominant social motive. These tend to be people from Latin American cultures and China, where decision making depends on context. They do not like the social motives measure.

2. In terms of negotiating high net value integrative agreements, negotiators who are cooperative and negotiators who are indi-

vidualists are about equally successful, but negotiators who are competitive are significantly less successful.[15]

3. Cooperators and individualists use different negotiation strategies to reach their high net value outcomes.[16]

As noted earlier, there are basically two types of negotiation strategy: distributive strategy (behaviors that serve to divide resources) and integrative strategy (behaviors that serve to maximize and also divide resources). Behaviors that support distributive strategy focus on seeking to influence: persuading the other party to make concessions, substantiating positions (argument), making threats, and committing to positions. Behaviors that support integrative strategy focus on seeking and using information: generating information about parties' priorities and interests and proposing outcomes that capitalize on differences. Research generally confirms the theoretical distinction between integrative and distributive strategy with the caveats that some behaviors may serve both integrative and distributive functions depending on how they are employed, and that negotiators may use both integrative and distributive strategies in the same negotiation.

When negotiators on both sides of the table share the same social motives, we can predict negotiation strategy with some certainty. Two cooperative negotiators use integrative strategy more and distributive strategy less than two individualistic negotiators; and two individualistic negotiators use distributive strategy more and integrative strategy less than two cooperative negotiators.

These findings suggest how to start negotiations regardless of what the other party's social motive is: signal willingness to cooperate. You may have to do this several times if the other party is an individualist and wants to engage in bargaining over positions rather than interests. You may have to engage in some distributive bargaining yourself. However, keep going back to integrative bargaining. Negotiators tend to reciprocate each others' strategic behaviors. If you persist, you should be able to get the other to engage in integrative bargaining.

Finished with the Basics

In this opening chapter, we've reviewed the basics of negotiation, focusing on the differences between distributive versus integrative deal making, understanding BATNAs, and what it means to negotiate a high net value deal. We've also gotten a taste of the additional complexities involved in negotiating across cultural or national borders. In Chapter Two, we cover the basics of how culture impinges on negotiation, seeing even more ways in which successful global negotiation requires understanding cultural contexts.

Chapter Two

Culture and Negotiation

Joe Romano found out on a business trip to Taiwan how close a one-syllable slip of the tongue can come to torpedoing a deal. . . . Mr. Romano, a partner of High Ground, Inc., an emerging technology-marketing company in Boston, has been traveling to Asia for 10 years and speaks fluent Mandarin and Taiwanese. Or so he thought, until he nearly blew an important deal when he met the chief executive of a major Taiwanese manufacturer. "You're supposed to say 'Au-ban,' which means basically, 'Hello No. 1 Boss,'" Mr. Romano explained. "But being nervous, I slipped and said 'Lau-ban ya,' which means, 'Hello, wife of the boss.' So I basically called him a woman in front of 20 senior Taiwanese executives, who all laughed," he said. "He looked at me like he was going to kill me because in Asia, guys are hung up on being seen as very manly. I had to keep asking them to forgive 'the stupid American' before the C.E.O. would accept my apologies."[1]

Language mistakes and violations of local protocol are difficult to avoid when negotiating globally, but they are seldom deal breakers. As Mr. Romano learned, a groveling apology can go a long way toward mending relationships.

The real cultural deal breakers are embedded in failures to take culture into account at two critical points: when planning the negotiation and when choosing strategy. Three of my students discovered this for themselves in the course of researching Lafarge's first and second attempts to establish a foothold as a major cement manufacturer in Yunnan province in China. Lafarge, a French company, is the world leader in building materials, holding top positions in each of four areas: cement, aggregates and concrete, roofing, and gypsum.[2]

Lafarge's planning gaffe involved a failure to understand the Chinese government's interests. Lafarge wanted to enter the Yunnan market profitably and quickly by taking full ownership of two state-owned cement manufacturers. Lafarge assumed the government would be willing to sell, if the price was right. But Lafarge was wrong. The government's interests were less in money than in access to Lafarge's state of the art cement-manufacturing processes. In 2004, the time of this negotiation, the Chinese government had plenty of foreign capital; what it needed was a means of upgrading its inefficient construction manufacturing industry, while maintaining jobs and ensuring a steady supply of construction materials. The government also knew that transferring state-owned entities to local interests would be viewed more favorably from a public relations perspective than would a direct sale to a foreign company.

Lafarge's *strategic* gaffe involved the choice of whom to send to Yunnan to negotiate. Lafarge initially sent two fairly junior members of their investment team to talk to the heads of the two Yunnan cement companies. Although Lafarge may have thought that they were simply engaging in some due diligence research—were these the right companies to buy—the Chinese were miffed that a potential business partner would send analysts to talk to business directors. According to Sanjeev Krishna (investment officer for emerging markets at Health Sciences, International Finance Corporation—World Bank) the due diligence process in China is far different than in the West. In China, he advises, one needs to develop a solid relationship before embarking on the due diligence process. In the West typically a lot of due diligence is conducted prior to an entity even deciding to develop a relationship.

The end of this story is that Lafarge is in Yunnan province and technical know-how is being transferred to the Chinese cement companies, but the ultimate deal was not quite what Lafarge had

envisioned. Lafarge formed a joint venture with a Hong Kong company to purchase 80 percent of the Yunnan cement business. As a
result, Lafarge's ultimate share was only half of that (40 percent),
not the 100 percent it initially sought.

This chapter is about how culture affects negotiation. It begins
with an introduction to ways of characterizing different dimensions
and types of cultures. It goes on to describe a general framework
that illustrates how culture affects negotiation. The framework can
be used with the Negotiation Planning Document and strategic
choices discussed in Chapter One to incorporate cultural consider-
ations into preparations for negotiation.

Although it is filled with examples of negotiating in different
parts of the world, keep in mind that the chapter is not about protocol and not about how to negotiate in individual specific places, such
as China. The reason for this will be explained more thoroughly in
the section on cultural prototypes and cultural stereotypes. But in
brief the reason is that even experience within a culture does not
guarantee future negotiating success. Mr. Romano had ten years of
experience negotiating in Asia. Lafarge started doing business in
China in 1994. Ten years later, when Lafarge opened negotiations in
Yunnan province it already had cement operations in Sichuan
province. To adequately integrate cultural knowledge into negotiation strategy requires more than experience; it requires an understanding of how and why culture affects negotiations.

What Is Culture?

Culture is the distinct character of a social group.[3] It emerges from
the patterned ways that people in a group respond to the fundamental problems of social interaction.[4]

A useful metaphor for describing culture is an iceberg. Just like
with an iceberg there is more to culture below the surface than
above, and just like an iceberg, culture is not static, it drifts and
shifts. Exhibit 2.1 illustrates the cultural iceberg. Visible above the
squiggly "waterline" of the cultural iceberg are behaviors and

Exhibit 2.1. Culture as an Iceberg.

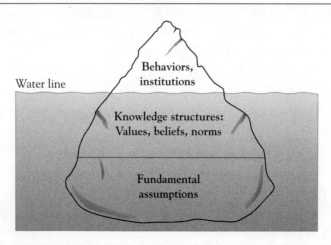

institutions. Below the waterline are two deeper, psychological levels. Each of the following sections examines one level.

Behaviors and Institutions

Above the iceberg's waterline are the characteristic *behavior* patterns of cultural members, as well as the culture's overt institutions.
Some of the most obvious cultural behavioral differences are differences in greetings. For example, in Japan people bow; in India they
may press hands together in *namaste;* in Latin America they grab
each other's upper arms; and in France, Italy, and Spain they kiss on
the cheeks. Although it is always polite to respect another culture's
greeting protocols, and there are many Websites with good advice
about what to do in Rome and so on,[5] it is not always necessary to
engage in them when negotiating cross culturally. You are after all
a cultural outsider. Even with significant cultural experience you
will probably never get the inclination of the Japanese bow right,
because the degree of inclination depends on the status of the person you are bowing to.

Interpreting the behaviors that you may see at the negotiation table is of greater importance. The risk is that you will jeopardize the negotiation by interpreting these behaviors through the lens of your own culture. For example, the first time I watched a class of Indian managers negotiate, I was startled by their side-to-side head movements. Side-to-side head movements in U.S. culture mean no, no, no! I thought negotiations were not going well, and I was really upset when many in the class continued this behavior during my debriefing. I asked my host professor, "What went wrong, they hated the class, how can we fix it for tomorrow?" He replied, "Why do you think that?" I said, "They shook their heads no, no, no all afternoon." "Oh," he said, "That means 'I'm listening.'"

I cannot anticipate all the behaviors that you are likely to encounter across the negotiation table. I can assure you that it is normal to interpret those behaviors through the lens of your own culture, and that such interpretation is frequently erroneous and may affect negotiation relationships and ultimately outcomes. To avoid these cultural biases when negotiating globally, you need a cultural interpreter, someone who not only knows the language but also can interpret the body language and the strategic behavior being exhibited across the table. Your cultural expert should also be able to help you understand the cultural context of the negotiation, for example, the institutional environment in which the negotiation is embedded.

Institutions on the iceberg figure stands for economic, social, political, legal, religious institutional environments that may affect the negotiation. Culture is manifested in institutional choices, such as whether there is a free-market economy or a communist political system, and it is embedded in the institutions' *ideologies*—the set of principles and precepts underlying institutional choices.

These cultural institutions provide social structures for nation-states, which is why in this book we are interested primarily in culture contained within national boundaries. Nation-states have their own unique institutional cultures that negotiators must navigate. Consider the aftermath of the Arcelor acquisition by Mittal. Ultimately,

Arcelor shareholders preferred selling to Mittal, a company registered in Rotterdam, incorporated within EU laws, and run by an Indian living in London, rather than selling to Severstal, a Russian company lead by a Russian oligarch, Alexsei Mordashov. Why? Mittal's EU-based political, legal, and economic environment apparently was viewed by shareholders as much less risky than Severstal's.[6]

Another reason to be concerned with the institutional structure of nation-states is that governments have interests that derive from their institutional ideologies and are reflected in their approach to negotiations. As we saw in the Lafarge example, the Chinese government, although encouraging foreign investment, nevertheless had strong institutional interests that included maintaining some local ownership, acquiring state-of-the-art technology, maintaining employment, and availability of construction materials.

In fact, one of the most important realities about negotiating globally is that governments are frequently at or close to the table. Western and Eastern companies alike, regardless of their negotiation experience, too frequently stumble badly when they try to do business in a new cultural environment. A recent example is China National Offshore Oil Company's 2005 failed bid for Unocal, which was ultimately bought domestically by Chevron.[7] CNOOC failed to take into account the risk that their acquisition could be blocked by the U.S. Congress. When Congressional approval appeared to be unlikely, CNOOC let Chevron outbid them for Unocal. Failing to understand the institutional environment in which the negotiation is occurring can sabotage negotiations. In Chapter Nine, you will read much more about government at and around the negotiating table.

Cultural Values, Beliefs, Norms, and Knowledge Structures

The behaviors and institutions that one can see above the cultural iceberg's waterline are supported underwater by a culturally shared psychology of values, beliefs, norms, and knowledge structures. It is convenient to characterize a culture by its values or norms, but there are two important traps to avoid when doing so.

The first trap to avoid is confounding a cultural *prototype* (a central tendency) with a cultural *stereotype* (the idea that everyone in a culture is the same; that there is no distribution around the mean). Keep in mind this distinction between prototypes and stereotypes. There is always variance within a culture.

The second trap is failing to understand that cultures are characterized by features measured at the individual level but then aggregated (averaged across cultural group members) to create a cultural prototype. It is at the cultural group level that we are most likely to find relationships between group-level psychological elements of culture and negotiation behaviors and outcomes. Individual-level cultural values seldom explain individual-level negotiation behavior or outcomes.

Exhibit 2.2 may help you to visualize the meaning of each of the traps. Each bell curve in Exhibit 2.2 illustrates a different culture's distribution on a psychological characteristic. The lines dropped from the height of the curve illustrate the cultural prototype. Note that there is a distribution around each culture's prototype and each distribution has "tails." Also notice that there are plenty of members from both cultures in the central, overlapping region of the curves. Not everyone in culture 2 is more extreme on the cultural

Exhibit 2.2. Cultural Prototypes and Cultural Stereotypes.

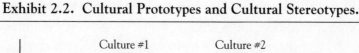

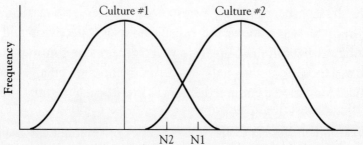

variable than everyone in culture 1. In fact, N1, a negotiator from culture 1, is actually closer to the culture 2 prototype than N2, a negotiator form culture 2. These cultural overlaps help explain why psychological elements of culture measured at the individual level do not predict negotiation behaviors or other types of outcomes.[8]

So why bother studying psychological characteristics of culture if you cannot see them, if they do not characterize everyone in the culture, and if, at least at the individual level, they do not predict negotiation outcomes very well, if at all? Even though psychological characteristics are below the surface of the cultural iceberg, you often can see them reflected in the culture's institutional ideology and in the patterns of behavior characteristic of people from that culture. Even though not every cultural member is going to be like the cultural prototype, because of the nature of the bell curve, more cultural members will fall under the central bell than in the tails of the curve. This means that unless a culture is extremely heterogeneous (the curve is very flat), anyone you negotiate with is more likely to come from the cultural center than from the tails. In addition, knowing cultural prototypes helps you anticipate the other party's interests as you prepare your planning document. It also helps you anticipate their likely strategic behaviors as you make your own strategic choices.

Cultural Values

A *value* is a judgment of what is important in social interaction. A cultural value is a judgment shared by a group. National cultures differ in terms of shared values,[9] two such differences seem particularly important for negotiations: individualism versus collectivism and hierarchy versus egalitarianism. (However, other value continuums— such as a focus on traditional ways versus openness to change—may account for national cultural differences in particular negotiations.)[10]

Individualism Versus Collectivism. The continuum *individualism versus collectivism* distinguishes between cultures that generally place individuals' interests above those of the collective and cultures that generally place collective needs above those of individuals. In individualist cultures social, economic, and legal institutions promote the autonomy of individuals, reward individual accomplishment, and protect individual rights. In collective cultures institutions promote interdependency of individuals with the others in their families, work establishments, and communities by emphasizing social obligations. Individual accomplishment reflects back on others with whom the individual is interdependent. Legal institutions support collective interests above individual interests.

Research generally categorizes nations in North America (excluding Mexico) and Western Europe as individualist cultures and pretty much the rest of the world as more or less collective, especially East Asia and Latin America. No one has studied Africa.[11]

Coming from a culture that is high on individualism or high on collectivism may affect negotiators' interests, goals, and so on—elements of their planning as well as their strategic choices. For example, individualistic cultures promote and condone self-interest, which may be reflected in negotiators' targets and their strategic use of argument; collective cultures' emphasis on social obligations may be reflected in negotiators' choices for indirect confrontation and face saving.

An example illustrates that there are cultural differences in negotiation strategy even between cultures that are in many ways similar. A U.S. software engineer working on a project for an Israeli client reported how much he was challenged by the different ways of approaching issues and discussing them: "There is something pretty common to the Israeli culture, they like to argue. I tend to try and collaborate more, and it got very stressful for me until I figured out how to kind of merge the cultures."[12]

According to my own research, Israeli managers are more likely to have individualistic social motives than are managers from any other culture I have studied (see Chapter One for more about social motives and "Norms for Managers' Social Motives" on the CD-ROM for data on Israelis).

However, you may find much less in this book about individualism versus collectivism than you might have expected, considering that this is the cultural value most widely studied by psychologists.[13] Although some commentators claim that the difference between individualism and collectivism influences basic psychological processes, these same commentators admit "the empirical basis for this conclusion is not as firm as might be desired."[14] Even in the 2004 *Handbook of Negotiation and Culture* (edited by Michele Gelfand and yours truly), individualism versus collectivism dominates the chapters on culture. But a review of the research cited in these chapters attempting to link individualism versus collectivism to negotiation processes and outcomes is disappointing. In the negotiation contexts of deal making, dispute resolution, and negotiating decisions in multicultural teams, I simply do not see evidence of a link, beyond a possible difference in the level of self-interest and concern for relationships. Only in the negotiation context of social dilemmas is there clear research evidence of an effect associated with individualistic versus collective cultural differences. In social dilemmas, people from collective cultures *are* more cooperative than those from individualist cultures.[15] (There will be more about this in Chapter Eight.)

In sum, the cultural value of considering individualism versus collectivism does not give us a great deal of leverage in understanding culture's effects on negotiation. This may be because individualism and collectivism do not act in isolation from other elements of culture. Psychological culture is an amalgam of values, beliefs, norms, and knowledge structures. Just knowing that a culture is more or less individualistic does not tell us enough to do more than make very general statements about likely behavior in negotiations. We have to look at more elements of culture.

Hierarchy Versus Egalitarianism. The continuum *hierarchy versus egalitarianism* distinguishes between cultures that are differentiated into closed and inflexible social ranks and cultures in which social structure is relatively flat, open, and malleable. In hierarchical cultures, social status determines social power, and social power generally transfers across situations. In egalitarian cultures, social boundaries are more permeable, and social status may be both short-lived and variable across situations.

Western cultures, especially Northern European nations, tend to be egalitarian. As you move south in Europe and on to Africa and south from North America to Central and South America, culture tends to be more hierarchical. Asian cultures are usually classified as hierarchical.[16]

In a study of multicultural teams, Kristin Behfar, Mary Kern, and I found that hierarchical-egalitarian value differences were a pervasive challenge, in some cases limiting some team members' participation in negotiating team decisions. A manager reared in India told us about being on a team that was trying to standardize a process across a U.S. company's sites in Belgium, Mexico, Canada, and the United States. He said, "In India, if you had a senior business person [on the team], just by age you would give them more respect and the reporting relationships [would stay] pretty much intact [even when on a team together]. You don't call your director by his first name. You usually refer to him as Sir XYZ. And I think the people in Mexico are also like that to a large extent. I felt like they also watch very carefully what they say in terms of who they address and how they say it and how forceful they are. . . . But I think that's asking a little too much of the Americans. . . . their reporting relationships are still there, but when you're in a meeting they usually consider everybody as an equal. . . ."[17]

In hierarchical cultures the reluctance to confront higher-status people may stem from concern for maintaining and using social hierarchies. When conflict does occur in hierarchical cultures, such as in the Chapter One example of the American who asked his Chinese counterpart for data, the conflict is more likely to be handled indirectly by a social superior than by direct confrontation.[18] When a higher-status third party gets involved in a dispute, that party's decision reinforces its authority without one party having to concede to the other, hence losing social status. In contrast, in an egalitarian culture, success in *direct* negotiations can lead to differentiated status, but not likely to *permanent* changes in social status, since a negotiated agreement in an egalitarian culture is unlikely to be an avenue for setting precedents.

Within hierarchical cultures, social relations are bound by a web of responsibilities and obligations that are mostly absent from egalitarian cultures. For example, in hierarchical cultures social inferiors are expected to defer to social superiors, who in return for the power and privilege conferred on them by right of their status have an obligation to look out for the well-being of lower-status parties.[19] No such obligations exist in egalitarian cultures. In the 1990s, for example, Rubbermaid (now Newell Rubbermaid) was the leading brand-name maker of plastic kitchenware and household items such as laundry baskets, yet definitely of lower business status than Wal-Mart. When the price for the main component in its products, resin, more than tripled between 1994 and 1996, Wal-Mart (Rubbermaid's biggest customer) balked at paying increased prices. When Rubbermaid insisted, Wal-Mart relegated the manufacturer's items to undesirable shelf space and used its market power to promote a Rubbermaid rival.[20]

The web of responsibility and obligation that engulfs social relationships in hierarchical cultures reflects a rather fixed distribution of power in those cultures. The concept of BATNA is not unheard of in hierarchical cultures, but it is much less important than determining parties' relative status, which then translates to responsibilities and obligations and the distribution of resources in a negotiated agreement.[21]

How negotiators from hierarchical cultures determine power is sometimes lost on Western culture negotiators. A Brazilian manager working for a Latin American division of a U.S. company that sources a lot of products in Asia told us about a negotiation he attended on the buyer's side along with his U.S. boss. On the seller's side sat four Koreans. He says, "In the meetings . . . the Koreans were trying to put things very carefully in an ornate manner. And this guy (the U.S. boss) didn't want to know the introductions or the small issues. He wanted the issues that were really going to close or make or break the business. The Koreans were shocked, as they wanted to go through the small stuff to warm up the negotiation first." No doubt underneath the "small stuff" in this warm-up to the negotiation was information about the company and the products that the Koreans thought was important in order to establish their status in the negotiation.[22]

In contrast, the concept of BATNA fits well with the conceptualization of power in egalitarian cultures. BATNAs are situational and flexible. If a negotiator is unhappy with his or her BATNA, he or she may be able to improve it.

Beliefs

A *belief* is an expectation. Culture has the very nice effect of helping cultural members navigate social life without having to negotiate every move. If I'm in Great Britain, Japan, or Australia with my friend Mara, she drives. Mara is Australian, she knows the rules of the road for left-side driving, and, more important, she believes that the other drivers on those roads also know the rules. Mara's beliefs allow her to anticipate other drivers' actions and get us safely to our destination. In the United States, Europe, or North Africa, I drive. In China and India we take taxis.

Beliefs permeate negotiations: beliefs about the other party's interests and priorities; beliefs about their power, be it from status or BATNA; beliefs about their reservation price and about the strategic choices they are likely to make.

Beliefs about trust are very important in negotiations because they underlie the strategic choice of negotiating distributively or integratively. Without trust negotiators are not likely to share information about interests and priorities that is necessary for high net value integrative agreements. *Trust* in negotiation is the willingness to make yourself vulnerable to the other party, usually by sharing information.[23] *Quick trust* is the belief that the other party is trustworthy until he or she proves to be untrustworthy.[24] Quick trust is characteristic of U.S. negotiators. In contrast, *slow trust* is characteristic of negotiators who wish to build strong relationships prior to sharing information in negotiation that might make them vulnerable to the other party. Slow trust is the belief that the other party has to prove that he or she is trustworthy. In slow-trust cultures, trust and trustworthiness are qualities that are held in great esteem and not easily earned, but rather must be built gradually.

A French lawyer working for an American company told me about her company's interest in developing business in Morocco. The company's area managers identified a Tunisian partner and began developing a relationship with him. He wanted assurance that the American company was serious, so the area managers arranged to bring in the regional European head for a meeting. However, the regional manager's expectations about what was going to be accomplished at the meeting were very different from those of the potential Moroccan partner. The Moroccan partner greeted the regional manager upon arrival, engaged him in social conversation, then departed with him for a lunch that took three hours and pushed the regional manager up against a flight deadline. He was furious; he had come to Morocco to talk business. From his perspective, nothing had been accomplished. But the French observer speculates that the Moroccan partner was *also* disappointed in the meeting because no relationship was built with the high-status regional manager.[25]

Negotiators from Western cultures may believe that engaging in small talk at the beginning of a new negotiation relationship is a waste of time. But negotiators from relationship-oriented cultures such as Tunisia, an Arabic-speaking, Muslim culture, may use such conversation to consolidate knowledge about the extent to which the other party is to be trusted. Recall the earlier example about the Brazilian observing his American boss trying to get negotiations started with the Koreans; small talk may contain important information about power and status that a party is trying to convey. If the recipient of the small talk does not understand the subtext, perhaps the listener is not worthy of trust.

Norms for Directness of Communication

Norms are standards of appropriate and inappropriate behavior in a cultural context. Norms are functional because they reduce the number of choices people have to make about how to behave. And, like beliefs, norms that provide guidance about how you should behave also provide insight into how others in the culture are likely to behave.

Norms regarding directness or indirectness of communication are important when negotiating globally. When people communicate indirectly, the same words take on different meanings depending on the context in which they are spoken. People in indirect-communication cultures (also called *high-context cultures*) understand each other because they share the social context with the speaker. In high-context cultures people interpret words together with the context in which the words were conveyed. It's no surprise then that these indirect-communication cultures tend also to be collective cultures in which people share common social contexts. By contrast, in direct-communication cultures information is communicated explicitly; meaning is on the surface of the message, not embedded in its context. People in direct-communication cultures (also called *low-context cultures*) understand each other because they share a vocabulary. Although they, too, share a social context they do not need to pay attention to that context to interpret a communication. Direct communication cultures also tend to be individualistic.

The research by Edward T. Hall and others indicates pretty clearly that non-Western cultures (for example Japanese, Russian, and Arab cultures) use indirect communication more than Western cultures, such as Germany, the United States, and Switzerland.[26]

Negotiators with experience in Japan know that a Japanese "yes" (*hai*) doesn't necessarily mean "yes." An Indian manager working out of Singapore for a Fortune 500 company on an eBusiness project learned this the hard way. He told us about negotiating with team members who were in Japan:

So . . . we would fly in there and . . . say, "Okay, this is what . . . the businesses priority [is] across Asia, and do the projects in Japan align with the same priorities?" . . . and so on . . . What would typically happen is . . . we would pretty much get a "yes," [and] on the face of it we would feel that we got a consensus, [and that] they bought into the priorities of the projects and . . . where [the dollars] should be spent on these projects. . . . [W]e thought we achieved a lot . . . However, in terms of their actions, we would . . . not see the same, . . . and their projects would still be focused on things which we believed . . . the Japan team felt were high priority for them. Their spending on the projects would continue in the same way. So what we were seeing was that we would walk into this meeting, we would have a consensus, they would say yes, [but] when we would come back [to Singapore] it would not be reflected in their actions."[27]

Determining whether or not parties had an agreement was a major challenge that surfaced when Kristin Behfar, Mary Kern, and I interviewed members of multicultural teams about the challenges they faced. Parties from high-context cultures are frequently simply reluctant to say "no,"[28] and parties from low-context cultures that want a "yes" are very good at hearing what they want to hear and not very good at interpreting a high-context "yes."

Interpreting high- and low-context communication in negotiations goes beyond understanding when yes means no. If negotiators are going to reach integrative agreements, they need to share information about interests and priorities.[29]

The latest research shows that negotiators from low- and high-context cultures negotiate in rather different ways.[30] Low-context-culture negotiators generally use a questioning strategy that culminates rather far into the negotiation with a settlement offer that links the issues. They ask the other party questions about interests and priorities, assume that the party is telling the truth, and reciprocate with information about their own interests and priorities. As this process unfolds during the first half to two-thirds of the negotiation, low-context-culture negotiators slowly build an understanding of the trade-offs possible in negotiations, then they start using this information to make offers to capture the trade-offs. In contrast, high-context-culture negotiators use a more indirect strategy to gain information about the other side's interests and priorities. The strategy is to make and receive both single- and multi-issue offers. On the surface, this negotiation strategy seems pretty direct: I tell you what I want, and you tell me what you want. But the information about interests and priorities is not on the surface of the offers; instead, it is embedded *between* them. I slowly build an understanding of your interests and priorities by drawing inferences about them from the way you change my offer. There is much more about how to manage these cultural differences in information exchange in Chapter Four.

Low- versus high-context cultural norms not only predispose negotiators to use either the questioning or the offer strategy, they also may inhibit full understanding of the other party's interests and priorities. The high-context-culture negotiator should be able to understand the direct communications of the low-context negotiator, but the low-context negotiator may not be sufficiently experienced with high-context communication to draw inferences about interests and priorities from a pattern of offers and counteroffers. This may be particularly true when issues are offered one at a time, rather than in a package.

Regardless of the research showing that low- and high-context cultures respectively favor the questioning and offer strategies, in principle, negotiators from low-context cultures should be able to use the offer strategy and negotiators from high-context cultures should be able to use the questioning strategy. Some psychologists argue that all human behaviors are available to people in all cultures,[31] it's just that characteristics of different cultures cue different means of fulfilling a social function, such as negotiation. But cultural psychologists are just beginning to study when culturally normative behavior occurs and when it does not.[32]

Knowledge Structures

A *knowledge structure* is a cognitive construction. It is an implicit theory, a mental model, an actor's script for a specific domain of thought or action. Knowledge structures are important because they guide judgments and decisions, and direct actions in specific domains such as negotiation. Negotiators' knowledge structures contain the answer to the question, What does a person like me do in a situation like this?[33]

It is useful to address knowledge structures at this point of our inquiry into culture and negotiation because knowledge structures integrate cultural values, beliefs, and norms that are relevant to a particular context of negotiation. The question has two parts: "What does *a person like me* do in *a situation like this?*" Both parts rely on culture. A *person like me* is defined by the context of the psychological elements of the values, beliefs, and norms of one's cultural identity group. A *situation like this* is likewise viewed through a normative cultural lens: "What is appropriate behavior in this situation?"

Using cultural values to predict negotiation behavior is pretty simple: if you know the value prototype of a culture, you can make a straightforward prediction, for example, that the culture is individualistic and therefore the negotiator will only care about his or her own interests. (Except, of course, as we discussed previously, such predictions are frequently off the mark.) Using knowledge structures to predict negotiation behavior is not at all simple. It requires knowing something about the person's cultural background *and* about the negotiation situation and how people in a culture react to different situations. For example, in a study of managers acting as third parties in dispute resolution, U.S. and Japanese third parties acted pretty much as one might predict given knowledge that the U.S. culture tends to be egalitarian and the Japanese culture to be hierarchical. U.S. third parties tended to involve the disputants in the decision to resolve the dispute regardless of whether they were bosses or peers. Japanese third parties tended to make the decision to resolve the dispute themselves. But Chinese third parties intervened very differently depending on their role as boss or peer. When the Chinese were in the role of boss, they acted like the Japanese. When the Chinese were in the role of peer, they acted like the Americans.[34]

Despite being hard to use to make predictions, knowledge structures are extremely useful because they integrate multiple influences of culture and they take into account characteristics of the negotiation contexts in which we find ourselves. Knowledge structures help us plan our global negotiations and make strategic choices.[35]

Cultural Assumptions

An *assumption* is an unproven supposition. Assumptions form the broad base of our cultural iceberg (Exhibit 2.1). They are linked to cultural members' knowledge structures and the ideologies underlying cultural institutions.

Cultural assumptions are widely held by members of a culture. Yet many times people are unaware of the assumptions that guide their own behavior, only realizing what those assumptions are when they try negotiating with someone whose assumptions are different. The assumptions in Exhibit 2.3 were articulated by a Japanese software engineer to be used as part of a cultural training program for his company, Infosys, a global leader in IT and business consulting. (See also "System Modification for Japan" on the CD-ROM.)

Recognizing differences in fundamental cultural assumptions is the first step toward developing a working relationship that respects and uses those differences. A multicultural team member told us what happened when the members of the U.K.-U.S. financial services team began working together.[36] He said that the U.S. approach to problem solving was to *forge ahead and start trying to rip apart things and let's do this and that*, whereas the U.K. members of the team took a more pragmatic approach: *let's not hurry up, let's think about this*. At first these different approaches to problem solving generated conflict, but when they didn't go away, the group not only learned to live with their differences but also realized that

Exhibit 2.3. Assumptions of
Indian and Japanese Software Engineers.

Assumption	Indian Engineer	Japanese Engineer
Self-concept	I am superior.	I am inferior.
Customer	Customer is a partner, an adult	Customer is God or a child
Words	Words are not final. Some are less important.	Words are final. They are commitment.
Commitment	I cannot say I do not know.	I cannot say I know.
Communication	I talk.	I listen.
Expertise	I am an expert after ten days.	I am an expert after ten years.
Teamwork	The team is there for me.	I am here for the team.
Decision making	I make a decision.	The team makes a decision.
Time	I value my time.	I value your time.
Negotiation	I convince you. I present my position.	I sympathize with you. I represent your position.
Silence	Silence is emptiness of the mind. (weakness)	Silence is consolidation of the mind. (strength)
Comprehension	I focus on the big picture.	I focus on the details.
Rules	Rule can be applicable. Some are less important.	Rule is a rule. No exception. All are important.
Suggestion	No. This is a better way. I will give you solution.	Yes but . . . Maybe, this is a better way. How do you think?
Risk	Risk is to be managed.	Risk is to be avoided.
Emotion	Emotion is to share.	Emotion is to hide, or explode.
Quality	I achieve the goal. 90 percent is completed.	I achieve the goal. 120 percent is completed.
Relationship	I spoke to him once. He is a friend of mine.	I spoke to him ten times. I just know him.

Exhibit 2.3. Assumptions of
Indian and Japanese Software Engineers, Cont'd.

Assumption	Indian Engineer	Japanese Engineer
Schedule	It takes five days. Therefore, it takes a week.	It takes five days. Therefore, it does not take a week.
Explanation	It is information.	It is an excuse.
Hierarchy	I obey my boss and act accordingly.	I obey my boss, but may act differently.
Arguing	It adds values. It is enjoyable.	It damages the relationship. It is uncomfortable.
Information	I share any information. I like quantitative info.	I share necessary information only. I like qualitative info.

Source: Used with permission of Junichi Yoshida and Infosys.

their cultural differences provided good checks and balances for teamwork.

In Chapter Seven we'll take up this example again and label the teams' negotiated decision-making process *fusion* (like fusion cooking, in which chefs may substitute a spice or sauce or cooking technique from an Asian culture in a French or Italian recipe). Fusion allows for the coexistence of both culture's approaches.[37] Fusion is being discussed seriously now by political scientists and government officials who are faced with multicultural populations that desire to protect their cultural differences rather than integrate or assimilate. Perhaps one of the reasons why Infosys has become "one of the jewels of the Indian information technology world"[38] is that the company is willing to recognize, confront, and negotiate cultural differences in order to get work done!

A Model of How Culture Affects Negotiation

Exhibit 2.4 illustrates how culture affects a two-party negotiation.

Exhibit 2.4. Culture in a Two-Party Negotiation.

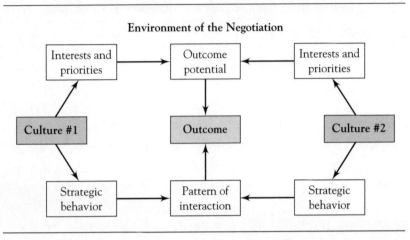

The exhibit shows that negotiators from each culture come to the negotiating table with interests and priorities that are culturally based. In the negotiation between the Chinese government and Lafarge, the Chinese government had three interests: local control, updating technology, and uninterrupted delivery of cement. These interests and the high priority placed on them compared with simply attracting more foreign investment illustrate how culture affects interests. Despite rapid economic growth and membership in the World Trade Organization, China remains a planned economy; in the case of Lafarge, economic planning took precedence over foreign investment. Lafarge had two interests entering the Yunnan market: speed and profitability. These interests, too, were cultural. Lafarge is a for-profit enterprise. Its investments in China are motivated by its desire to make money for its shareholders. Lafarge was interested in bringing new cement technology to these plants in Yunnan province not because it is altruistic but because with new technology production would be more profitable. Note that neither the Chinese government nor Lafarge's interests required that Lafarge own 100 percent of the cement plants, even though Lafarge set out to do so. The fit between negotiators' priorities and interests is what generates potential.[39]

Culture also may affect negotiators' strategic behavior: their confrontational style, their social motivation, and their integrative or distributive strategic approach to negotiation. We know a little about strategic behavior in the Lafarge negotiation. Lafarge's initial confrontational strategy was direct, motivated by its goal to accumulate economic capital. It sent financial analysts to Yunnan Province to do due diligence, collecting information that would allow Lafarge to develop a target price that would ensure profitability. In contrast, leadership of the Chinese cement companies no doubt preferred a less direct strategy that engaged first in relationship-building with high-level peers from Lafarge. They probably were concerned for their jobs. Financial analysts could not provide the relationship assurances they were likely seeking.

Exhibit 2.4 shows that negotiators' strategies generate a pattern of interaction in negotiation. That interaction can be functional and facilitate capturing the potential for an agreement; or, as in the Lafarge negotiation in Yunnan province, it can be dysfunctional and lead to an impasse.

Exhibit 2.4 illustrates one more important aspect of negotiating globally: the environment in which the negotiation is embedded. Environment refers to the context of negotiation and encompasses all the pressures and parties who are not at the table but nevertheless have an impact on negotiation. In Lafarge's case, the negotiation environment included the fact that China had a communist government, that China was engaged in a period of rapid growth and development of infrastructure (for example, constructing roads and buildings that require cement), and that the commitment to market economics was not uniform throughout China.

Culture and the Negotiation Planning Document

Chapter One closed with a discussion of strategic planning for negotiation. Now that we know more about culture, we can expand planning for a negotiation to include culture.

We have already discussed how institutional and psychological culture affect parties' interests and priorities. Analysis of cultural bases for interests and priorities can be incorporated directly into the Negotiation Planning Document.

Incorporating Cultural Parties. The Negotiation Planning Document can be extended as illustrated in Exhibit 2.5 by adding columns to represent multiple parties. In the previous section, the Chinese party in the Lafarge negotiation was represented as the directors of the two Yunnan province cement companies, but it would be more correct to represent the Chinese party with three faces: the company directors, the Yunnan province government, and the central Chinese government. It also may be that the two directors have different interests and should be separated for the purpose of planning. By adding a column for each party and analyzing each of the parties' positions, interests, and priorities, we incorporate culture into planning for negotiation.

Incorporating Cultural BATNAs. BATNAs too may be cultural. Consider Lafarge's BATNA to buying 100 percent of the Yunnan cement plants. This was China. Buying land and building one's own plant was not an option, but there was the option of entering into a rather complex joint venture agreement with a third party from Hong Kong. The joint venture ultimately bought 80 percent of the cement plants. There are lots of corporate strategic reasons for entering into joint ventures. In this case, those reasons had to do with the economic and political environment of the negotiation.

Negotiation Strategy and Culture

Culture should also be on your mind as you make choices about negotiation strategy. There is plenty of discussion, but not much formal research, concerning cultural differences in direct versus indirect confrontation. Negotiators from cultures that are collective—and

Exhibit 2.5. Negotiation Planning Document for Lafarge.

Issue	Lafarge			Company Directors			Yunnan Province Government			Chinese Central Government		
	Priority	Position	Interests	Priority	Position	Interests	Priority	Position	Interests	Priority	Position	Interests
Example		Position	Interests		Position	Interests		Position	Interests		Position	Interests
Price	1	Low	Make money	4	Indifferent	Not owners	2	High	Owners	4	High	Precedent
Speed	2	Rapid	Make money	3	Slow	Retain control	5	Slow	Manage employment	5	Medium	Manage employment, production, gain technology
Local Control and Jobs	5	No	Manage productively	1	Yes	Retain jobs	1	Yes	Retain prestige, employment	3	Some	Manage employment, gain technology
Technology	3	Yes	Efficiency	2	Yes, but	Threatened, don't know how to manage with Lafarge technology	3	Yes, but	Not cause a loss of jobs	2	Yes	And train locals to use it
Uninterrupted Delivery of Cement	4	Yes	Make money	5	Don't care	Not their job	4	Yes	Do not want to slow down local projects	1	Yes	Meet national needs
BATNA		Joint venture			Keep running the plants			Sell to another buyer			Sell to another buyer	

that engage in slow-trust and high-context communication—tend to prefer relationship-building prior to substantive negotiating. Since this pattern covers a large part of the world, it may be wise to plan to build relationships early when negotiating globally. Lafarge will never know whether the structure of its ultimate deal might have been better if the company had sent high-level managers to Yunnan province to build relationships with the directors of the cement companies, and possibly also with local officials.

Research does not support the idea that negotiators from some cultures primarily use integrative strategy and those in other cultures primarily use distributive strategy. There are three reasons: first, although negotiators themselves may have a preferred strategy, research indicates that they systematically alternate distributive and integrative strategies during negotiations. Second, there is substantial variation within cultures in the ability to use integrative strategy (and variation in how it is used). Third, savvy integrative negotiators can direct even diehard distributive negotiators to high joint-net-gain outcomes. How to do all these things is covered thoroughly in Chapters Three and Four. Here, however, let's look a bit further at what's involved in setting aside one's own culturally dominant negotiation strategies in the interest of getting an agreement. Let's ask, What are the risks in conceding to the other party's *micro-level strategy*?

Micro-level strategy refers to procedural issues such as where the negotiation takes place; whether the issues are discussed in a one-at-a-time agenda format; who is at the table; and what the negotiating medium is, for example, face-to-face, conference call, or e-mail. Recall the example in Chapter One of the negotiation between a U.S. company and a Saudi company in which messengers were employed. In further describing that negotiation, Darren Wee pointed out that in his previous experience, his company had never before negotiated with agents with no authority to make commitments. He said, "The Saudis wanted a list of questions and points that we wanted to cover and they would get back to us preapproving some questions and indicating others were not approved. They even dictated the seating chart at each meeting and wanted names and positions of all participants. . . ." "We had to concede all the process, and a significant amount of value to do the deal."[40] Ultimately, Darren Wee's company reached an agreement with the Saudis with margins that were acceptable to top management. Should they have conceded "all the process"? Would they have reached agreement if they had not?

Does making concessions on the micro-level process signal weakness? It certainly does signal flexibility and interest in the negotiation. It may help build relationships—"Okay, let's try it your way." However, it may also signal weakness in a hierarchical culture in which it may be taken as evidence of deference to a more powerful party—deference that would be expected to generalize across process and outcome. In contrast, the innate flexibility of an egalitarian culture implies that being flexible about the process should not necessarily signal substantive weakness.

A Complex Link

It would be helpful if the relationships between culture and negotiation were simple and straightforward, if one could say when in Rome use this strategy, when in Beijing use that one. The research to date indicates quite clearly that the link between culture and negotiation is complex. Look back at Exhibit 2.2 to see again the two reasons why this link between culture and negotiation is not straightforward: not all members of a culture behave like the cultural prototype, and cultural profiles overlap.

A third reason for the complexity of relationship between culture and negotiation is that cultures are not composed of single features. Cultures have profiles of features. Single cultural features may be more or less important, depending on the profile in which they are embedded. Given the state of the research, we can make only general statements about single cultural features and negotiation strategy.

A fourth reason why negotiation strategy is not perfectly related to culture is that knowledge structures that encompass cultural effects are nevertheless contextually cued: *What does a person like me do in a situation like this?*

Fifth and finally, there is the influence of the other negotiators at the table. Negotiators are quite likely to reciprocate each other's strategies.[41] When all negotiators are from the same culture, reciprocity reinforces culturally normative negotiation behaviors. When negotiators are from different cultures, reciprocity may help negotiators adjust their strategies to each other, but the resulting negotiation process may be a fusion of culturally different strategies.[42]

Anticipating cultural differences at the negotiation table helps negotiators make sense of those differences when they appear and adjust their own behaviors to reinforce or to block the other party's strategy. Excellent global negotiators proceed slowly, testing their assumptions about what strategy will be effective with the other party. They are willing to adjust their use of negotiation strategy to achieve their interests.

The next two chapters develop effective planning and execution of a deal-making negotiating strategy in a global environment. These chapters rely heavily on data my colleagues and I have collected working with negotiators around the world as they use their culturally normative negotiation strategies to try to create and claim value in a challenging negotiation simulation.

Chapter Three

Culture and Integrative Deals

Markets are becoming global at an astonishing rate, as suppliers look for new outlets with less competition and buyers look for variety in quality and price. North Americans buy South American fresh fruits and vegetables. South Americans watch television shows and films produced in North America. People in developing countries sew the shoes, footballs, and clothes used by consumers at their leisure in developed countries. Engineering-construction companies compete for contracts to build infrastructure in developing countries. Corporations are merging to realize global efficiencies that come with size. All these transactions involve negotiating globally.

Global deals are being done. Why then be concerned about negotiating globally? There are three reasons. First, some deals turn out poorly because in the rush to go global, negotiators fail to pay attention to their alternatives and lack clear standards for evaluating global deals. Second, opportunities are being lost because negotiators assume that bargaining is bargaining regardless of culture. Third, money is being left on the table either because negotiators do not know how to negotiate integrative agreements or because they are unable to do so when negotiating across cultures. Information is crucial to the search for integrative agreements, and negotiators from different cultures handle information rather differently. Skilled negotiators can avoid making poor global deals by paying attention to standards for evaluating global deals and by learning how culture affects the path to distributive outcomes and integrative agreements.

This chapter introduces Cartoon, a negotiation simulation that we have used extensively for the past ten years to help managers around the world evaluate their negotiation skills. The simulation also provides a sort of laboratory for us to study the strategies and outcomes of negotiators from different cultures. This chapter will take you in-depth into the process of negotiating high net value integrative deals. When you have finished reading about the Cartoon exercise, test your skills with the case "A Scandinavian Scare," which is on the CD-ROM. By the end of the chapter we will be analyzing cultural differences in negotiating integratively.

Before we talk about Cartoon, let's look a bit further at criteria for deciding whether deals are good or bad.

Three Criteria for Good Deals Versus Bad Deals

You're already familiar with the first criterion, net value. The second is the transaction costs of negotiating, including developing relationships. The third involves the long-term realization of anticipated gains.

Net Value for Both Parties—Joint Gains

Recall from Chapter One that a net value deal is one that is better than the negotiator's best alternative if no agreement is reached at the negotiating table. Negotiators need to be concerned about *joint gains*—their own and the other party's net value—for two reasons. First, an offer that produces net value for one negotiator and not the other will not generate a deal. Second, when negotiators fail to pay attention to the other party's net value, they leave money on the table that no one gets. Why is this so, you may ask? The short answer is that when negotiators fail to pay attention to each other's interests and to incorporate those interests into offers that trade off positions on low-priority issues for positions on high-priority issues, they do not take advantage of the maximum potential in their deal. The example developed in this chapter illustrates leaving money on the table. It also explains how to use strategy in global negotiations to generate high individual and joint net value deals.

Transaction Costs of Negotiating and Relationship Building

Transaction costs are the time, money, and energy consumed when negotiating. Negotiating globally is likely to generate higher transaction costs than negotiating domestically. New business relationships almost always call for face-to-face negotiations. When partners are from different parts of the world, negotiations may require substantial investments of time and money.

High transaction costs can be justified, but only if good deals get done. But the opposite situation too often occurs: negotiators get engaged in protracted negotiations, unsure whether they should cut their losses and get out or continue to try to work with the other party. As a general rule, in direct confrontation cultures such as the United States, the more time and energy it takes to negotiate the deal, the less net value there is likely to be in the deal. But this rule of transaction costs may not hold in cultures in which great emphasis is placed on building relationships. Then, the time spent building relationships ultimately may pay off in high net value deals.

Good management of transaction costs is illustrated by the way the artist Christo and his wife, Jeanne-Claude, have negotiated with private and public officials around the world for permission to mount projects that usually involve large amounts of public space and fabric.[1] These installation artists negotiated off and on with New York City for more than two decades before installing more than 7,500 saffron fabric-draped gates in New York's Central Park in February 2005. While waiting for New York City to say yes, Christo and Jeanne-Claude surrounded eleven islands in Biscayne Bay with pink fabric, wrapped the Reichstag with gold fabric (his offer was turned down twice before the German government came to him), and installed miles of blue parasols in Japan and yellow ones in the United States. These artists understand the transaction costs of negotiating and that building relationships takes time. They also understand the value of their time, and are willing to put a project aside, though not necessarily abandon it forever, when the transaction costs mount too high.

Long-Term Realization of Anticipated Gains

The purpose of deal making is not just to generate a net value deal but to realize long-term gains. Many aspects of deals are unpredictable. Markets get misread in the rush to gain access to new consumers. Political, economic, social, and technological environments change. So do aspects of cultures. This means that some deals that seemed to generate net value when agreement was reached fail to produce anticipated actual gains. Companies then have two choices: they can commit more resources to the problem or cut their losses and get out. Committing more resources requires dispassionate evidence that the situation will turn around with more resources. There is strong research evidence that at least Western culture decision makers and negotiators get overcommitted to even obviously losing courses of action. They are reluctant to admit they were wrong, and they believe they can turn situations around.[2] Getting out requires being willing to admit to having made a mistake. Wal-Mart does not make many mistakes, but it cut its losses and closed its businesses in South Korea and Germany in the second quarter of 2006 because it was unable to capture sufficient market share in either culture.[3]

The Link Between Net Value Deals and Long-Term Gains

It seems obvious that if you negotiate a negative net value deal you are not going to produce long-term gains. But as the Internet and telecommunications bubbles illustrated, managers caught in the exuberance of potential market growth sometimes forget that no amount of volume compensates for negative-margin deals. You might fool the markets in the short term—Enron certainly did—but you cannot fool them forever. Barring an unpredicted event, such as currency fluctuation in your favor, if you negotiate a negative net value deal you are not going to produce long-term gains.

Being an excellent negotiator means being able to walk away from a deal when net value and long-term gains are in doubt. For example, in May 2001 Henry Schacht, chairman of Lucent, walked away from a potential merger with Alcatel. Lucent is a U.S. company that designs and delivers systems and software for communications networks. Alcatel is a French company that provides voice, data, and video communications applications. Their planned merger in 2001 was estimated to potentially save the two companies $4 billion in annual costs on combined sales of roughly $50 billion. After seemingly friendly and successful negotiations Schacht called off the deal ostensibly over board representation. However, the real reason may have been uncertainty about Alcatel's financial situation. The day after merger talks ended, Alcatel issued an "unexpected and severe" profit warning amounting to a $2.57 billion second-quarter loss. Presumably, Schacht was concerned that putting together two weak companies would jeopardize the combination in the long term.[4]

Fortunately, the 2006 end of this story also illustrates the value of relationships built during the 2001 negotiations. In April 2006 Alcatel and Lucent announced a merger agreement. Serge Tchuruk, chairman and CEO of Alcatel, who led the 2001 negotiations with Lucent, came back to Lucent with a new offer. This one was acceptable to Lucent's board and chief, Patricia Russo, who then became the CEO of the merged companies.

Cartoon: A Simulation for Studying Deal-Making Negotiation Behavior

One of the best ways to learn about negotiation is to put yourself in a simulation and negotiate. When we teach managers negotiation skills, we do not start off telling them how to negotiate. We assign them a role, as buyer or seller, and an opposite role partner. We give buyers and sellers some confidential information about the issues to be negotiated, as well as interests and priorities, and each has information about his or her alternatives. We give everyone time to prepare and a quiet place to negotiate. We encourage participants to use what they already know about negotiating to see how far their current skills take them. We tell them we will post everyone's results, and we often ask them to make an audiorecording, for us to listen to and for them to take home and evaluate after the course.

A simulation is a very good way to evaluate your negotiation skills and identify areas for improvement, because *what* is being negotiated is a constant, making *how* it is negotiated the only variable. Few deal makers get the same deals, and few use the same strategies. By looking at all the different deals that are reached and discussing all the different strategies that were used, negotiators can gain a lot of insight into their own negotiating strengths and weaknesses.

For the same reason that simulations provide an excellent source of feedback, they also provide a very good way to learn about how people from different cultures negotiate. When my colleague Tetsushi Okumura and I began to study deal-making negotiations across cultures, we changed the product in a preexisting deal-making simulation[5] to a cartoon because cartoons are produced in many different countries and are quite easy to sell in the global marketplace because dubbing in a new language is inexpensive.

The negotiation involves a film company as seller and a TV station as buyer and concerns the rights to broadcast one hundred episodes of a half-hour animated cartoon called *Ultra Rangers* (think of a racially heterogeneous team of high school students who call on supernatural powers to save the earth from danger).

Managers around the world find the Cartoon simulation challenging. Most get deals that are better than their BATNAs, but most of those deals leave a minimum of $1 million on the table. Negotiators from some cultures leave closer to $1.5 million of unclaimed value. With a clearer understanding of the fundamentals of integrative and distributive negotiation, they might have negotiated a better deal.

The rest of this chapter uses Cartoon to illustrate integrative negotiation and what negotiators must do to realize integrative potential and avoid leaving money (value) on the table. There is some data on culture and outcomes in this chapter, but Chapter Four takes Cartoon globally, discussing in more detail how managers from different cultures negotiate deals with integrative potential.

All deal-making negotiations require the distribution of resources; some, like Cartoon, provide the opportunity to integrate as well. Attempting to integrate is important in two ways. First, if you do not integrate there may be no deal, or no satisfactory deal (recall my pumpkin rind-seed deal with Mme. Petit in Chapter One). Second, if you don't integrate you will leave value on the table from which no one profits. No negotiator intentionally leaves value on the table. Some do it unintentionally because they don't believe there is any further value to be had. But in most negotiations there are multiple issues, and in most the opposing parties' priorities are not the same across all issues, so in most negotiations there is potential integrative value. Other negotiators leave value on the table because they do not know how to identify that value. Still others avoid sharing the information necessary to create integrative value, because they fear that sharing will make them vulnerable to the other party.

As you learn about the Cartoon negotiation simulation, you will see how to analyze a negotiation for its integrative value. You will also see how integrative skills apply to contingent contracts, which are sometimes useful when the time comes to determine how to distribute value.

Analyzing the Cartoon
Negotiation for Integrative Value

Exhibit 3.1 puts together the confidential information that we provide the buyers in Cartoon with the confidential information that we provide the sellers. There are three issues in Cartoon that must be negotiated if agreement is to be reached:

1. *Price per episode.* How much the buyer is going to pay for the right to show the Cartoon episodes

2. *Runs-per-episode adjustment.* How much showing each episode more or less frequently will cost or save the buyer and seller

3. *Financing costs or savings.* How much financing the purchase over time will cost or save the buyer and seller

Note that buyers and sellers are given price aspirations and limits, and that the limits of $35,000 (the least the seller will take per episode) and $60,000 (the most the buyer will pay per episode) provide a very large bargaining range for agreement. Negotiators are given various options of four to eight runs and the cost or savings associated with each. The financing calculation is somewhat more complicated, but again buyers and sellers are given the options of paying 100 percent of the cost up-front versus financing some of the cost over years 1–5.

Exhibit 3.1 also shows that there is second cartoon, *Strums* (think of small imaginary creatures whose antics entertain young children), that can be included in the deal but is not required. For the one hundred episodes of *Strums*, negotiators are given a reservation price. Buyers cannot pay more than $20,000 per episode of *Strums* because they can get alternative programming for that price. Sellers cannot take any less than $10,000 per episode of *Strums* because they have another purchaser who has offered that amount. As we learned in Chapter One, the reservation price is based on the BATNA.

The final information in Exhibit 3.1 is about ratings. A rating in industry jargon is the percentage of all TV households watching a particular show (number of households watching divided by total number of TV households). The information about the different ratings from 2–3 to 6–7 was generated by the negotiators' companies and is the likelihood that the show will receive a particular level of rating in the buyer's local market.

Exhibit 3.1. Preferences in Cartoon.

Issue	Buyer	Seller
Revenue	$8.4 million	n.a.
Price per Episode		
Limit	$60,000	$35,000
Aspiration	$30,000	$70,000
Runs-per-Episode Adjustment		
4	$(1,680,000)	$500,000
5	$(840,000)	$250,000
6	$0	$0
7	$840,000	$(250,000)
8	$1,680,000	$(500,000)
Financing Savings or Cost		
Year 1	10%	−20%
Year 2	20%	−35%
Year 3	30%	−50%
Year 4	40%	−60%
Year 5	50%	−70%
Strums		
Reservation Price	$20,000	$10,000
Ratings (Estimated Likelihood)[a]		
2–3	20%	10%
3–4	50%	10%
4–5	10%	10%
5–6	10%	50%
6–7	10%	20%
BATNA	$3.0 million	$2.5 million

[a] A rating point is the percentage of all TV households watching a particular show (number of households watching divided by total number of TV households).

Source: J. M. Brett and T. Okumura, based on the Moms.com exercise by A. E. Tenbrunsel and M. H. Bazerman. In J. M. Brett (ed.), *Negotiation, Teamwork, and Decision-Making Exercises* (compact disk) (Evanston, Ill.: Dispute Resolution Research Center, Northwestern University, 2006). Reprinted by permission.

Integrative potential in deal-making negotiations is embedded in the differential interests and priorities of the buyer and seller. To find the integrative potential in Exhibit 3.1, look at the "Runs-per-Episode Adjustment" and "Financing Savings or Cost" rows. Notice that the *buyer gains* significant revenue from showing *Ultra Rangers* more than six times, because the buyer receives advertising revenue each time an episode is shown. By contrast, the *seller loses* future revenue if *Ultra Rangers* episodes are shown too many times, because after many showings interest in *Ultra Rangers* may wane, and the seller may not receive as much the next time it is sold in that same market. However, the estimated loss to the seller is much less than the estimated gain to the buyer. Of course, the negotiators do not know each other's interests unless they share this information.

Now look at the "Financing Savings or Cost" row. This information indicates that the cost of capital is different for the buyer and the seller. Here the seller is more sensitive to financing than the buyer is. The buyer would like to put off paying for *Ultra Rangers* as long as possible, but the seller really needs the cash at the time of the sale.

Exhibit 3.2 plots buyers' and sellers' net values for three different agreements or outcomes. Outcome A illustrates money being left on the table—$1.7 million to be exact! The price per episode for outcome A is $46,000, the parties agreed on six runs, and 25 percent of the purchase price was paid immediately, with the rest paid annually in three equal parts. The net value for the buyer is $1.5 million and for the seller, $0.9 million. Joint gains are $2.4 million. Exhibits 3.3 and 3.4 show the math for figuring the buyer's and seller's net value for outcome A.

Now look at outcomes B and C in the graph in Exhibit 3.2. Both outcomes B and C move the runs and financing to the extremes: eight runs and 100 percent of the money paid up-front. Outcomes B and C both generate $4.10 million in joint gains (buyer's net value plus seller's net value) and so are better than outcome A. Negotiators have created integrative value by trading off

Exhibit 3.2. Net Values in Three Different Cartoon Outcomes.

Outcome	Net Values for Buyer/Seller	Joint Gains	Price	Runs	Financing
A	$1.5/$0.9	$2.4	$46,000	6	25% years 0–3
B	$1.6/$2.5	$4.10	$55,000	8	100% year 0
C	$3.1/$1.0	$4.10	$40,000	8	100% year 0

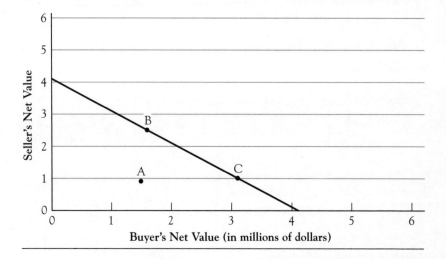

low-priority issues for high-priority issues. In fact, any agreement for eight runs and all the money up-front could be plotted on the B-C line in Exhibit 3.2.

Note too that both outcome B and outcome C are slightly better in terms of net values for buyer and seller than outcome A. B is better than A for the seller by $1.6 million and for the buyer by $.1 million. The reverse is true for C. C is better than A for the seller by $.1 million and better than A for the buyer by $1.6 million. Thus, both parties should be willing to choose either B or C over A. Of course the seller will prefer B and the buyer will prefer C.

Exactly where on the B-C line the agreement falls depends on how the integrative value is distributed, and this depends on what

Exhibit 3.3. Buyer's Outcome A for Cartoon.

Offer: $46,000 per episode, 6 runs, financing 25 percent up front and 25 percent equal payments in Years 1–3. No runs adjustment.

Revenue
= Expected Revenue + Runs Adjustment
= $8.4 million + $0
= $8.4 million

Price of Cartoon
= $46,000 per episode × 100
= $4.6 million

Payments Savings Calculation:

Year	Percent Paid	Amount Paid ($ million)	Savings (%)	Savings (million $)
0	25%	$1.15	0	0
1	25%	$1.15	10%	$0.115
2	25%	$1.15	20%	$0.230
3	25%	$1.15	30%	$0.345
			Total:	$0.69

Payment Savings
= $0.69 million

Net Price of Cartoon
= Price of Cartoon – Payment Savings
= $4.6 million – $.69 million
= $3.91 million

Net Profit of Cartoon
= Revenue – Net Price + Other
= $8.4 million – $3.91 million + $0
= $4.49 million

Net Value of the Agreement
= Net Profit – BATNA
= $4.49 million – $3.0 million
= $1.49 million

Exhibit 3.4. Seller's Outcome A for Cartoon.

Offer: $46,000 per episode, 6 runs, financing 25 percent up front and 25 percent equal payments in Years 1–3. No runs adjustment.

Revenue

= $46,000 per episode × 100

= $4.6 million

Financing Cost Savings Calculation

Year	Percent Paid	Amount Paid ($ million)	Savings (%)	Savings ($ million)
0	25%	$1.15	0%	$0
1	25%	$1.15	–20%	–$0.23
2	25%	$1.15	–35%	–$0.4025
3	25%	$1.15	–50%	–$0.575
			Total:	–$1.2075

Financing Cost Savings

= $1.2075 million

Net Revenue from Cartoon

= Revenue – (Costs + Other)

= $4.6 million – ($1.2075 million + $0)

= $3.3925 million

Net Value of the Agreement

= Net Revenue – BATNA

= $3.3925 million – $2.5 million

= $0.8925 million

---

price per episode the parties agree to. In outcome B, the price of $55,000 per episode results in a deal that is better for the seller than the buyer. In outcome C, the price of $40,000 per episode results in a deal that is better for the buyer than the seller. Exhibit 3.2 makes clear that deal makers need to be concerned about integrative value, or they will end up with a deal like outcome A that leaves money on the table. Exhibit 3.2 also makes clear that deal makers need to be concerned with distributive outcomes or, as illustrated by the case of the seller in outcomes A and C, all or most of the integrative value will go to the buyer.

There is another source of integrative value in the Cartoon simulation. Buyers and sellers have compatible interests in a second animated cartoon series—one hundred episodes of *Strums*. The seller would also like to sell *Strums*, and the buyer has an available time slot for another cartoon. Exhibit 3.1 shows that the buyer has a reservation price for *Strums* of $20,000 per episode.

The seller's reservation price is $10,000 per episode. Although it is not necessary to include *Strums* in a deal for *Ultra Rangers*, if the negotiators can agree to a price within the range of their reservation prices, *Strums* adds $1 million in integrative value to be distributed.[6]

Recall that adding the runs-financing trade-off in Exhibit 3.2 added $1.7 million in additional revenue to be shared. Exhibit 3.5 illustrates the $1 million effect of adding *Strums* at a price of $15,000 per episode. Maximum joint gains in Cartoon is $5.1 million. Although there is nothing "right" about splitting the difference, the example makes it easy to see that the effect is to add $500,000 to each party's net profit. If the price were lower, say, $12,000 per episode, the buyer would gain more, $0.8 million, and the seller less, $0.2 million.

Negotiating Across Cultures:
The Cartoon Outcome Study

Just how well do managers negotiating Cartoon do in terms of creating and claiming value? Getting cross-cultural negotiation data is particularly difficult because negotiators need to speak a common language and be face-to-face. However, our research has let us gather such data. The following describes what we've found in the course of what we call our "Cartoon Outcome Study."

Over the past ten years my colleagues and I have been collecting data on managers' strategies and outcomes when they negotiate

Exhibit 3.5. Net Values Adding a Compatible Issue.

Outcome	Net Values for Buyer/Seller	Joint Gains	Price	Runs	Financing	Strums
A	$1.5/$0.9	$2.4	$46,000	6	25% years 0–3	
B	$1.6/$2.5	$4.10	$55,000	8	100% year 0	
C	$3.1/$1.0	$4.10	$40,000	8	100% year 0	
D	$2.1/$3.0	$5.10	$55,000	8	100% year 0	$15,000
E	$3.6/$1.5	$5.10	$40,000	8	100% year 0	$15,000

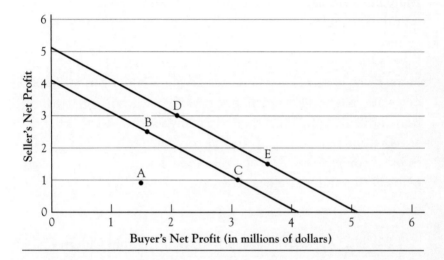

Cartoon as the first exercise in their negotiation training workshop. Our database includes managers from Brazil, China (PRC), France, Germany, Hong Kong, India, Israel, Japan, Russia, Thailand, and the United States. These managers all have ten or more years of work experience and they are interested in improving their negotiation skills! We use a very standard and brief introduction to the class that tells them what to expect, but not how to negotiate. Then we give them a role, time to prepare and an opposite role partner with whom to negotiate. They have seventy-five minutes to negotiate, and we are strict about the time.

Distributive and Integrative Outcomes
Within and Across Cultures

Exhibit 3.6 shows buyer, seller, and joint gains in Cartoon for negotiations within cultures. The buyer gains are the lighter lower part of each bar and the seller gains are the darker higher part of each bar. Let's look first at individual gains for buyers and sellers, and then turn to joint gains.

Individual Gains. On average across cultures, buyers and sellers split the resources in Cartoon 50–50. There are significant between-culture differences.[7] For example, French buyers claim about 58 percent of the value, whereas Thai buyers claim about 44 percent, and Hong Kong buyers claim 43 percent. Value claiming in real-world negotiations is largely a function of BATNA, which in turn is a function of the market. When there are many sellers, buyers' BATNAs are good and buyers should, other factors being equal, claim proportionately more value. The opposite should be true when there are many buyers and few sellers. The data suggest that in the Cartoon

Exhibit 3.6. Individual and Joint Gains Within Cultures.

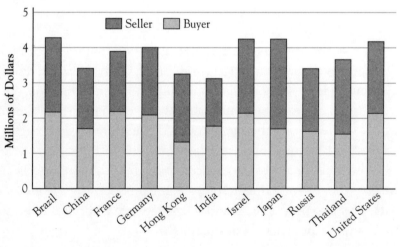

simulation, the case writers were successful in balancing the power distribution between buyer and seller.

Joint Gains. The joint gains in Exhibit 3.6 are far more interesting to interpret than are the individual gains. The joint gains are represented by the height of the bars in the exhibit. Recall that maximum possible joint gains are $5.1 million. On average everyone leaves money on the table! Across cultures, average joint gains were $3.808 million. There are significant statistical differences between cultures.[8] Some things to notice: first, there is no U.S. hegemony in negotiating integrative agreements. U.S. managers negotiate about the same level of joint gains as managers from Brazil, Germany, Israel, and Japan. The Hong Kong Chinese, the Russians, and the Indians have the most difficulty negotiating joint gains. The major reason is that negotiators from these cultures tend to leave *Strums* for a later meeting. They view meeting again to negotiate *Strums* as a fine opportunity to build their relationship. You can see this in Exhibit 3.7, which shows the percentage of negotiators who included *Strums* in

Exhibit 3.7. Percentage Including *Strums* by Culture.

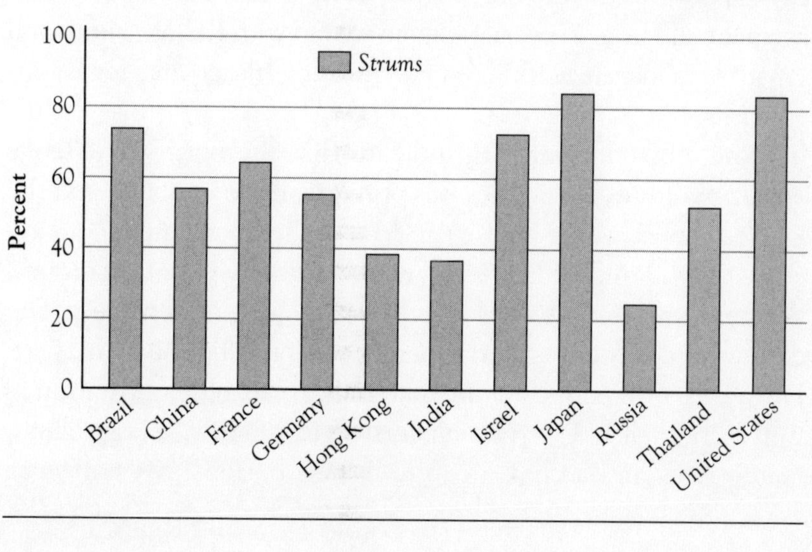

their agreement (Hong Kong Chinese, 38 percent; Indians, 36 percent; and Russians, 24 percent). Recall that including *Strums* in the deal adds $1 million in joint value, so even with a cultural reason for leaving *Strums* off the table, negotiators from some cultures had a much more difficult time finding the trade-offs in Cartoon than did others. Look at the joint gains for the Chinese ($3.56 million), the Hong Kong Chinese ($3.19 million), the Indians ($3.07 million), and the Russians ($3.37 million).

In the first edition of this book it was the Israelis who were the most successful in negotiating joint gains. Six years later, the Israelis are still performing very well in the Cartoon exercise, but they are not performing better than their counterparts from Brazil, Germany, Japan, or the United States. Notice that of these high-performing cultures, the German negotiators are including *Strums* only about 55 percent of the time, compared to over 72 percent in the other high-performing cultures. This suggests the Germans get the trade-off award in this edition!

Cross-Cultural Individual and Joint Gains

The cross-cultural data in Exhibit 3.8 come mostly from managers participating in the EMBA program at the Kellogg School of Management and from a special program we ran with Kellogg alums and Japanese managers working in the greater Chicago area for Japanese firms.

The cross-cultural data indicate that the biggest challenge crossing cultural boundaries was primarily between Japan and the United States, where gains were $3.5 million compared to an average of $4.0 million across all intercultural negotiation groups. We have analyzed these U.S.-Japan data rather extensively. The data were collected at two separate sessions about a year apart. Japanese participants had the materials in Japanese translation as well as in English. U.S. participants were primarily Kellogg alums, many of whom had had a course in negotiations! My colleague

**Exhibit 3.8. Individual and Joint
Gains in Between–Culture Negotiations.**

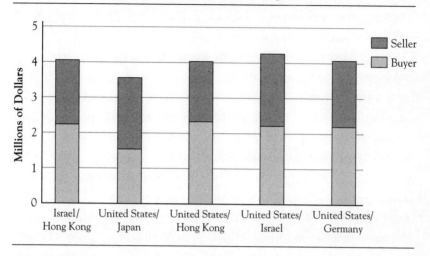

Tetsushi Okumura and I watched these negotiations carefully; the negotiations were not acrimonious! Just the opposite, everyone was being so polite that they seemed to be engaged in *satisficing*; that is, they accepted an offer as soon as it was better than their reservation price, rather than pushing for net value or joint gains. Negotiators both left *Strums* out of the deal and failed to trade off runs and financing.

The other interesting finding in Exhibit 3.8 is what happens to the Hong Kong Chinese when they negotiate with the U.S. negotiators. Recall from Exhibit 3.6 that within culture, Hong Kong Chinese negotiators created on average $3.18 million in value, and only 38 percent included *Strums*. Exhibit 3.8 shows that when they negotiate with Israeli or U.S. managers, the value they create is indistinguishable from the cross-cultural U.S.-Israeli or the U.S.-German negotiations, which average $4 million. The Hong Kong Chinese were able to adjust in the intercultural negotiations in ways that the Japanese were not.

Contingent Contracts

There is one more source of value to analyze that is embedded within the structure of the Cartoon negotiation. This is distributive value associated with a better- or worse-than-expected future that can be captured by a *contingent contract*. It does not represent any increased integrative value for the deal as a whole, but it affects the distribution, and developing a contingent contract requires applying integrative negotiating skills.

A contingent contract is an agreement to change the negotiated outcome in a specific way on the basis of the occurrence of a future event. In Cartoon, a contingent contract can be based on the buyer's and seller's differing expectations of future ratings the series will receive, and the ratings' effects on advertising revenue. The ratings information in Exhibit 3.9 shows that the buyer is pessimistic about the ratings, anticipating with a 50 percent likelihood that the ratings will be on the order of 3 and 4. The seller (Exhibit 3.10) is more optimistic, anticipating with a 50 percent likelihood that the ratings will be between 6 and 7.

Exhibit 3.9. Net Advertising Revenue Calculations in Cartoon—Buyer's Perspective.

Ratings	Likelihood	Net Advertising Revenue
2–3	20%	$7 million
3–4	50%	$8 million
4–5	10%	$9 million
5–6	10%	$10 million
6–7	10%	$11 million

Expected-value calculation: Assuming that each episode will be run six times, the buyer's overall estimate of the net advertising revenue from the series is calculated as follows:

$$(0.20 \times \$7 \text{ million}) + (0.50 \times \$8 \text{ million}) + (0.10 \times \$9 \text{ million}) + (0.10 \times \$10 \text{ million}) + (0.10 \times \$11 \text{ million}) = \$8.4 \text{ million}.$$

**Exhibit 3.10. Net Advertising Revenue
Calculations in Cartoon—Seller's Perspective.**

Ratings	Likelihood	Net Advertising Revenue
2–3	10%	$7 million
3–4	10%	$8 million
4–5	10%	$9 million
5–6	50%	$10 million
6–7	20%	$11 million

Expected-value calculation: Assuming that each episode will be run six times, the seller's overall estimate of the net advertising revenue from the series is calculated as follows:

$$(0.10 \times \$7 \text{ million}) + (0.10 \times \$8 \text{ million}) + (0.10 \times \$9 \text{ million}) + (0.50 \times \$10 \text{ million}) + (0.20 \times \$11 \text{ million}) = \$9.6 \text{ million}.$$

The buyer anticipates that it can sell $1 million of advertising for each rating point. Exhibit 3.9 shows that the buyer's overall estimate of the net advertising revenue for the series is $8.4 million. This is simply an expected value calculated as shown in the exhibit.

If we use the same math but insert the optimistic seller's estimates of the likelihood of each rating category, the expected revenue using the seller's expected ratings is $9.6 million. If the seller is correct, the buyer's revenue will be $1.2 million greater than was anticipated at the time of the negotiation. Exhibit 3.10 illustrates this calculation.

The seller would like to share this additional revenue if it materializes. The seller proposes a contingent contract: if the ratings are greater than 5, the buyer will pay the seller an additional $1 million. The buyer, still conservative and not expecting to have to pay, agrees, provided the seller will provide a $1 million rebate if the ratings come below 4. Exhibit 3.11 shows how each side calculates its expected value for this contingent contract. But this is only one of many possible contingent agreements that could be made on the buyer and seller's different expectations of ratings in Cartoon.

Exhibit 3.11. Example of a Contingent Contract.

If ratings are < 4, Buyer receives $1 million rebate from seller.

If ratings are > 5, Buyer pays $1 million surcharge to seller.

Expected Value:

Buyer .7($1MM) + .1($0) + .2(–$1MM) = $500,000

Seller .2($–1MM) + .1($0) + .7($1MM) = $500,000

By this time, you may recognize clearly why negotiating contingent contracts requires integrative negotiation skills: these contracts are built on expected differences; the same type of information required to integrate is required to make bets contingent on future events.

As we noted earlier, contingent contracts affect distribution value; they do not increase integrative value. In the example from Cartoon, no new value was created. The contract simply shared with the seller value resulting from greater demand for *Ultra Rangers* than the buyer anticipated. Without the contingent contract, if the ratings came in at 5 or above, the buyer would have kept all the additional advertising revenue. Why, then, would the buyer enter into such a contract? Possibly because the buyer could negotiate a lower price per episode, if willing to share advertising revenue with the seller in the event of such high ratings. If the seller really believes his own analysts, the contingent contract would be equivalent to receiving $50,000 per episode rather than the $40,000 per episode in, for example, alternative C in Exhibit 3.5.

Both risk and challenge are involved in negotiating contingent contracts. The risk is that the factor on which the contract is contingent is not objective. (Ratings in our example are reported by a third party.) When negotiations are cross-cultural and companies have different accounting methods, finding an objective factor on which to make contracts contingent may be difficult. When contingent factors are not objective, parties can legitimately have different opinions on whether or not the contract has been met, and a dispute can ensue. In general, it is unwise to negotiate a deal that you fear may generate future disputes.

Relatively few managers negotiating Cartoon incorporate contingent contracts in their deals. Even when buyers and sellers recognize that they have different priorities among the issues, they almost always fail to recognize that they also have different expectations of the ratings.

Moving Through the Normal Stages of Negotiation

Preparing to negotiate requires analyzing what is negotiable—not just what issues have to be in the deal, but what issues can be in the deal. That's what this chapter has been largely about. The Negotiation Planning Document introduced in Chapter One can serve as a guide, recording what is negotiable and helping you identify integrative potential. Once preparation is done, of course, you must execute a negotiation strategy to capture that value and distribute it. Executing a strategy through the stages of a negotiation is the theme of Chapter Four. This section simply introduces the general rationale for discussing negotiation in terms of stages.

Negotiations normally move through stages, each with a character of its own. Even in negotiations as short as the Cartoon simulation there are identifiable stages. In negotiations that stretch over weeks or months it is relatively easy to see movement from one stage to another as negotiators change from an emphasis on distributive to integrative strategy and vice versa.

The Arcelor-Mittal Steel merger talks that were described in Chapters One and Two provide a real-world example of a negotiation moving through stages. It was face-to-face meetings between lower-level executives that helped restart negotiations after five months of acrimony, finally leading to a merger valued at €26.5 billion. These meetings, led by the two companies' chief financial officers, were set up after Lakshmi Mittal wrote the Arcelor board providing new information about Mittal's status and vision for the combined companies. The first face-to-face meeting discussed technical questions related to the business plan. Then Lakshmi Mittal responded quickly in writing to the Arcelor board. With those questions resolved, the two negotiating teams met several more times, ultimately reaching the conclusion that "we do have a common vision, a common industrial plan, and we can realize these synergies," according to Aditya Mittal, who was the Mittal team's lead negotiator and CFO of the company.[9] Notably missing from the podium when the chairmen of the two companies announced the merger was the Arcelor CEO Dollé. When publicly rejecting Mittal's first offer, Dollé had used French slang roughly translated as "monkey money," which was widely viewed as a racial slur. He also tried to engineer a competing offer from Severstal to block Mittal, an offer that Arcelor shareholders widely criticized and rejected. As of this writing Dollé was not expected to remain with the company.

After Dollé's public and personal rejection, Lakshmi Mittal did not appear in person at the negotiating table until it was time to announce the merger. Nevertheless, he was in written communication with the Arcelor board, and he sent his son to the table, signaling the level at which negotiations between the two companies should proceed and his own close involvement.

The Arcelor-Mittal negotiation illustrates the normal stages that negotiations usually pass through. They normally start with a stage characterized by distributive strategy focused on posturing and positioning, such as Dollé's posturing when Mittal first made an offer in February 2006. This first-stage strategic approach defines the negotiators' differences but it does nothing to integrate those differences. So negotiators move on to a second stage of integrative strategy focused on information sharing, for example, Mittal's letter to the Arcelor board outlining his strategy for combining the two companies. The third stage tends to be a strategic mix. Negotiators use integrative strategy to continue to gather information, but also to put information into offers. In this stage negotiators also use distributive strategy to persuade the other party to accept an offer, such as the series of meetings between CFOs. In the final stage of a successful negotiation, parties weigh offers against their alternatives and select among offers for one that generates net value to each. The final stage of negotiation can also lead to impasse, if no offer surpasses a negotiator's reservation price.

Keep in mind that negotiation is a process of social interaction. Negotiators can move the negotiation from one stage to the other but to do so effectively they must take into account the strategic behavior of the other party, and that often depends on culture. In the next (and final) chapter that specifically focuses on negotiating deals, we will see how cultural differences in negotiation strategy play out with regard to the natural stages of negotiation.

Chapter Four

Executing Negotiation Strategy

In the previous chapter we saw how to analyze a negotiation and discover its integrative potential. In this chapter we focus on how to execute negotiation strategy to create integrative value and claim it, using the integrative and distributive negotiation strategies introduced in Chapter One.

Distributive negotiations with a single issue and fixed pie of resources normally take a straightforward application of distributive negotiation strategy. (Unless, as in the pumpkin example, you can transform a single issue into multiple issues.) Negotiations with integrative potential, such as the Cartoon simulation we analyzed in Chapter Three, and realistically almost any negotiation with multiple issues, do not take a straightforward application of integrative strategy. Instead negotiations with integrative potential, such as the one at the end of Chapter Three between Arcelor and Mittal, normally move through stages in which distributive and integrative strategies share dominance. And not surprisingly, culture matters. Choices about negotiation strategy depend on where one is in the normal progression of negotiations from beginning to end and the need to move negotiations ahead from one stage to another. Choices also depend on the strategic behavior of the other party, and that is influenced by culture.

Edward T. Hall, the high-context versus low-context communication theorist, was standing in a Mexican marketplace watching people from three different cultures interacting:

Unfolding before my very eyes was a perpetual ballet. Each culture, of course, was choreographed in its own way with its own beat, tempo, and rhythm. Beyond this there were individual performances, pairs dancing out their own dramas.[1]

Although everyone in this Mexican market was going through the universal stages of negotiating, the rhythms and steps of the negotiation dance varied depending on the cultural backgrounds of the negotiators.

Recall from Chapter Two that people in high-context cultures (such as Japan and Russia) tend to communicate indirectly. They understand each other because they read meaning from the social context in which the message is delivered. By contrast, people in low-context cultures (such as Germany or Israel) tend to communicate directly. They understand each other because they share a vocabulary. They do not need to read meaning from the social context in which the message is delivered.

In our study of negotiation strategy using Cartoon, Wendi Adair and I picked up on Hall's dance metaphor to explain how high-context, low-context, and mixed-context negotiators enacted the four stages of the negotiation dance described at the end of Chapter Three.[2] The results of this strategy study illustrate the relationships between culture, stages, and negotiators' strategies. Results also identify relationships between use of integrative and distributive strategies and outcomes.

The "Cartoon Strategy Study" uses some different participants than those in the Cartoon Outcome Study, the results of which were reported in Chapter Three. This is because we used data from audiotapes of the negotiations in the Strategy Study, and we do not have recordings of all the negotiations in the Outcome Study. We'll begin by describing participants, data collection, and coding strategies in the Strategy Study. After that, we'll look at how cultural groups differed in terms of their uses of information and influence strategies, and we will link negotiation strategy to outcomes. Throughout this chapter there is advice for gaining information and using influence in negotiations.

Participants, Data Collection, and Coding Strategies

Exhibit 4.1 describes the negotiators we studied with our Cartoon simulation: 89 pairs of managers from low-context-communication cultures including Germany, Israel, Sweden, and the United States; 102 pairs of managers (Japan, Hong Kong) and M.B.A. students (Russia, Thailand) from high-context-communication cultures; and 45 pairs with mixed-context-communication culture from the United States and Japan, and the United States and Hong Kong.[3]

We studied these managers and M.B.A. students using the same procedures as described in Chapter Three, with one difference. We asked them to record their negotiations. The recordings were transcribed. (Russian and Japanese recordings were translated into English and transcribed.) We trained four coders and checked their inter-rater reliability repeatedly over the two years that the coding

Exhibit 4.1. Participants in the Cartoon Strategy Study.

Context or Culture	Pairs	Level	Language
Low Context			
Germany	20	Manager	English
Israel	18	Manager	English
Sweden	24	Manager	English
United States	27	Manager	English
High Context			
Hong Kong	18	M.B.A. and Manager	English
Japan	24	Manager	Japanese (translated)
Russia	36	M.B.A.	Russian (translated)
Thailand	24	M.B.A.	English
Mixed Context			
United States–Japan	24	Manager	English
United States–Hong Kong	21	Manager	English

took place. The coders coded each subject-verb thought unit in each transcript with regard to distributive and integrative strategy. Coders coded integrative strategy statements as either of two types of information: asking questions or making offers. Coders coded distributive strategy statements into two types of influence strategy: posturing and persuasion. Exhibit 4.2 shows wording and instructions we gave to our coders to guide them in their coding.

We looked at sequences or pairs of coded behaviors, as in what you say and what I respond. Sequences are a really good way of studying negotiators' behaviors because they represent what is going on *between* negotiators. We studied three different types of sequences:

- *Reciprocal sequence:* You say something (for example, make an offer), and I respond with a coded behavior that is in the same specific strategic category as what you just said (for example, a counteroffer).
- *Complementary sequence:* You say something (for example, provide information) and I respond with a coded behavior that is in the same general strategic category as what you just said (for example, an offer).
- *Structural sequence:* You say something and I respond with a coded behavior that is in a different general strategic category. In other words, I am attempting to restructure or redirect the dialogue.

We also counted the total number of behaviors in a negotiation and then divided each negotiation into quarters. We counted the frequencies of each type of sequence in each quarter of each negotiation. From that, we calculated the proportion of each type of sequence in each quarter of each negotiation. Then because proportions have some peculiar characteristics that make them difficult to use in standard statistical analyses (the mean and variance are related), we log-transformed the proportions. To present the results we added a constant. These transformed proportions form the y axis in the exhibits showing the results (such as Exhibit 4.3).[4]

Exhibit 4.2. Cartoon Coding Categories and Examples.

General Strategy/ Specific Strategy	Code Category	Example	Explanation
	Integrative Strategy—Direct Information		
Priorities and Interests	Preference for a negotiable issue, option, relative importance of issues, assertion of interest	"We prefer to have the money up-front." "Runs are really important to us."	Priority and interest information are explicitly conveyed.
Reactions	Positive, negative, or neutral reaction; Positive acceptance of offer; affirming what other said	"If possible we'd like to broadcast your . . ." "That is too risky for us." "We think that this is a nice line-up." "We may be able to do that." "Yes, runs are important to us."	Yes or no reactions to other party's offers also provide information on one's own priorities.
Mutuality	Noting common or mutual interests	"We need a new show in our line-up and you need to sell this contract, so this deal can have benefits for both of us."	One's own and the other's interests and priorities are conveyed.
	Noting differences	"We don't see the ratings at 6 but at 3."	Information about differences is conveyed.
	Integrative Strategy—Indirect Information		
Offers	Single-issue offer or counteroffer	"We're offering to pay 40 percent up-front." "What do you think about five runs?"	Information about interests is embedded in the differences between offers.

Exhibit 4.2. Cartoon Coding Categories and Examples, Cont'd.

General Strategy/ Specific Strategy	Code Category	Example	Explanation
	Multiple-issue offer without trade-off (often phrased using *and*)	"Would you consider eight runs and $50,000 per title?"	Priorities and interests are revealed in the pattern of multiple-issue offers and in the differences between multiple-issue offers.
	Multiple-issue offer with trade-off (often phrased using *if-then*)	"With that type of payment schedule and for a six-run deal, I really think I still need to ask you for $70,000 per episode."	Priorities and interests are revealed in the trade-offs in these offers.
	Distributive Strategy—Posturing		
Affective Posturing	Sympathy (you do this or this is good for you because of how it affects me or my company) [reference to something negative for me]	"We cannot exceed our budget. Right now it's really tight—if you could find a way to share the risk, it would be very helpful for us." "We've got to make a profit." For seller: "We need to have cash up front because of all of our expenses."	An appeal is made to the other's emotions or norms of fairness.
	Information about competitors (other stations, other cartoons or shows, other suppliers)	"We are looking for programs from other companies as well."	Reference is made to competitors using contextual information in order to influence.

Exhibit 4.2. Cartoon Coding Categories and Examples, Cont'd.

General Strategy/ Specific Strategy	Code Category	Example	Explanation
	Information about own company (strategic plan, profitability, long-term relationships, reputation, power)	"We are planning to introduce some other cartoons in the future." "Hollyfilm [seller] is a leader in the industry."	Referring to the status or prestige of oneself or one's company appeals to social norms to defer to those with high power or status.

Distributive Strategy—Persuasion

General Strategy/ Specific Strategy	Code Category	Example	Explanation
Rational Persuasion	Reference to minimal acceptable price or conditions (reservation price) [implicit offer here]	"If you could provide us with the product at $45,000, that is the limit we can afford to spend."	Inability to make more concessions is conveyed.
	Substantiation (you do this or this is good for you because of how it affects you or your company)	"This is a good opportunity for your company to get in the market."	Information is provided.
	Argument or persuasion (we need . . . because . . .; informational persuasion) [reference to something positive for me, you, us]	"We're confident that there's a worldwide appeal." "We think *Ultra Rangers* is worth $80,000 a show. It has strong proven demographics."	Information is provided.
	Reference to BATNA—what we do if we don't reach an agreement; general other offer, or specific numbers [implicit threat here]	"We've received an offer from one of your competitors." "We already have an offer with a price better than what you are offering."	Information is provided about alternatives.

Exhibit 4.3. Reciprocal Questioning Over Time.

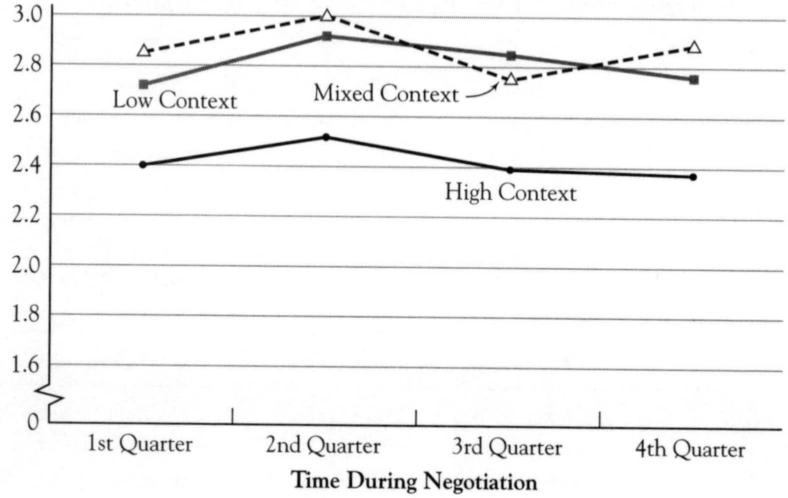

Integrative Strategies, Time, and Joint Gains

In this section we look at how two integrative strategies are used during the four stages of negotiation in the Cartoon simulation. Negotiators want information about the other party's interests and priorities to combine with their own interests and priorities, construct trade-offs, and create integrative value. But at the same time negotiators are reluctant to reveal information about their own interests and priorities. Remember, sharing information in negotiation makes you vulnerable; when you share information about your interests and priorities, the other party knows what you are willing to give up and what you must have.

With this dilemma in mind, let's compare the experiences of negotiators who were more and less successful in reaching integrative outcomes. Cartoon negotiators who were less successful—for example, outcome A in Exhibit 3.2—lacked information, typically having only the vaguest idea about the other party's interests and priorities. They agreed because the offer was better than their BATNAs, but they remained uncertain about whether the agreement was as good as it could have been. They typically had difficulty explaining the choices they made for runs and financing.

Cartoon negotiators who reached more integrative agreements had two characteristics in common. They were very interested in information during negotiation, and they had a strategy for getting it. Our research has identified two rather different strategies for acquiring the necessary information to reach integrative agreements.[5] One is a questioning strategy, the other an offer strategy. These strategies are not used with the same frequency in all cultures. However, either strategy can lead negotiators to integrative agreements that leave no money on the negotiating table.

The Questioning Strategy—Direct Information

Sharing information directly could be a series of reciprocal sequences of questions and answers, comments on mutual interests and differences, or feedback about the correctness of a negotiator's inference.[6] One party asks a question about the other party's interests; the other party answers honestly and asks a question in return. Negotiators might comment on which issues seem to be in their mutual interest and which issues are more important to one party than the other, and correct erroneous conclusions. In the Cartoon negotiation a series of questions about interests and priorities might reveal that runs are more important to the buyer and financing more important to the seller. Further questioning might reveal that both parties were also interested in the sale of rights for the second cartoon, *Strums*.

Exhibit 4.3 shows the pattern of reciprocal sequences of the questioning strategy over time in the Cartoon negotiation for negotiators from low- and high-context cultures when they negotiate against their own kind (for example, low-context facing low-context) and when they negotiate against their opposite (low-context facing high-context). The first thing to notice is that high-context negotiators are reciprocating the questioning strategy less than the low-context or mixed-context negotiators at all four time periods. This effect is what statisticians call "significant," and it is very important. High-context culture negotiators just do not like to share information directly.

The second thing to notice about Exhibit 4.3 is that high-context negotiators can share information directly when negotiating with a low-context negotiator. There are no significant differences in Exhibit 4.3 between low- and mixed-context negotiators. This shows that high-context negotiators have a questioning strategy knowledge structure (a mental model or script) that gets activated when they are negotiating with a low-context negotiator.

The third thing to notice is that reciprocal questioning increases in the second quarter of the negotiations. This pattern is consistent with prior research and theorizing, which suggest that negotiations start out distributive focusing on positions and then shift to integrative in the second quarter; this happens as negotiators, realizing there is no agreement between their positions, turn their attention to the issues, and to interests and priorities.[7] The reciprocal questioning strategy eases off a bit in the third quarter because, with information about interests and priorities now available, negotiators can turn to putting the information to work in offers.

Joint Gains from the Reciprocal Questioning Strategies. The rise in reciprocal use of the questioning strategy in the second quarter of negotiations is very important for reaching an integrative agreement. Negotiators who failed to make the transition to reciprocal information sharing in the second quarter had significantly lower joint gains than those who did. This means it is important to know how to use the questioning strategy effectively.

This research also provides a solid basis for advice about using the questioning strategy: negotiators need to ask and answer questions about issues, interests, and priorities. They need to give each other feedback: "Yes that will work for me," or "No, that won't work for me because . . ." They need to be explicit about sharing knowledge about similar and divergent interests and priorities. Reciprocating the other negotiator's direct information sharing builds trust.[8]

It says, "It's safe to share with me, because I'm sharing with you." It also sends the message, "I'm trustworthy because I'm listening to you." Here is some advice for sharing information directly:

- Ask questions about interests or priorities. Asking questions has two purposes: getting information and building trust. In general, ask questions about things that you would be willing to share information about in return. If you are not willing to reciprocate information, the other party will notice and quickly stop answering.

- Give a little information about your own interests or priorities and then ask the question. This gives the other party something in advance of answering the question. It shows that you are willing to make yourself a little vulnerable. It sends the signal, "I'm trustworthy."

- When you cannot answer a question because it would give away too much strategic information, be honest about it and give some other information that you can share: "I'm sorry, I cannot give you that information at this point, but I can tell you . . ."

The Offer Strategy—Indirect Information

Most of what we know about offers comes from research in Western (low-context, direct) cultures on distributive negotiation, when negotiators typically are focusing upon a single issue and using offers to state positions and stake a claim.[9] This prior research illustrates the value-claiming function of offers in distributive negotiations. We know that first offers can act as an anchor or reference point from which negotiators make subsequent concessions and adjustments. We also know that negotiators make more offers and more concessions as deadlines approach.[10]

When we were studying U.S. and Japanese managers negotiating Cartoon, Wendi Adair, Tetsushi Okumura, and I got the idea that offers could also be part of an information-search strategy in integrative bargaining. The Japanese and U.S. negotiators achieved the same level of joint gains, but the Japanese were using questioning less and single- and multiple-issue offers more than the U.S. negotiators.[11] We knew the Japanese were high-context communicators and that social interaction in high-context cultures hones skills in using the context of a communication for the purpose of conveying meaning beyond the open meaning of the content.[12]

In studying the transcripts of the Japanese negotiations, we began to see how offers might be used to glean information about the other party's interests and priorities. The offer strategy involves plotting how offers change over time, and from the changes drawing inferences about the other party's interests and priorities. Take a look at Exhibit 4.4, which illustrates how single-issue offers are assessed within the context of previous offers and can be used to effectively identify trade-offs. The table reveals information about priorities embedded in a series of single issue offers. In offer 1, the buyer starts with a low offer on price. In offer 2, the seller responds by asking for 100 percent of the financing up front, but without an alternative offer on price. Thus, the price of $35,000 is still on the table. Then, in offer 3 the buyer proposes eight runs, without questioning the 100 percent up-front financing or changing the price. Thus the content of offers 1 and 2 are implicit in offer 3. The ne-

Exhibit 4.4. Information Embedded in a Series of Single-Issue Offers.

Issue	Buyer Offer 1	Seller Offer 2	Buyer Offer 3	Seller Offer 4	Buyer Offer 5
Price	**$35,000**	$35,000	$35,000	**$50,000**	$50,000
Runs		8	8		8
Financing		**100% cash**	100% cash	100% cash	100% cash
Strums					**$10,000**

Note: Explicit offers are shown in bold.

gotiation continues in a similar manner until all five issues are on the table.

Exhibit 4.4 involved single-issue offers. Exhibit 4.5 illustrates the same general principle at work in a series of multi-issue offers. In offer 1, the buyer indicates a low price for *Ultra Rangers* and *Strums*, plus eight runs, and financing spread out over time. In offer 2, the seller comes back asking for more money for each show and 100 percent up-front financing, but leaves the eight runs intact. The implicit message is, "If I am going to give you eight runs, you are going to have to pay me 100 percent up front, and I need more money." The buyer's offer 3 indicates that the buyer got the message about the trade-off of runs and financing, and that he or she is willing to pay $15,000 for *Strums*, but not so much for *Ultra Rangers*.

Once we figured out how the Japanese might be extracting information about interests and priorities from offer patterns, we wondered, "Is it just the Japanese who do this, or do negotiators from other high-context cultures also use offers in this way?" The answer is illustrated in Exhibit 4.6. It is not just the Japanese! Negotiators from Russia, Thailand, and Hong Kong (all high-context cultures) also reciprocate offers more than do low-context culture negotiators.

A second thing to notice in Exhibit 4.6 is that high-context negotiators start off reciprocating each others' offers at a significantly higher rate than low- or mixed-context negotiators. This is consistent with our previous research into the frequencies of offers among Japanese negotiators.[13]

Exhibit 4.5. Information Embedded in a Series of Multi-Issue Offers.

Issue	Buyer Offer 1	Seller Offer 2	Buyer Offer 3	Seller Offer 4
Price	$35,000	$70,000	$45,000	$60,000
Runs	8	8	8	8
Financing	25% per year 1–4	100% cash	100% cash	100% cash
Strums	$10,000	$15,000	$15,000	$15,000

Exhibit 4.6. Reciprocal Offers Over Time.

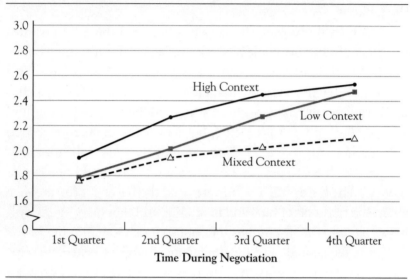

The third thing to notice is that the reciprocation of offers increases over time for all groups of negotiators. This is consistent with prior research that shows that in the fourth quarter negotiators work to reduce alternatives and move toward a final decision.[14] By that final stage, negotiators should have sufficient information to construct offers and be quite confident that agreement is possible. Offers in the fourth quarter serve two purposes: to reach an agreement and to try to get as much net value as possible out of that agreement for oneself.

Two final things to notice in Exhibit 4.6 are that by the fourth quarter there is no statistical difference between low- and high-context negotiators' reciprocation of offers, but mixed-context negotiators start lagging behind the low-context negotiators in reciprocating offers as early as the second quarter. That lag becomes significant in the third and fourth quarters. We know from Exhibit 4.3 that the low- and mixed-context negotiators are sharing information directly throughout the negotiations. However, the mixed-context negotiators do not seem to be able to engage in the fourth-quarter dance of putting that information together in a series of offers and counteroffers at the same rate as high- and low-context negotiators facing partners of their own type.

The patterns in Exhibits 4.3 and 4.6 are consistent with the interpretation that high-context negotiators are using offers early in the negotiation to search for information and later in the negotiation to consolidate that information in agreements that maximize joint gains. In subsequent research, back with just the Japanese and U.S. negotiators, Wendi Adair, Laurie Weingart, and I tried another way to demonstrate that Japanese and U.S. same-culture negotiators were using offers differently: we would show that failure to follow a culturally normative approach to negotiations could interfere with performance. In fact, we found that early, explicit offers actually interfered with negotiators' joint gains in same-culture U.S. negotiations.[15] We believe this happened because early offers blocked the search for information that leads to integrative agreements. The block grew out of the fact that the early offers acted as anchors that fixated negotiators on one outcome rather than on the search for better outcomes. We also found lower joint gains among Japanese negotiators who made their initial offers too late without engaging in prior direct information sharing. These negotiators were posturing early in the negotiation, talking about their own company's status rather than talking about the issues and making offers.

This evidence showing that failing to engage in culturally normative information sharing early in the negotiation hurt joint gains really underscores the importance of negotiators being facile with both high-context and low-context styles of information sharing. Negotiators need to be able to acquire information via both direct question and answer and indirect interpretation of offer patterns. They also need to understand the importance of consolidating that information into agreements using multi-issue offers.

The Hidden Powers of Reciprocal Offer Strategies and the Problem for the Low-Context Side. Multiple-issue offers have some hidden powers. They minimize the need for trust in negotiation. They also link integrative and distributive outcomes. But it's a nice question whether you have to be Japanese or from another high-context culture to use the offer strategy to gather information about the other negotiator's interests and priorities. Let's explore the hidden powers further, then consider some caveats for negotiators from low-context cultures.

There are two reasons why multiple-issue offers minimize the need for trust in negotiation. First, they do not require parties to reveal priorities on single issues as is done in the questioning strategy. Second, they do not engender distrust, which sometimes occurs when single-issue interests or priorities are revealed. An example may help. I knew the first time that I went to teach negotiations in China that negotiators from high-context cultures used lots of offers, but I did not fully understand the implication of offers for trust until I was debriefing my E.M.B.A. class, which had just negotiated Cartoon. When I got to the third point in my questioning-strategy slide (about asking questions, sharing a little information, and so on), a hand went up in the back of the room. "Why would we do that, professor?" I was asked. Being an experienced teacher of negotiations, I asked, "Why *wouldn't* you do it?" The student replied, "I wouldn't trust anything the other party said to me." I then checked his outcome, which was fully integrative, and asked, "Well, what did you do?" "I made him an offer," he said. Then I turned to his negotiating partner and asked, "What did you do?" The partner said, "That offer was just terrible for me, so I made him a counteroffer." The reason that multiple-issue offers avoid the trust problem is that negotiators do not make offers that they are not willing to accept as a final agreement. Multiple-issue offers are a truth serum.

Multi-issue offers link integrative and distributive outcomes and therefore help negotiators avoid two negotiation traps that regularly lead to impasse. The first trap is separating the integrative and distributive parts of the negotiation. When negotiators integrate without distributing resources, they tend to get greedy when they see how large the joint resources are; as a result they hit an impasse when they try to divide the resources.

The second trap is negotiating one issue at a time, agreeing on the easy ones, setting aside the hard ones, and getting to the end of the agenda with nothing to trade off. Many negotiations are complex with many issues, many options, and lots of details to work out. Low-context-culture negotiators like to work from agendas and check off accomplishments; high-context-culture negotiators like to see the big picture before they agree to resolve individual issues. Recall the example in Chapter Two of the Latin American division of a U.S. company negotiating with a Korean supplier. Once the parties got through the small talk and got down to negotiating they ran into another micro-strategic clash. The manager we interviewed on the U.S. side told us, "[On the] first day we agreed on three points and on the second day, we wanted to start with point four, but the Korean side wanted to go back and rediscuss point one through point three. . . . my boss (U.S.) almost had an attack." You may be surprised at how these U.S. and Korean negotiators got through this micro-strategy clash. The U.S. buyer had a draft of a proposed multi-issue contract, which he then put on the table. Now the Koreans could see the scope of the negotiation and were willing to talk about the issues.[16]

Thus far, a multi-issue offer strategy finesses the trust problem that is endemic to the questioning strategy. Because it imposes a distribution on an integrative outcome, it also avoids the traps of integrating before distributing and of issue-by-issue bargaining that may lead to impasse. But at the same time, negotiators from low-context backgrounds may need some additional help with two problems: a tendency to get anchored on early offers and a lack of skill interpreting the contextual meanings of communications.

To avoid anchoring on early offers, the recommendation in Chapter One was to counteroffer. This still seems like a good strategic response. However, the most recent research suggests that, to avoid anchoring on offers, low-context negotiators need to develop a knowledge structure or script that combines early offers with searching for interests and priorities; this knowledge structure needs to replace the knowledge structure they may already have, which combines early offers with anchoring.

Regarding the second general problem of interpreting meaning, additional help is also in order. Low-context negotiators probably do not have high-context interpretive skills to make the search between early offers fruitful, but one helpful technique for reading interests and priorities from offers is to plot offers as in Exhibits 4.4 and 4.5. Plotting helps negotiators read between the columns and draw inferences about interests and priorities that can be further tested in the next offer. Although the Japanese appear to be able to infer information from a series of single-issue offers as in Exhibit 4.4, low-context negotiators may find it easier to understand interests and priorities when the offers are multi-issue, as in Exhibit 4.5.

Two More Tools for Inferring Information from Offers. One other tool for inferring information from offers is equivalent proposals. Another is second agreements.

Equivalent Proposals. Advancing equivalent proposals can help negotiators infer information from offers. *Equivalent proposals* are two or more multi-issue offers that are presented at the same time.[17] Exhibit 4.7 illustrates a set of two equivalent proposals offered by a seller in the Cartoon negotiation. Note that the seller's net value is the same for both offers, but the offers are differentially configured. The seller might use this set of proposals if the buyer has been saying that the buyer absolutely has to finance 20 percent of the deal. In the equivalent proposal, the buyer can see that the combination of dropping the price and giving 100 percent of the money up front is worth $90,000.

Exhibit 4.7. A Seller's Equivalent Offers for Cartoon.

Offer	Net Value Buyer/Seller (in millions)	Price of Ultra Rangers	Runs	Financing
A	$2.67/$1.32	$45,000	8	80% Y(0) 20% Y(1)
B	$2.76/$1.32	$43,200	8	100% Y(0)

Note that in Exhibit 4.7 all the additional gains generated by the offering of equivalent proposals go to the other party. There is nothing to do about this, unless you have already negotiated in advance to split the gains generated by the trade-off. Thus it is particularly important when using equivalent proposals to keep your target in mind. The seller could just as easily have made equivalent proposals that generated more net value for him- or herself by pricing *Ultra Rangers* higher.

Equivalent proposals are not just good for getting information from negotiators who are reluctant to share, or from negotiators who don't fully understand their own priorities. They are also very good for dealing with negotiators you think are lying about priorities and negotiators who come up with "just one more thing" when you thought the negotiation was over. In either case, make one proposal that you think should be acceptable and another that integrates the new issue or gives more on the issue for which you think the other party has falsified a priority. Make sure the proposals are equivalent to you and anchored to give you as high a net value as you think is possible. Whether the other party did not understand his or her own priorities or was lying about them is really irrelevant because, once the other party has made a choice between your equivalent proposals, *you* understand his or her priorities.

Second Agreements. The other additional offer strategy for generating information about interests and priorities is to try to negotiate a second agreement (also known as a post-settlement settlement). The process requires both parties to agree that once a first agreement has been reached, they will share information fully and try to move to a more integrative second agreement, in effect a post-settlement settlement. The rule for negotiating second agreements is that the first agreement stands unless parties jointly identify another agreement as good or better for each of them.[18]

Second agreements have some negative characteristics. One problem is that as full information is shared, the parties may learn that one of them was more forthcoming or more honest than the other was. The party who shared naturally feels taken advantage of and mistrustful. Had there been no provision for a second agreement, the level of differential disclosure might never have surfaced. If you have interests or information that you do not want the other party to know, a second agreement is not a wise strategy. The mistake sometimes occurs during acquisitions. The seller, anxious to get the best price, presents her financials in the best possible light. An agreement is reached, the seller gives the buyer full access to information in the expectation that new synergies between the merged companies will be revealed, and a second agreement can be reached. Instead, the buyer is surprised and unhappy when given full access to the seller's financial information. Not only does the buyer see no further synergies, but he believes he has overpaid for what he is getting.

Another problem with second agreements is how to distribute the additional value found by full sharing of information. If negotiators in Cartoon shared their confidential information, essentially making all the information in Exhibit 3.1 available to both negotiators, they would see that there is an additional $2 million to be gained and distributed by integrating runs and financing and adding *Strums* to their agreement. How should that additional value be distributed? Negotiators sometimes reach impasse over this problem because second agreements separate the integrative and distributive outcomes of negotiation. A better strategy is to agree to the distribution of integrative value before going looking for it in a second agreement.

A Summary of Advice About Offers. Following is a summary of advice about using offers in negotiation, including a few points not mentioned earlier:

- You can use offers to gather and to consolidate information for integrative agreements.
- When using offers to gather information, make sure you are using your offer-search knowledge structure (or mental script), not your offer-anchor knowledge structure.
- When using offers to consolidate, make multi-issue offers.

- Low-context negotiators will find it easier to get information from a series of multiple-issue offers than from a series of single-issue offers.

- Do not make offers that are unacceptable to you. The other party will assume that the offer is acceptable to you, or you would not have made it. If you back away from an offer, you lose credibility. Take time to construct and check your offer. Once you have offered something, it is hard to take it away unless you link the retraction to a concession elsewhere.

- Anchor offers so that you receive an adequate distributive outcome. This is especially important for equivalent proposals because they give all the additional integrative value to the other party. Make sure you are claiming adequate distributive value.

- Post offers visually on a flip chart or chalkboard, or write them on paper that you can hand to the other party. Make it easy for the other party to understand what you are offering.

- Make two or at most three equivalent proposals at a time. Don't overwhelm the other party.

- Have a computer and spreadsheet handy so that you can analyze offers quickly. Once you introduce offers into the negotiation, the other party is likely to do so too.

In this section we have seen that reaching an integrative agreement requires strategy for learning about the other party's interests and priorities, and for consolidating that information in offers that link integrative and distributive outcomes. In the next section we turn to distributive strategy to capture net value within an integrative agreement.

Distributive Strategies to Capture Net Value Within an Integrative Agreement

In multi-issue negotiations, distributive outcomes exist within integrative agreements. Here is what we already know about factors that affect distributive outcomes within integrative agreements:

- Early offers act as anchors, especially among low-context-culture negotiators.

- Anchoring may block the information search required for constructing integrative agreements.

- Separating integrative and distributive phases of the negotiation risks impasse if parties get greedy over distributing resources created by integrative bargaining.

- Negotiating one issue at a time jeopardizes the creation of integrative value and also separates integrative and distributive phases of the negotiation.

- Multi-issue offers link integrative and distributive outcomes.

In this section we address the question of how to claim as much net value as possible without leaving integrative value on the table and without risking an impasse. More specifically, we'll be looking at two distributive strategies: posturing and persuasion.

Posturing Strategy

According to the dictionary, to "posture" is to strike a pose, especially for an effect. When negotiators engage in posturing they are signaling, "I'm someone to deal with; this negotiation is going to take some effort on your part." Posturing is rather more subtle than just stating your positions on the issues. Posturing is conveying your status credentials for taking those positions. Exhibit 4.2 showed the two codes that we used to label statements that amount to posturing: information about one's own company and information about competitors. Above those two codes you can see also a code for "anti-status" statements—sympathy. Sympathy is an appeal to the other party's status: "I need you to do this for me because you have the ability to do it, and I don't."

Posturing is a rather indirect form of influence. Telling the other party about your status and asking for sympathy are both subtle influence attempts because both remind parties of their responsibilities in the social relationship. Thus we might expect negotiators from high-context, hierarchical cultures to engage in posturing.

Exhibit 4.8 shows the pattern of reciprocal posturing over time in the Cartoon negotiation for high-, low-, and mixed-context negotiators. The first thing to notice is that reciprocal posturing occurs in the first quarter and then drops off. This is consistent with theorizing about the stages of negotiation. Continuing to engage in reciprocal posturing after the first quarter would risk taking the negotiation into a no-win conflict spiral.[19] However, not posturing at all seems to violate knowledge structures of what negotiation is all about. Posturing plays a role in setting up the negotiation to proceed in the stage pattern we described at the start of this chapter.

The second thing to notice about Exhibit 4.8 is that it was the low-context negotiators who engaged in significantly more posturing in the first quarter than the high- or mixed-context negotiators. This frankly was a surprise to Wendi Adair and me; we had expected the opposite because of the cultural pattern of high context

Exhibit 4.8. Reciprocal Posturing Over Time.

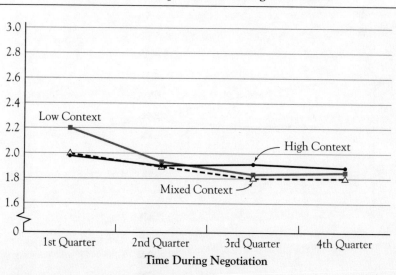

and hierarchy. But we're not inclined to jump to new conclusions based on these results. When results surprise researchers, it means more research is necessary! We are not ready to ignore a plethora of evidence outside this particular study that suggests that negotiators from high-context, hierarchical cultures open negotiations with posturing. It is possible, for example, that the Cartoon simulation does not provide enough status details to facilitate posturing by high-context negotiators.

The third thing to notice about Exhibit 4.8 is that after the first quarter there are no cultural differences in reciprocal posturing. In essence, Exhibit 4.8 tells us that reciprocal posturing across cultures occurs in the first quarter.

Exhibit 4.9 shows fewer occurrences of the structural *sequence* "Posture→Question" over time for low- and mixed-context negotiations. A structural sequence is a way to change the strategic direction of a negotiation.[20] The high-context negotiators did not engage in this transition. There are probably two reasons. First, as we have

Exhibit 4.9. Structural Sequences of Posturing→Questioning Over Time.

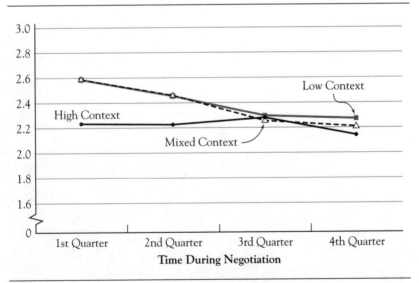

just seen in Exhibit 4.8, they engaged in less posturing in the first quarter then did low-context negotiators. Second, as we saw in Exhibit 4.3, they engaged in less questioning in the first quarter.

Posturing Strategy and Gains. As we know, distributive strategies such as posturing are motivated by the goal of claiming high net value. But distributive strategies may have opposite effects on negotiation outcomes when used in high- and low-context cultures. For example, we found that in low-context cultures, buyers' value-claiming motivated sellers to respond with information or offers. The result was just the opposite in high-context cultures. There, buyers' value-claiming motivated sellers to respond with posturing.

Earlier we discussed some reasons why distributive strategy may have a negative effect on joint gains. We also reported that counter-cultural strategizing (such as Japanese negotiators making first offers late or U.S. negotiators making first offers early) has a negative effect on joint gains. Two additional pieces of evidence that distributive strategy can have a negative effect on joint gains come from the Cartoon Strategy Study. Regardless of culture, negotiators who failed to make the transition from the distributive strategy of posturing to the integrative strategy of questioning in the second quarter of the negotiations generated significantly lower joint gains. They left money on the table. The same is true for negotiators who jeopardized their deals by using influence (any combination of posturing and persuasion) heavily in the fourth quarter. However, in the latter case, it seems likely negotiators using influence in the last quarter were desperately trying to get some movement from each other.

Advice for Using the Posturing Strategy. Even negotiations with integrative potential begin with posturing, but they will end in impasse or in low net value agreements unless posturing is transformed into information search. This structural strategic transition is particularly important for low-context negotiators. Here is some advice on how to make this transition:

- If you are going to posture be sure to accompany messages about status with positions on issues.

- If you are going to open the negotiations by posturing, be prepared to direct a structural strategic transition to questioning. Do this by asking a question about interests or priorities or by offering a little interest- or priority-based information about your own position.

Persuasion Strategy

Persuasion is our second distributive strategy. Persuasion is all about making rational arguments, as opposed to posturing, which is about making emotional appeals. Rational arguments may be telling the other party about your limits, telling why a concession is good for him or her, or telling why it is good for you. References to your own BATNA (what you will do if there is no agreement) are another form of rational argument, as are references to the other party's BATNA (for example, "Your alternative is not as good as you think it is because . . .").

Persuasion based on rational argument is direct communication. The meaning of the argument is in the words conveyed. A threat is also a rational argument, whether it is implicit, such as "My alternative is to make a deal with your competitor," or explicit: "If you do not concede on this point, then I will go ahead with negotiations with your competitor." It is always enlightening in a class to ask a negotiator, "Did you threaten the other party?" and get the answer, "No I just told him about my BATNA." When I ask the other party, "Did you perceive a threat?" I often get the answer, "Absolutely!" Because rational arguments are not subtle, we can expect low-context negotiators to be comfortable making them.

Persuasion is unlike posturing in that persuasion requires some understanding of the other party's positions. Until parties have exchanged at least some rudimentary positional information, they don't know what to persuade the other party to concede. This is another reason why posturing is most likely to occur in the first stage of the negotiation and persuasion comes later after some information has been exchanged via questioning or offers.

Exhibit 4.10 shows the pattern of structural sequences of persuasion and offers over time. Note the sequence here: negotiators are responding to persuasion by making offers that presumably are concessions. The direction of this pattern, persuasion→offer, suggests that rational argument works in terms of generating concessions. However, we did not see this pattern generating higher net value for buyers; at the same time, it does not generate lower net value either. This suggests that responding to persuasion with offers, especially in the later stages of the negotiation, moves the negotiation toward an outcome, but not necessarily a particularly good outcome.

Another thing to notice in Exhibit 4.10 is that the frequency of these persuasion→offer sequences increases with time, for both low- and high-context negotiators. This pattern is consistent with the idea that to be persuasive you first have to get some information about the other party's priorities and interests. The pattern is also

Exhibit 4.10. Structural Sequences of Persuasion→Offers Over Time.

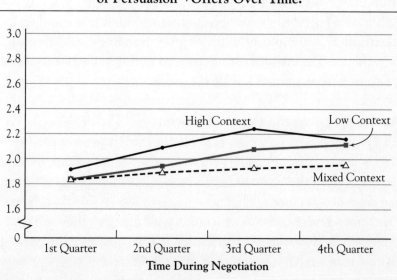

consistent with the evidence in Exhibit 4.6 that high-context-culture negotiators get information about positions via offers early in the negotiation.

Sequences, whether reciprocal or structural, bring regularity to the negotiation. When negotiators are engaged in sequencing they can predict each other's response. The flat pattern for the mixed-context negotiators is another indicator that these negotiators are engaged neither in a high- nor a low-context dance. The relatively low and flat pattern of mixed-context-culture negotiators in Exhibit 4.10 is consistent with their pattern in Exhibit 4.6. These mixed-context-culture negotiators are having problems dancing together. Interestingly, engaging in patterned behavior in mixed-culture pairs helps them create joint value and at the same time helps buyers claim value. This was true for both information sharing and influence attempts, further indication that the main challenge mixed-culture negotiators had was in generating patterned sequences of any type of behavior. When they did sequence information and influence attempts, their outcomes were better.

Do not interpret Exhibit 4.10 as suggesting that low-context negotiators do not use persuasion. Remember, Exhibit 4.10 shows structural *sequences* of persuasion and offers. Remember, too (from Exhibit 4.6), that high-context-culture negotiators use and reciprocate offers at significantly higher rates than low-context-culture negotiators. Thus this structural pattern in Exhibit 4.10 is not just a function of persuasion but also of offers.

Advice for Using the Persuasion Strategy. The evidence in Exhibit 4.10 is clear: persuasion peaks in the third quarter of the negotiation when parties are using persuasion to seek concessions. Impasse occurs rarely in the Cartoon negotiation, since there is a large potential zone of agreement. Therefore it seems reasonable that, by the third quarter, negotiators have a pretty good idea that they will reach agreement and so engage in persuasion to try to generate the greatest net value from that agreement. Stating limits and engaging in substantiation and argument at this stage are probably pretty low risk, especially if they generate concessions. However, discussing BATNA at this stage may stimulate a conflict spiral, especially in situations in which the zone of potential agreement is smaller than it is in the Cartoon simulation. If you are going to discuss BATNA, the Strategy Study data are very clear: get it over with in the third quarter. If you wait until the fourth quarter you will jeopardize your joint gains! Here is some advice for using the persuasion strategy:

- If you are going to engage in persuasion, get the sequence right. Wait for a concession after your persuasion attempt.

- Don't make references to limits such as reservation price too early in the negotiation. Once you have provided the other negotiator with this information, the negotiator will know exactly how much he or she will have to concede to get you to say yes.

- Use your BATNA only sparingly as a tactic of persuasion. Just providing information about your BATNA is likely to be viewed as a threat. The time to use your BATNA is when negotiations have stalled and you really are considering turning to your BATNA rather than continuing to negotiate.

Now that you understand how negotiation strategy plays out over the course of a negotiation, make a recording of one of your own negotiations and use the "Guide to Listening to Your Negotiation Audio Recording" on the CD-ROM to evaluate your own use of strategy.

Culture, Stage, Strategy, and Outcomes

Throughout the previous sections on using information and influence strategies, we have been discussing outcomes. In this section we pull together those important findings and generate advice for when and how to use strategy to generate individual and joint net value. We'll look at two aspects of outcomes: joint gains and the buyer's proportion of those gains.[21]

Exhibit 4.11 shows the mean level of joint and buyer gain for high-, low-, and mixed-context negotiations. High-context negotiators generated $3.5 million in joint gains, and buyers claimed $1.68

Exhibit 4.11. Individual and Joint Gain for
High-, Low-, and Mixed-Context Negotiations.

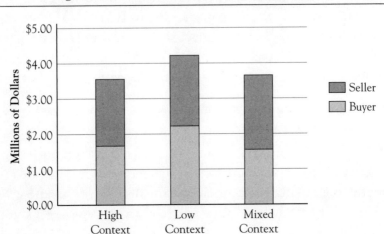

million in value. Low-context negotiators generated $4.2 million
in joint gains, and low-context buyers claimed $2.22 million in
value. Mixed-context negotiators generated $3.7 million in joint
gains, and mixed-context buyers claimed $1.56 million in value.

In summarizing, we'll begin with advice that applies to both low-
and high-context cultures, then move on to specific advice for each.

Strategy and Outcomes Regardless of Culture

Here's what the data from the Cartoon Strategy Study suggest you
should be doing to negotiate high joint gains:

- Get information sharing going immediately. Use the question-
  and-answer strategy or use the offer strategy, but in either case
  get started. Negotiators who are sharing less information in
  the first half of the negotiation are doomed to leave money on
  the table!
- Do not sabotage your deal in the fourth quarter by trying to
  influence each other using posturing and persuasion.

Here's what the data indicate buyers should be doing if they want to claim value:

- Reciprocate information sharing. Buyers who claimed value were in pairs that engaged in information sharing from the first quarter.

- Respond to posturing with information. This helps turn the negotiation toward integrative strategy.

Strategy for High-Context Negotiators

Here's what to do to maximize joint gains in a high-context negotiation:

- Avoid reciprocating questions and answers at stage 1.
- Don't jeopardize your deal by engaging in influence attempts in stage 4.

Here's what to do to claim value in a high-context negotiation:

- Don't respond to posturing with information in stage 2 or stage 3.

Strategy for Low-Context Negotiators

Here's what to do to claim value in low-context negotiation:

- Share information using questions and answers, and offers, especially in stage 1.
- Respond to posturing with offers.

Strategy for Mixed-Context Negotiators

Here's what to do to claim value in a mixed-context negotiation:

- Engage in reciprocal information sharing at all time periods.
- Respond to posturing with information or an offer.

Using Stages of Negotiation to Judge Progress

Negotiations generally move through stages of positioning, information gathering, generating solutions via information consolidation and persuasion, and reaching agreement. What negotiators do in the first half of the negotiations has significant implications for the joint gains that they generate at the end. Negotiators who understand the temporal nature of the negotiation process should be able to use the stage model to judge the progress of their negotiation. Just as negotiators use their BATNAs to evaluate offers, they can use the stage model to evaluate their progress. Finding progress lacking, negotiators can use structural transitions to move the negotiation to the next stage.

A Culturally Informed Model

Exhibit 4.12 summarizes the strategic activity that we found occurring in the Cartoon simulation. Note that information gathering goes on throughout the negotiation. Negotiators who do not get information sharing going during the first quarter are significantly more likely to leave money on the table. Negotiators across cultures begin to get serious about information consolidation in the third and fourth quarters using offers to integrate the information that they have acquired earlier in the negotiation. Influence attempts occur throughout the negotiation, but they become patterned in the first quarter with posturing and questioning among low-context negotiators and with persuasion and offers in the third and fourth quarters.

Exhibit 4.12 also indicates how negotiations are culturally specific in that different types of cultures enact integrative tasks differently. For example, negotiators from high-context cultures reciprocated the offer strategy more and the questioning strategy less than did negotiators from low-context cultures.

Finally, Exhibit 4.12 summarizes how negotiators shift between distributive and integrative strategies in culturally specific ways. For

Exhibit 4.12. A Culturally Informed Stage Model of Negotiations.

Strategy	Cultural Context	Stage 1	Stage 2	Stage 3	Stage 4
Information Gathering	Low	Q & A	Q & A	Q & A	Q & A
	Mixed	Q & A	Q & A	Q & A	Q & A
	High	Offers	Offers	Offers	Offers
Information Consolidation	Low	—	—	Offers	Offers
	Mixed	—	—	Offers	Offers
	High	—	—	Offers	Offers
Posturing	Low	Posturing → Questioning	Posturing → Questioning	—	—
	Mixed	Posturing → Questioning	Posturing → Questioning	—	—
	High	—	—	—	—
Persuading	Low	—	—	—	—
	Mixed	—	—	—	—
	High	—	—	Persuading → Offers	—

example, negotiators from low-context and mixed-context cultures sequenced posturing with questioning more than did those from high-context cultures (especially in the first and second quarters), and negotiators from high-context cultures sequenced persuasion and offers more than did negotiators from low-context cultures in the third quarter.

The Ongoing Challenge of Mixed-Culture Negotiating

The Cartoon Strategy Study data show that culturally unique uses of negotiation strategy are fine so long as negotiators remain within their own cultures. What happens when negotiations cross cultural boundaries is well illustrated by the mixed-culture groups in our study.

They only develop systematic sequencing of questioning behaviors. They do not seem able to make transitions, from information search to information consolidation, as the low-context-culture negotiators do, or from persuasion to offers, as the high-context-culture negotiators do. Mixed-culture negotiations appear unpatterned compared with either the low- or high-context-culture negotiations. The mixed-context-culture negotiators do not appear to have knowledge structures that become accessible when they realize they are negotiating across cultural boundaries. Instead they appear to be building those knowledge structures as they go—a formidable task to accomplish at the same time as trying to negotiate a multiple-issue agreement. What to do?

In a mixed-culture negotiation that lasts from a few weeks to a few months, it is unlikely that negotiators are going to generate knowledge structures that fuse their cultural differences. It seems more likely that one or the other is going to have to abandon a culturally familiar strategic negotiation style and take up as much as possible the other party's strategic negotiation style. Clearly, taking up a low-context negotiation style requires more than reciprocating questioning. It also requires learning how to make the transition from questioning to consolidation of information into offers. And taking up a high-context negotiation style requires more than making early offers. It requires using offers to search as opposed to using offers to anchor negotiations. Excellent global negotiators need to be prepared with both high- and low-context knowledge structures for negotiation.

Consolidating Knowledge About Negotiation Strategy

The next chapters turn to different negotiating venues: dispute resolution, teams, and social dilemmas. Everything in the first four chapters of this book is relevant to negotiating in those venues, so let's review what we've covered:

In Chapter One we became familiar with all the basic building blocks of negotiation strategy: parties, positions, issues, interests, priorities, BATNAs, reservation price, and target. We learned how to use all these concepts to produce a Negotiation Planning Document. We learned a little about integrative and distributive negotiation strategy.

In Chapter Two we acquired an in-depth understanding of culture and also worked with a model that explains how culture affects negotiators' interests, priorities, and negotiation strategies.

In Chapter Three we took a close look at criteria for good and bad deals and then plunged into how to analyze a negotiation for integrative potential. Looking at some cultural differences in integrative and distributive outcomes underlined the importance of going after integrative value.

In this chapter we have learned how to do that. We saw that negotiators have two strategic compulsions: the need for information and the need to influence. We also saw that negotiators from high- and low-context cultures enact those compulsions rather differently.

As we move to see how negotiation strategy works in the venues of dispute resolution, teams, and social dilemmas, we will rely on and extend our understanding of deal-making negotiations.

Chapter Five

Resolving Disputes

Conflict is the perception of opposing interests. Conflict occurs when people are interdependent, need to share resources, and find that they have opposing interests concerning how those resources should be distributed.[1] For example, Shuji Nakamura, the inventor of the Blue LED, received ¥20,000 (about $200) for his invention. Court records estimate that Nichia Corporation, his employer at the time of the invention, would generate ¥120.8 billion (about $120.8 million) over the lifetime of the patents. Nakamura asked for more, which he expressed as the claim, "You owe me more compensation." Nichia rejected his claim, saying, "No, we already paid you all the compensation you are entitled to."[2]

At this point the conflict between Nakamura and Nichia Corporation became a *dispute*. A conflict is the perception of opposing interests; a dispute is a rejected claim.[3] In the continuation of this dispute, Nakamura filed a lawsuit claiming ownership of the patent and requesting ¥2 billion (about $200 million) in compensation (see "Nichia Corporation Versus Shuji Nakamura" on the CD-ROM).

No culture is immune from conflicts and disputes. People everywhere in the world experience conflict, make and reject claims, and try to resolve disputes. How they do so varies systematically with culture. Culture affects which claims are made, why they are rejected, and how disputes are resolved. The cross-cultural negotiator, armed with a fundamental understanding of dispute resolution and sensitivity to culture, should be prepared to negotiate the resolution of disputes regardless of where in the world the dispute occurs.

This chapter begins by explaining how disputes arise and why they tend to escalate. Then it introduces three approaches to resolving disputes: interests, rights, and power. Within that discussion, it also discusses options for confronting conflict directly or indirectly and when each option is culturally appropriate.

How Disputes Arise and Escalate

Not all conflicts turn into disputes. Contracts are carefully crafted and relationships carefully cultivated to minimize misunderstandings that lead to disputes. Yet neither the contractual nor the relationship approach to minimizing disputes is foolproof within cultures, much less across cultures. Claims are made and rejected because not every contingency can be anticipated at the time a contract is signed and not every difference in interpretation can be identified and resolved in advance. Claims are made and rejected also because not all relationships are strong enough to overcome the cost and disappointment of an unfulfilled expectation.

Too, disputing is often emotional. People tend to take the rejection of their claims personally. Deal making can become emotional, but deal-making negotiations do not normally start out with outraged, angry, hurt, unhappy negotiators. Dispute resolution negotiations often do. Disputes over goals and resources (called *task conflict*) and disputes over means, including the dispute resolution process itself (called *procedural conflict*), may easily spill over into *interpersonal conflict*, with each party blaming the other. When claims are made and rejected, peoples' self-respect is affronted—for example, "How dare Nichia claim that the patents were a corporate-wide effort?" Once an event is framed as an insult, emotions are engaged and dispute resolution negotiations may not only have to resolve the issues in dispute but also have to restore the honor and self-respect of the disputants. Let's look at three basic approaches to dealing with these difficult situations.

Interests, Rights, and Power:
Three Approaches to Resolving Disputes

There are three approaches to resolving disputes: negotiators can identify their *interests* and integrate them; they can try to determine who has *rights* under some standard of rules, contract, law, or precedent; or they can determine who has more *power* and the weak party can concede. Exhibit 5.1 shows these three approaches to dispute resolution as concentric circles, with interests embedded within rights and rights embedded within power.[4] The concentric circles indicate that negotiations focused on interests occur within the context of who is right and who is wrong under some rights standard. Negotiations focused on the rights occur within the context of who is more powerful.

Negotiating to resolve a dispute via integrating interests, determining rights, or relying on power is a dynamic process. It can start in the interests, the rights, or the power circle, but it does not necessarily stay in the circle in which it begins.

Exhibit 5.1. Three Approaches to Resolving Disputes.

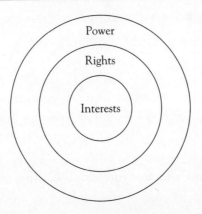

Source: W. L. Ury, J. M. Brett, and S. B. Goldberg, *Getting Disputes Resolved: Designing a System to Cut the Costs of Conflict* (Cambridge, Mass.: Program on Negotiation, Harvard Law School, 1993). Reprinted by permission of John Wiley & Sons, Inc.

As an example of this kind of shift, recall the dispute described in Chapter One between the U.S. and Chinese joint venture managers over data. When the U.S. manager realized the report was not providing the data he had expected he called his Chinese counterpart to ask for a meeting to discuss his data needs. She politely put him off. A day later he was called into her manager's office and told that there was no problem with the report: it was exactly as it had always been, and would not be changed. The U.S. manager, who had not been angry at his Chinese counterpart, was now furious. From his cultural perspective his counterpart's behavior—refusing to meet with him and then getting her superior involved, was inappropriate. He had wanted to talk about his interests; she had escalated the dispute to power by involving her superior. She was content with this culturally appropriate approach. She had maintained harmony. He was offended, worried about always having to work through her boss to work with her in the future, and concerned that if his U.S. superiors learned that he could not manage conflict with his joint-venture peers, his career would be affected. From her perspective the conflict was resolved; from his, it was ongoing.

The next three sections elaborate on interests, rights, and power as approaches to resolving disputes. They illustrate how each of these approaches is used in different cultures. They also give advice for analyzing a dispute from each of these three perspectives.

Uncovering Interests

Interests are the reasons why claims are made and rejected. They are the needs and concerns underlying parties' positions on the issues in dispute.

Self-Interests and Collective Interests.   Culture affects the relative importance of self-interests versus collective interests.[5] People all over the world are concerned with realizing their goals and being respected by others, as well as with achieving the goals of the social groups to which they belong and acting in ways that reflect positively on those groups. In individualist cultures, self-interests generally take precedence over collective interests. In collective cultures, collective interests generally take precedence over self-interests. Of course, people from collective cultures have self-interests and people from individualist cultures have collective interests; it is just that when they act within their own culture, the stimuli of everyday life cue culturally consistent behavior. When one disputant is from a collective culture and the other is from an individualist culture, there may be an opportunity to trade self-interests off against collective interests. But there may also be frustration and misunderstanding, because a primary focus on self-interests as opposed to a primary focus on collective interests can lead to different outcomes.

In one of our studies using a dispute simulation called Summer Interns, we compared the way Hong Kong Chinese and U.S. managers resolved a dispute between the director of human resources and the director of engineering for a heavy-construction company.[6] The dispute was over the hiring of summer interns. Companies in many cultures hire university students as summer interns. The primary purpose of these programs is long-term recruiting. Summer internships provide both students and companies with information on which to base a postgraduation offer of permanent employment. A secondary purpose of summer internships is relatively low-cost temporary labor. In our Summer Interns scenario, Engineering asked for summer interns early because Engineering had work for them. HR was not able to supply the interns, and Engineering went out and hired two on its own. HR then claimed that the two interns hired by Engineering would not be part of the summer interns program and that Engineering would have to pay for them itself. Thus there were two interrelated issues that needed to be resolved immediately: who was going to pay for the two summer interns that Engineering had already hired and whether these two employees were going to be participating in all of HR's summer interns programs, such as orientation and mentorship. There were numerous other issues, including how and when future interns would be hired.

Most of the Hong Kong Chinese managers were uncomfortable in the Summer Interns dispute resolution simulation. They told us they would prefer to discuss the problem with their boss. But since we did not provide a boss, they tended to resolve the two immediate issues and direct the other issues to a committee of peers who also used summer interns in their departments. Most of the U.S. managers negotiated fairly elaborate agreements, often resolving first how they were going to interact with each other in the future over summer interns and then deciding what to do about the immediate problem.

Different patterns of interests generate different outcomes. Which outcome do you prefer, the Hong Kong Chinese managers' agreements that took into account the collective interests of those not at the table or the U.S. managers' agreements that resolved all the issues at one meeting? It depends a little on your perspective, doesn't it? If you were the Engineering manager and your interests were met, the multifaceted U.S. solution would be both expedient and best. If your interests were not met, involving your peers in other departments in a thorough evaluation of the program might result in a better, if less expedient, outcome. If you were one of these managers' peers and the resolution of their dispute would likely set a precedent for your future summer interns, would you prefer the U.S. or the Hong Kong Chinese model?

Advice for Analyzing Interests. When negotiating with disputants from collective cultures, disputants from individualist cultures are most likely to err by underestimating the extent of concern for the collective on the part of the collective-culture disputants. Disputants from individualist cultures need to keep in mind that managers in collective cultures share many similarities to union leaders and political leaders, whose continuity in office depends on their ability to deliver value to their constituencies. In collective cultures, future social status depends on the maintenance of relationships and harmony within the social group. When a negotiation process or outcome imperils relationships or harmony, social well-being is threatened. No wonder disputants from collective cultures are so concerned about the collective interest.

Recall the Negotiation Planning Document first presented in Chapter One. When adapting it to analyze a dispute that crosses collective-individualist boundaries, it may be wise to add a column representing the positions, interests, and priorities of the collective, in addition to columns for each of the parties at the negotiating table.

It may be difficult to guess negotiators' interests. Sometimes historical and cultural information can help. In the Blue LED example that opened this chapter, the inventor, Nakamura, wanted to be compensated for his invention commensurate with his contribution. Underlying that position may have been a collective interest as well. The Blue LED was a major breakthrough, perhaps worthy of a Nobel Prize. If any Japanese inventor was in a position to challenge the ambiguity of Japanese patent law that seems to provide nonexclusive rights for the employee for his invention, it was Nakamura.[7]

In thinking about uncovering interests, keep the following thoughts in mind:

- Culture affects the relative importance of self-interests and collective interests, and the relative importance of these two different types of interests can lead to different outcomes.

- Do not underestimate the importance of collective interests when negotiating with a disputant from a collective culture or the importance of self-interests when negotiating with a disputant from an individualist culture.

- Why and why not (as in "Why are you rejecting my claim?" and "Why can't you grant my request?") are the fundamental questions for uncovering interests across cultures. Negotiators from high-context cultures, however, may be uncomfortable with direct questions, and you may be better off making proposals to uncover their interests.

Integrative Agreements for Resolving Disputes

Once you know the other disputant's interests, there are a number of ways to identify integrative solutions besides trading off low-valued interests for high-valued ones. Some disputes can be resolved if the party rejecting the claim will take a onetime, non-precedent-setting step. Reconsider our joint venture example. The Chinese manager might have been willing to provide the requested data on a onetime basis, giving the U.S. manager time to look for other sources for the information he needed. Or perhaps the Chinese manager rejected the U.S. manager's claim because he felt that the data requested would be unreliable and hence of little value. A limited-duration experiment with criteria for evaluation would have met such an interest quite nicely. Often disputes uncover fundamental problems, and disputants are satisfied with a plan to work on those problems. The Chinese manager might have said, "I'd be happy to give you that information if I could get it using the software that we've got, but I can't. Can you help me make a case for purchasing a new software package so we can get the information you need?" Finally, sometimes a short-term fix is enough. The Chinese manager might have offered, "I can't give you exactly what you want, but I could give you something similar." Exhibit 5.2 identifies six different types of integrative agreements for resolving disputes. Knowing interests may lead to non-precedent-setting solutions, limited-duration experiments, or the discovery of fundamental problems that both parties agree need to be managed more effectively.

Determining Right and Wrong

Rights are embedded in standards of fairness, corporate rules, contract, law, or precedent. As compared to interests, rights are abstract, generalized principles. Disputants justify making and rejecting claims with a variety of rights standards. The U.S. manager requesting new data used an implied fairness standard: "I need these data to . . ." The Chinese boss, in rejecting the claim, relied

Exhibit 5.2. Integrative Agreements for Resolving Disputes.

Type of Agreement	Description
Trade-off agreement	Agreement in which parties make concessions on low-priority issues in order to gain more on high-priority issues
Narrowly focused agreement	Agreement that focuses on the particular circumstances of the dispute, as opposed to the general principle underlying the dispute
Limited-duration agreement	Agreement to try something for a limited time and then evaluate before continuing
Contingent agreement	Agreement that depends on another event, usually in the future
Broadly focused agreement	Agreement that focuses on the interests underlying the dispute
Future-based agreement	Agreement that deals with the future before dealing with the past

on precedent: "The report contains what it has always contained." He could have used a fairness justification: "You should have asked for what you wanted before the report was compiled. It's not fair that she be asked to rerun the report for some after-the-fact notion of yours." When the dispute between Nichia and Nakamura transformed into a lawsuit, the claim and its rejection rested on differing interpretations of Japanese patent law. Nakamura took the position that the law provided nonexclusive rights to the employee for his invention, and Nichia claimed that it owned the patent because it had paid Nakamura ¥20,000 in compensation.

Rights standards endow claims with legitimacy, and in principle, legitimate claims should be easier to accept. In fact, three characteristics of rights standards make rights-based dispute resolution problematic. First, a single standard may be interpreted in contradictory relevant ways. Second, several relevant potential rights standards may contradict each other about what the outcome (for example, who wins) should be. Third, imposing a rights standard on a dispute generates a win-lose, distributive outcome. People resist negotiating losses. Instead, they agree to disagree about who is right and who is wrong and escalate the dispute to a greater degree within the rights circle (for example, by going to court); or beyond rights to the wider context of power.

Some rights standards are explicit, like laws and contracts that result from negotiations in which parties agree to terms and conditions to govern their interactions. Other rights standards are implicit, as in the case of norms such as deference to status or age, and standards of fairness, such as equity and equality. Explicit standards are codified and enforced by social institutions such as organizational hierarchies, the police, and the courts. Implicit standards are embedded in the cultures of social groups and enforced by social acceptance and social ostracism.

Using Rights in Different Cultures. The basic principle of fairness as a justification for making and rejecting claims extends across cultures. However, reliance on one versus another standard of fairness varies with culture because values (what is important) and norms (what is appropriate) extend only to the boundaries of social groups.[8]

Catherine Tinsley audiotaped and transcribed managers from Germany, the United States, and Japan as they tried to resolve the Summer Interns dispute.[9] She coded every argument and justification used during the forty-five minutes allowed for negotiation. Exhibit 5.3 shows her definitions and some examples of explicit rules, implicit rules, future rules, and precedent. Exhibits 5.4 through 5.7 illustrate her findings with respect to various rights standards. The data in these figures illustrate significant differences from what would be expected if culture did not matter. Technically, they are called residuals from expected values. If managers in a cultural group are using a behavior as frequently as expected (given what else they are discussing), the residual will be zero. If they are using it more than expected, the residual is positive, and if using it less than expected, the residual is negative.[10]

RESOLVING DISPUTES 125

Exhibit 5.3. Coding Rights Standards in the Summer Interns Study.

Code	Statement Type	Example	Explanation
Explicit rules	References to explicit rules, procedures, or regulations	"Did you post the job for 48 hours?" "I consider that I am due two interns."	Provides a standard with organizational legitimacy on which to base an agreement
Implicit rules	References to implied rules, standards, and norms. Statements about fairness or "rightness or wrongness" of actions.	"You're setting a bad example." "I don't think that's a fair distribution." "You are not supposed to hire on your own."	Provides a standard with social legitimacy on which to base an agreement
Precedent	Salient actions that happened in the past	"SIP always starts in June." "This is similar to last year's case."	Provides a historical precedent on which to base an agreement
Future rules	Proposals to create future rules to govern the relationship	"From now on I promise interns within three weeks." "Next year, how about if I come to you?"	Provides standards for how the problem will be dealt with in the future; may be coupled with a withdrawal of the current claim

Source: Courtesy of Catherine H. Tinsley. See also Catherine H. Tinsley, "How We Get to Yes: Predicting the Constellation of Strategies Used Across Cultures to Negotiate Conflict," *Journal of Applied Psychology*, 2001, 83, 316–323. Reprinted by permission.

Exhibits 5.4 through 5.7 show a very interesting pattern of cultural differences in the use of rights standards. Exhibits 5.4 and 5.5 show that the German managers were more likely to use explicit and implicit rights standards when negotiating than were the U.S. managers. The U.S. managers, in contrast, were more likely than German or Japanese managers to set up rules to govern future interaction (how the summer interns would be hired in the future) when negotiating (see Exhibit 5.6). Exhibit 5.7 shows that the Japanese managers were more likely to rely on precedent when negotiating than were German or U.S. managers. In short, the data suggest that when resolving disputes the Germans look to rules, the Americans to the future, and the Japanese to the past.

Using Rights to Resolve Disputes. Trying to use rights standards to resolve disputes can be extremely frustrating. Often one standard is used to justify a claim and another to justify rejecting it. Which standard should prevail? If the two parties agreed on the rights standard, they would not have a dispute in the first place. The process

Exhibit 5.4. References to Explicit Rules, Procedures, Regulations, and Jurisdictions in the Summer Interns Study.

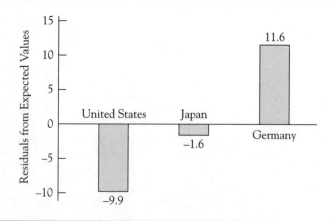

Source: Courtesy of Catherine H. Tinsley. Reprinted by permission.

Exhibit 5.5. Statements About Fairness and Norms in the Summer Interns Study.

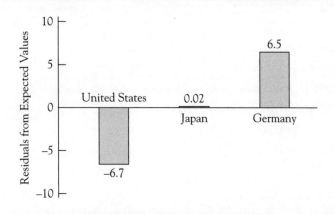

Source: Courtesy of Catherine H. Tinsley. Reprinted by permission.

Exhibit 5.6. Establishing Future Rules in the Summer Interns Study.

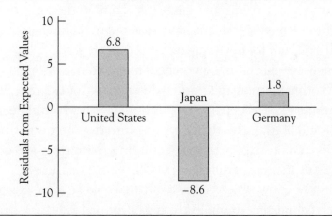

Source: Courtesy of Catherine H. Tinsley. Reprinted by permission.

Exhibit 5.7. Reliance on Precedent in the Summer Interns Study.

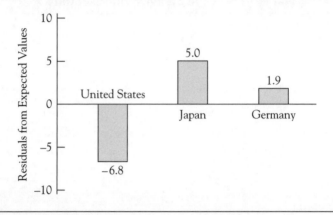

Source: Courtesy of Catherine H. Tinsley. Reprinted by permission.

of rights-based dispute resolution is one of searching for an acceptable rights-based standard. But any standard suggested by one party will be viewed as self-serving by the other party.[11] The U.S. manager in the joint-venture dispute made his claim on the basis of need. The Chinese manager might have rejected his claim based on equity: "It's not fair for me to have to rerun the report."

When we add cultural differences in preferences for rights standards to other cultural and normal differences (for example, which rights standard best supports my position, versus which rights standard should apply), the rights approach to dispute resolution becomes even more frustrating and confusing. Within a given culture there is still an array of different possible fairness standards, making it difficult to know which rights standard would be most acceptable in which culture. For example, the major cultural influences on Chinese negotiating style suggest that there are actually *three* "normative" standards in China: need, equality, and equity.[12] The Confucian legacy in China, which emphasizes hierarchy and tradition and teaches social responsibility, supports the need standard. Chairman Mao's vision of communism supports the equality norm. Sun-Tzu's ancient principles in *The Art of War*, which emphasize strategy, deception, and taking advantage of an adversary's misfortune, support an equity principle, that is, the strong will prevail.[13]

What to do?

- Realize that when suggesting a rights standard for resolving a dispute, you and the other party are each going to suggest a standard that results in a self-beneficial outcome.
- When weighing potential rights standards, think about what the other party might consider fair.
- Recognize that using a rights standard to resolve a dispute ordinarily means that one party will win and the other will lose. This makes it difficult for disputants to agree on which standard to apply.

Rights-based negotiation strategies do settle some disputes. Disputants may change their positions when new credible information becomes available to interpret a situation or a standard. Lawyers, for example, seek evidence and search for legal precedents. New evidence that is credible and clear may encourage disputants to withdraw claims or grant them. When new credible evidence makes the basis for claims uncertain, disputants may compromise, shift their dispute resolution focus and seek an interests-based settlement, or seek to clarify the rights standard.

Rights-based settlements may also occur after disputants consider their BATNA—what will happen if no agreement is reached. If a third party is likely to get involved, disputants may consider how persuasive their rights standard is likely to be with that third party. Concluding that your argument is not very persuasive may motivate you to concede to the other party's standard.

Intuitively, persuasion (rational argument, which we discussed thoroughly in Chapter Four) would seem to be an appropriate way to convince the other party that you are right and he or she is wrong under some rights standard. In fact, argument that does not contain new credible information is widely perceived as self-serving and is consequently ineffectual. When one party withdraws or grants a claim after a fierce argument in which no new information was exchanged, the concession is as likely motivated by a decision that pursuing the claim was not worth the costs or by a desire to restore harmony as by enlightenment.

In thinking about rights and culture, keep the following in mind:

- Culture affects how strongly disputants rely on rights standards and the standards they prefer to use.

- It is difficult to know which standard will be acceptable to the other disputant. This is so because there are so many different rights standards and because different aspects of culture support different standards.

- Rights standards are often suspect and therefore discounted. After all, disputants are unlikely to propose a rights standard that does not benefit them.

- The key to success in using rights standards to resolve disputes is either to propose a standard that the other disputant will agree is fair or to provide new credible information that makes the proposed standard appear fair. Without new credible information, argument is unlikely to work.

Using Power to Resolve Disputes

Power is the ability to get what you want from a dispute—to have your claim granted or your rejection upheld. Theoreticians talk about power in terms of dependency. In general, the more dependent you are, the less powerful you are. If you have good alternatives, you are less dependent and therefore more powerful.[14]

Understanding power in terms of dependency makes it easier to see how both status and BATNA are alternative indicators of power. As we discussed in Chapter Two, in hierarchical cultures high-status parties are viewed as powerful, because they have greater access to resources than do low-status parties. High-status parties can help low-status parties and culturally are expected to do so. In return, low-status parties defer to high-status parties. In Chapter One we pointed out that BATNA is a source of power because the better your BATNA the more you can demand of the other party, since you have a pretty good alternative to turn to.

In disputes, figuring out who is more powerful is not as easy as just determining who has the higher status or better BATNA. In disputes especially, parties evaluate their power through self-serving and cultural lenses. People do not like to lose; because admission is tantamount to conceding, people do not like to admit they are the low-power party in a negotiation. It is easy to see after the fact that the U.S. manager in the joint-venture example was not powerful. He did not get what he wanted. But what about before he made the claim? Had he known in advance that his request was not only hopeless but also risked censure he might not have made the claim in the first place. Surely he did not view his claim as without merit or himself as powerless to promote the claim.

Linked BATNAS. As mentioned in Chapter One, negotiators' BATNAs are usually linked in disputing. Just saying no in dispute resolution negotiations does not make the claim go away. The other party can continue to press the claim—to a boss, to peers, to the press, to court—and you have to deal with it.

The Blue LED example illustrates how BATNAs are linked in dispute resolution. When Nakamura could not reach a negotiated agreement with Nichia Corporation, he filed a lawsuit to gain control of the patent. Apparently Nakamura expected to win because Japanese law allows patents to be assigned to the individual inventor even when they are working for a firm. Nichia also no doubt expected to win because it had filed the patents and paid Nakamura the standard patent compensation. The court ruled that Nichia owned the patent but that Nakamura was entitled to reasonable compensation for his efforts.[15]

A lower court then awarded Nakamura the full $190 million that he sought. Nichia appealed. The higher court gave the parties three months to negotiate an agreement, saying that if they did not reach agreement by the deadline the court would decide. This time a negotiated agreement was reached. Nakamura got ¥843 billion (about $8.4 million) and Nichia got exclusive control over 159 other patents that had been developed by Nakamura while working for Nichia.[16]

In deal-making negotiations, it is wise to consider the other party's BATNA in order to understand his or her reservation price. In dispute resolution negotiations, it is critical to understand the other party's BATNA. Instead of focusing mainly on your own BATNA, think about the *other* party's BATNA. Besides knowing your best alternative, you need to know what your *worst* alternative is. What is the worst thing the other party can do to you? Nakamura's best alternative to an impasse in negotiations was to take Nichia to court and win. Nakamura's worst alternative was to take Nichia to court and lose. Since Nakamura neither had control over the Blue LED patents nor had received much compensation for them, he didn't have much more than time and legal costs to lose going to court. While such transaction costs of disputing were probably not trivial in this situation, Nakamura's decision to go to court is understandable even if he thought he had less than a 50–50 chance of prevailing. In contrast, Nichia had a lot to lose: patent control and a potentially huge cash payment. Given that exposure, Nichia would have to be awfully certain it would prevail before negotiating to an impasse with Nakamura. Of course, we'll never know if both parties in the Blue LED dispute had a clear vision of their BATNAs. But the failure to understand how BATNAs are linked and the failure to be able to see your BATNA without self-serving bias are probably the most common mistakes dispute resolution negotiators make.

Differences by Culture in the Use of Power in Disputes. Disputants from different cultures use power rather differently. In the Summer Interns study, Catherine Tinsley found that Japanese managers were more likely than either German or U.S. managers to use power-based strategies.[17] Exhibit 5.8 shows Tinsley's coding of three

Exhibit 5.8. Coding Power Tactics in the Summer Interns Study.

Code	Statement Type	Example	Explanation
Blaming and shaming	Accusatory, disapproving statement	"You make a sham out of this process."	Used to shame other into taking responsibility or making a concession
Threat, ultimatum	Statements that suggest negative consequences associated with continuing current behavior	"If it doesn't go as quickly as it should, then we are forced to take things into our own hands."	Used to intimidate other into making a concession to avoid threatened negative consequences
Powerful people	Suggesting that powerful people support your position	"Besides us, many other departments are unhappy." "Why don't we ask the board what it thinks?"	Suggests negative social sanctions unless concession is made

different power strategies: blaming and shaming, threats and ulti-matums, and involvement of powerful people.

Exhibits 5.9 through 5.11 show the significant patterns of dif-ferent uses of power among Germans, Japanese, and Americans doing the Summer Interns simulation. Recall that the bar graphs show deviations from expected values, represented by 0. A positive bar means the behavior was exhibited more than expected, a nega-tive bar that it was exhibited less than expected.

Tinsley suggests that the power strategy is more comfortably used in Asian than other cultures because of the hierarchical social strat-ification of those cultures.[18] This is certainly the pattern in Exhibits 5.9 through 5.11. Exhibit 5.9 shows that the Japanese engaged in more "blaming and shaming" than the Germans or Americans. In hierarchical cultures such acts remind a disputant of his or her role in society (which the claim and rejection indicate he or she forgot). According to one close observer of Japanese dispute resolution style,

**Exhibit 5.9. Blaming and Shaming
Power Tactics in the Summer Interns Study.**

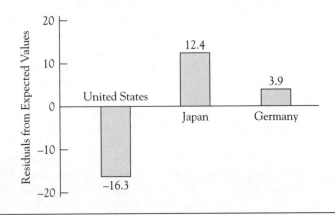

Source: Courtesy of Catherine H. Tinsley. Reprinted by permission.

the more emotional the appeal the more likely it is to be persuasive, because to refuse to concede in the face of such a plea, the recipient would have to ignore his or her role in society.[19]

Exhibit 5.10 shows the use of threats. Note that the scale here is much smaller than in the other exhibits. This indicates that threats were not used as much as the other power tactics. However the pattern in Exhibit 5.10 is the same as in Exhibit 5.9. The Japanese were more likely than the Americans to use threats. (There will be more about threats in the section that follows.)

Exhibit 5.11 shows that Japanese managers were also trying to enhance their power by alluding to the support of powerful others.[20] This too, is consistent with hierarchical culture. If you do not have the status yourself to bring about the other disputant's concession, perhaps the other disputant will concede when he or she realizes that you have a relationship with others who are powerful. It is not an empty threat. In hierarchical, high-context, collective cultures, conflict is not viewed as an isolated event. Therefore involving others who have a broader view of the context of the conflict makes perfect sense from this perspective.

Exhibit 5.10. Threats in the Summer Interns Study.

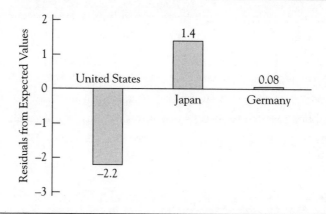

Source: Courtesy of Catherine H. Tinsley. Reprinted by permission.

Exhibit 5.11. Allusions to Powerful People in the Summer Interns Study.

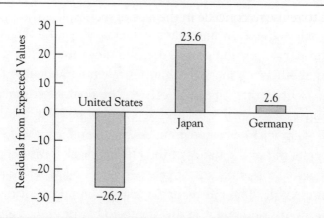

Source: Courtesy of Catherine H. Tinsley. Reprinted by permission.

Using Power to Win and Lose

An irony comes with using power: if you have to use power it costs you, and sometimes when you use power and win, you also lose.

Advice for Making Threats. The key to using power effectively is to make threats that you are willing to carry out but that you do not have to, because there are transaction costs and relationship costs of following through on threats. Here is some advice for making threats:

- Threaten the other party's interests. Get their attention.
- Be clear about what the other party needs to do to avoid the threat being acted on. "If you do not do _____, then I will do _____."
- Do not make threats you are unwilling to carry out. Following through should hurt them more than it costs you.

To understand these important elements of making threats, let's work through an example from the Summer Interns study. If the HR and engineering managers cannot reach an agreement, each has the ability to threaten the other. The engineering manager might threaten to involve his peer department heads in the dispute over the summer interns program, essentially taking the design of the program out of the hands of the HR manager. This is a potentially effective threat because it gets to the HR manager's interests, and it is credible. The HR manager wants to retain control of the summer interns program; the threat gets to her interests because it threatens her control. The threat is credible, because involving the other department heads is definitely something the engineering manager could do, even though it would cost him time and effort.

When Winning Is Losing. Any time there is an ongoing relationship between disputants or the potential for a future relationship, winning a power contest is likely to lose the relationship. Back to our Summer Interns example: if the engineering manager follows through on his threat, he is still going to have to continue working with the HR manager. If the engineering manager involves the other department heads and effectively takes control of the summer interns program away from the HR manager, she is likely to be very reluctant to cooperate with him on other future employment matters. Thus using power to win may turn out to be a rather empty victory when parties have to continue to work together.

Advice for Using Power

In thinking about power and culture, keep the following ideas in mind:

- Power in disputing is different from power in deal making in one key respect: disputants' BATNAs are linked. Instead of considering the best alternative for you if no agreement can be reached, it is important to consider what the other party can do to you if no agreement can be reached. Instead of your best alternative, consider your worst alternative to a negotiated agreement.
- Culture affects the choice of which power tactics are used. When negotiating with a disputant from a hierarchical culture, recognize that blaming and shaming tactics are reminding you of your social responsibilities; allusions to powerful people suggest power by association and potential social stigma if you do not concede.
- If you have to use power it costs you.
- When you "win" through power, you may also be losing in terms of an ongoing relationship or the potential for one.

Procedural Choices for Resolving Disputes

Now with a thorough understanding of interests, rights, and power it is useful to think about classifying procedures for resolving disputes not just by their focus on interests, rights, or power but also by their degree of directness. Procedures for resolving disputes can be direct or indirect. In Chapter One we pointed out that negotiations vary in terms of the degree to which parties whose interests are at stake in the negotiation are directly involved in the negotiation. At one extreme the principles may be at the table; at the other extreme there may be no contact at all between the parties, with all the negotiation occurring indirectly, for example, through the media.

Claims Not Worth Pursuing

Whether you choose to take a direct or an indirect approach to dispute resolution, you are confronting the matter, and you are presuming that, unless dealt with somehow, the dispute will have dysfunctional consequences. In the example of the rattling bicycles mentioned in Chapter One, the claimant, the U.S. buyer, feared that if he did nothing, his Chinese partner would ship the rattling bicycles and his German buyer would reject them. The U.S. buyer judged the cost of doing nothing as greater than the value of the likely outcome of doing something. He confronted, although indirectly.

Some claims, however, are not worth pursuing. In the example of the U.S. manager seeking different data from his Chinese counterpart's report, the U.S. manager might never have made the claim if he thought that the Chinese boss would get involved. He would rather live with the data he had than risk censure from a higher-level manager. Had his Chinese counterpart just said no, he might have done nothing further. What happened instead is a classic example of how disputants often lose control over their disputes and why just walking away is seldom an option in dispute resolution negotiation. The U.S. manager did not have the option of withdrawing his claim. His Chinese counterpart took it to the boss. Of course, if she had rejected the claim, she could not be sure that he would not pursue it with the boss. She may have reasoned that it was better to get there first.

In short, because BATNAs are linked in disputing, once a claim has been made, nonconfrontation is not often a viable option. In other words, the option for nonconfrontation—what is called *lumping it* in the language of dispute resolution—is all in the hands of the claimant. The claimant can decide to lump it before even making the claim. The claimant may also withdraw the claim and lump it at any time during the dispute resolution process, unless the claim has motivated a counterclaim.

The value of lumping it deserves some attention. Once a claim has been made it is difficult for the claimant to control the ramifications: revengeful counterclaims, public loss of face, or damage to the relationship. Societies simply would not function if people did not lump the petty, everyday annoyances of social life. The first consideration in dispute prevention is, therefore, "Should I make the claim, or lump it?" From here on, we assume that you have chosen to make and pursue the claim.

Cultural Preferences for Direct or Indirect Confrontation

When the other party uses a procedure that is not normative in your culture, you tend to take its choice personally—"She went to the boss because she wants to get me in trouble." Personal attributions about procedural choice escalate task conflict by extending the scope of the conflict from task to procedural and interpersonal. Recognizing that the other party's behavior is normative in that person's culture—"She went to the boss because that was the right thing to do in her culture"—does not resolve the task conflict. It also does not resolve the procedural differences. But it does keep conflict from becoming personal. Understanding cultural differences in preferences for procedures is the first step toward being able to resolve disputes across cultures.

Characteristics of Asian cultures (high-context communications, collective interests, hierarchical power distributions) encourage disputants to confront indirectly—as did the Chinese woman who went to her boss with the request for data. Characteristics of Western cultures (low-context communications, self-interest, and egalitarian power distributions) encourage disputants to confront directly. As with all cultural divides, this one is of relative emphasis, and no randomly selected disputant from a given culture is likely to have a preference structure that perfectly matches the cultural prototype. Still, it is well worth understanding these cultural differences in preference.

Direct confrontation is consistent with the action-oriented and solution-minded communication that is characteristic of low-context cultures.[21] It typically challenges the status quo—a right that is protected in egalitarian cultures but that is discouraged in hierarchical cultures. Direct confrontation disrupts harmony, a value protected in collectivist cultures.

Indirect confrontation is consistent with an underlying concern for face. Face refers to the self-image one projects to others—how people think about themselves in social situations.[22] People want the respect of others because such respect validates their own self-worth. Disrespect affronts face; respect confirms it.[23] Giving face in negotiations means signaling respect for the other person even when you do not agree with his or her positions. This is how it works: If I give face (signal respect to you), you feel personally validated. Then you are likely to reciprocate. Reciprocal respect should lead to a search for a resolution that takes the respect for the other into account. One good way to give face is to apologize. By apologizing, a person accepts that he or she has violated some social norms and implicitly accepts responsibility for doing do.[24]

In contrast, attacking face in negotiations means signaling disrespect for the person and disagreement with the person's positions. Attacking face might occur in association with expressing contempt when rejecting a claim.[25] If a disputant feels personally demeaned, he or she is likely to reciprocate, which in turn may lead to a hardening of position, an emphasis on persuasion, and a restricted search for alternatives. Such negotiation behavior is likely to lead to distributive agreements at best, and possibly to impasse.

Respect is important in all cultures. When parties are in conflict it is easy for conflict over issues to spill over into interpersonal conflict and issues of face. Although face is not unimportant to people from individualist and egalitarian societies, it seems to be more important to people from collectivist and hierarchical cultures because of the emphasis in those societies on interpersonal harmony.[26] Maintaining face both confirms the person's acceptance in a society (collectivism) and that person's status within the society (hierarchy). It is easier to maintain face using an indirect approach than a direct one. The difference is really whether you tell the other party directly what you think of his or her action or whether you tell the other party enough so that the party figures out what you think of his or her action.

When disputing is carried out indirectly through third parties, the disputants are buffered from each other. Third parties may also remind disputants, either directly or indirectly through their presence, of the importance of relationships and social harmony, factors that may be forgotten in the midst of emotional face-to-face negotiations.

Recent theorizing suggests that face and relationship issues are more important when conflict is between people within a social or cultural group than between people in different social or cultural groups. The disrespectful behavior of out-group members does not carry as much social identity information as the same behavior of in-group members.[27] However, commercial disputes are frequently carried out in a public forum. Publicity may affect a party's reputation within its own culture.

One example from the 1980s illustrates how a small U.S. company, which by the way is still going strong and slightly renamed as Fusion UV Systems, used negative publicity to get huge Mitsubishi Electric to the negotiating table. Fusion held patents in the United States and Japan for an ultraviolet lamp that had applications in the printing and silicon chip industries. Fusion claimed that Mitsubishi Electric violated its patent rights in Japan. Mitsubishi Electric rejected the claim, pointing out that it had recently won an industry award for its own ultraviolet technology. Fusion's response was a negative publicity campaign about this dispute in the American and Japanese business press. The publicity must have been extremely embarrassing to Mitsubishi Electric, because it appears to have brought Mitsubishi Electric to the negotiating table, though not to resolution.[28] It took ten years, and Fusion used every public relations pressure tactic it could muster from lobbying the U.S. Congress to getting Japanese patent law changed to shaming Mitsubishi repeatedly in articles in the business press. Finally, Fusion and Mitsubishi resolved their dispute privately. Their joint press release announced an agreement, but no terms were ever released— a face-saving decision.

Managers resolving disputes cross-culturally need the strategic flexibility to do so directly and indirectly. Claimants should be particularly sensitive to cultural preferences for direct versus indirect confrontation, because choosing an approach that is culturally offensive to the other party may cause the dispute to expand from the original claim and become procedural and interpersonal.

Advice for Choosing Direct Versus Indirect Confrontation. The following tips should be useful for choosing direct versus indirect confrontation:

- *Don't take the procedural choice personally.* It's likely to have been motivated by culture, not a personal vendetta.
- *Know the other disputant's cultural orientation.* Direct confrontation is consistent with the action-oriented and solution-minded communication that is consistent with low-context, individualistic cultures. Indirect confrontation is consistent with the concern for face and harmony characteristics of high-context, collective cultures.
- *Develop the flexibility to negotiate directly and indirectly.* Use Exhibit 5.12 to help you choose a procedure.

Confrontation and Approach

Exhibit 5.12 organizes a variety of dispute resolution procedures by their degree of directness and their focus on interests, rights, or power. As the chart suggests, negotiation can be a direct confronta-

Exhibit 5.12. Classification of Dispute Resolution
Procedures by Interests, Rights, and Power Approaches
and by Direct and Indirect Confrontation.

Approach	Direct Confrontation	Indirect Confrontation
Interests	Negotiation between principals Mediation	Negotiation between agents Shuttle mediation
Rights	Negotiation Bosses Advisory arbitration Arbitration Court	Seeking intervention by a boss Organizational change to remove legitimacy Legislation
Power	Negotiation using threats (including involving third parties) Boycotts, strikes Physical violence	Negotiation using blaming and shaming Negative publicity

tion procedure when engaged in by principals and more indirect
when principals are represented by agents. Negotiation can also take
an interests, rights, or power approach, and the approach can shift
during the negotiation. (There will be more discussion later about
when to take which approach and how to shift between them.)

In column 2 of the exhibit, mediation is third-party-assisted
negotiation, in which the third party has no authority to impose a
settlement on the disputants. Mediation is direct when parties are
always at the table with the mediator and indirect when the mediator engages in shuttle diplomacy. Mediation can be interests-based
but it can also focus on rights and fairness standards. Mediators
also may turn the spotlight on power to get the parties to realize
that winning is losing. (There will be more on mediation in Chapter Six.)

Also in column 2, arbitration is a quasi-judicial procedure in
which the parties try to convince the arbitrator of the "rightness" of

their positions using fairness norms, law, contract, precedent, and so on. Bosses, too, can act like arbitrators. The difference is that arbitrators are independent neutrals, and bosses have interests of their own. And whereas arbitrators are supposed to make decisions based on rights standards, bosses may use other criteria for making decisions. The difference between arbitration and court is primarily that arbitration is private and parties get to choose their arbitrator. Judicial proceedings are public and judges are assigned, not selected.

In column 3, there are two indirect procedures that merit some discussion: (1) organizational change to remove legitimacy and (2) legislation. Both of these procedures may be used when parties do not agree on what rule or law should prevail. Both can amount to engaging in indirect, rights-based negotiations by lobbying to have the rule or law changed.

In the bottom cell of column 2, note that in addition to using threats in negotiation, parties may act on their threats, cutting off social interaction via boycott or strikes, or engaging in physical violence such as war.

The bottom cell of column 3 refers to the kind of blaming and shaming that we saw occurring especially among the Japanese negotiating Summer Interns. Recall that the purpose is to remind parties of their social responsibilities. Negative publicity may also remind parties of their responsibilities; it may work also because it is just so onerous that the targeted party concedes in order to turn it off.

Recall how the interests, rights, and power circles in Exhibit 5.1 illustrated that negotiators' interests exist within the broader contexts of their rights and of power. The question we need to address next is when to take which of these three approaches. Unfortunately, there is very little U.S.-based research and essentially no cross-cultural research to inform our answer in the context of disputing. Lacking research, the best approach is to consider what message is being sent with an interests, rights, or power opening.

When to Use Interests

This may come as a surprise to you, but I want to caution you about opening dispute resolution negotiations with interests. There are two related reasons, one intuitive and the other based on empirical evidence. The intuitive reason is that if you open negotiations with interests you may be inadvertently sending a message of weakness. The empirical reason is that our research shows that when parties open with interests, the other party, thinking there is weakness to be exploited, may turn the negotiations toward rights or power. The interests-based negotiator in defense turns to rights or power and a conflict spiral ensues. Once this occurs—right and power are reciprocated—it seems to be very difficult to turn the negotiation back to interests.[29] This may be because the party opening with interests feels exploited and becomes defensive. In contrast, when negotiations open with rights or power and go nowhere, parties seem to get the rights and power posturing out of their systems, and become relieved to turn to interests, where there might be movement toward an agreement.

There may be some middle ground between opening with rights or power and opening with interests. Disputes are often about what happened—the facts of the situation. Disputants seldom agree about the facts, so this opening is not likely to lead to agreement (if there had not been disagreement about the facts there may not have been a dispute in the first place). But talking about the facts and agreeing to disagree may get the parties working together and signaling each other: "This dispute is important to me; you are going to have to participate to resolve it."

When to Use Rights

Focusing on rights suggests to the other disputant that you have in mind a distributive outcome in which you win and he or she loses. Of course, if the other party did not mind losing, he or she would most likely have granted your claim when you made it. Therefore opening negotiations by focusing on rights is unlikely to lead to a quick resolution of the dispute unless you have new credible rights information that the other party did not know when rejecting your claim. In fact, because disputants tend to reciprocate each other's rights arguments, opening with or directing the negotiation toward such arguments may at least for a time escalate the dispute rather than resolve it.[30]

Still, there are three very appropriate times to use rights arguments in negotiations:

- Use rights when you think that you have a standard that the other party has not considered and that, once the other party considers it, he or she will recognize the weakness of his or her own position and come to agreement.

- Use rights when you have a standard that you think the other party is likely to accept as fair. Presumably, this standard will also benefit you.

- Use rights when you want to make it clear that if the dispute cannot be resolved, you will go to a third party for resolution, and your argument to that party will be based on that same rights standard.

When to Use Power

Three factors impinge on the decision to use power: culture, emotions, and strategy.

Culture. As we discussed earlier in this chapter, negotiators from hierarchical cultures (such as Japanese) spend proportionately more time discussing power when resolving disputes than do negotiators from egalitarian cultures (such as U.S. and German). This may be because they are trying to determine who has the higher status and therefore who should defer to whom. It may also be that they are reminding each other of their social responsibilities. It is important to recognize that despite the focus on power the Japanese negotiators resolved the summer interns problem. Focusing on power did not lead the Japanese to impasse. Consider what might have happened if the U.S. or German negotiators had spent as much of their negotiation on power issues. Given that the power approach is counternormative for the latter groups, it seems likely that they would not have tolerated the power focus as well as the Japanese did. Here is some advice about culture and power:

- When resolving a dispute with someone from an egalitarian culture, keep in mind that that person may be more comfortable discussing interests than power.
- When negotiating with someone from a hierarchical culture, keep in mind that that person may use power repeatedly to try to get you to step up to your social responsibility.
- Also when negotiating with someone from a hierarchical culture, keep in mind that that person might wish to involve a third party.

Regardless of culture, when one negotiator focuses on power, the other is very likely to reciprocate.[31] This may escalate the conflict to encompass task, procedural, and interpersonal issues and lead to an impasse or a very one-sided agreement.[32] Of course, many negotiators would be quite satisfied with a one-sided agreement, so long as it benefits them and there are no relationship issues.

Emotions. When people become emotional, as they often do when disputing, they are likely to lose perspective and become less cooperative and less receptive to other ideas.[33] When people feel threatened, anxiety reduces their capacity for rational thinking, and when people become angry, their focus may shift from the task to retaliation.[34] A study we did monitoring the dispute resolution communications of eBay buyers and sellers illustrates these points nicely. The more angry the claimant, the more angry the respondent and, no surprise, the less likely the dispute was to settle.[35] But, holding anger constant, we also found that claimants who told the respondent what he or she should do (using words such as *should, ought,* or *must*) reduced their chances for settlement of their claim. In contrast, respondents who kept a cool head and provided a causal explanation for what went wrong increased the likelihood of settlement. We attributed these results to the effects of giving and affronting face.[36]

There are also people who use emotional outbursts or tantrums intentionally in negotiations. Their purpose is to get the other party to make a concession to turn off the tantrum. The effect, of course, is just the opposite. If you make a concession in the face of the other party's tantrum, you reinforce that party for using tantrums to negotiate!

The way to manage a negotiator who uses tantrums intentionally is to refuse to make concessions, but to keep negotiating. Put an offer on the table. See if you can change the focus. Take social responsibility in the face of tantrums; the more frequently you and others make concessions to tantrums, the more tantrums become a learned negotiating strategy.

Emotional outbursts may be more common in individualist cultures than in collectivist cultures, where values for harmony and concerns for face limit the display of emotion in negotiations. Yet signals of firmness are frequently used in collective cultures. No one loses face when a buyer walks away from a stall in an open-air market; yet a firm signal has been sent. In our eBay study, claimants (this time controlling for anger and commands) who communicated firmness (using words such as *interfere, withhold,* or *control*) increased their likelihood of dispute resolution.[37]

Tantrums may also have both emotional and strategic downsides. The emotional downside is that having tantrums takes its own emotional toll. In following up some interest-based negotiation training we did in a labor-management context, I was surprised to hear during a focus group with company representatives that "the relationship is much improved—Jeffrey [the union leader] doesn't throw tantrums anymore; he talks with us about interests." An hour later, Jeffrey told me he was "a new man." "In what way?" I asked. "You taught me how to negotiate using interests. You taught the others to listen and look for interests. I don't have to throw a tantrum to get them to the table, and I don't have to throw a tantrum to get them to engage in serious problem solving. You cannot imagine how my physical and mental health has improved!" I tell this story not to brag about our success in this instance but to point out that this negotiator was using tantrums strategically. He knew it, and the company people with whom he had to interact knew it. Moreover, doing so was taking a mental and physical toll on him—and probably on them too.

The strategic downside of using emotion at the bargaining table is that many people try to avoid negotiating with those who have a reputation for using emotion intentionally. This is easier to do in deal making than in resolving disputes, when BATNAs are linked. In disputing, over time, people learn to manage the other side's emotional outbursts by just saying no regardless of the merit of the claim. This escalates the costs of dispute resolution. Using emotion intentionally is a risky use of power at the bargaining table.

Here is some advice about using emotions at the bargaining table:

- *Don't reciprocate an emotional outburst.* Failing to confront anger with anger does not make you appear weak. The effect is just the opposite. Reciprocating the other disputant's emotional outburst draws you into his or her strategy and away from your own. It makes you appear unable to sustain your own strategic approach.
- *Don't take an emotional outburst personally.* Attributing an emotional outburst to something you did will only make you defensive and distract you from your preferred strategic approach. Attributing rejections to situational factors, such as understaffing, or to stable characteristics of the person ("She never says yes to anyone the first time") depersonalizes the rejection and should reduce emotions.

- *Consider putting the party's behavior on the table.* Tell the other party directly that his or her emotional behavior is interfering with dispute resolution. Ask if there is something you can do to help reduce the emotional tension.

- *Try apologizing for the other party's emotional state.* "I'm very sorry you are so upset" goes a long way toward diffusing a hot emotional standoff.

- *Call for a cooling-off period.* Suggest taking a break from negotiations. You may need it as much as the other party.

- *Suggest involving a third party.* Third parties can often act to buffer disputants who seem to bring out the worst in each other.

Using Power Strategically. There are times when you will want to use power in dispute resolution negotiations. When you cannot get the other party to the table to talk, using power may convince him or her to come to the table. Recall that in the Blue LED example, the Japanese court finally told Nichia Corporation and Nakamura to negotiate a settlement or the court would impose one.

You may also find it useful to resort to power when negotiations have broken down and all other attempts to restart them have failed. Recall Fusion's negative publicity campaign against Mitsubishi Electric when Mitsubishi rejected Fusion's claim that Mitsubishi had violated Fusion's Japanese patents. Fusion's options at the time it instigated the negative publicity campaign were extremely limited. It could lump the claim, living with the risk that Mitsubishi Electric would take market share away from Fusion in Japan, or demand royalty payments for Fusion's alleged violations of Mitsubishi Electric's patents. It could file its claim in the Japanese court system. Fusion's strategic decision was to choose the option that was most likely to encourage Mitsubishi Electric to come to the negotiating table. Clearly, when your BATNA is poor and you cannot get the other party to the table, using or threatening to use power may be strategically justifiable. Using power—or threatening to use it—communicates to the other party that the situation is no better than your BATNA and that you will be forced to go to your BATNA unless negotiations can be restarted.

It is not obvious whether disputants can talk about power in a purely informative way without one party inferring that the other is making threats. The U.S. bicycle buyer could have said to the Chinese manufacturer, "You know, I still owe you money," without defining the conditions under which the money would be withheld. People do make these statements about power in dispute resolution negotiations. We see it throughout the transcripts of the Japanese disputants in the Summer Interns negotiation.[38] We also see it at the beginning and particularly right after the midpoint of the transcripts of U.S. disputants resolving a different dispute.[39] The timing in the U.S. transcripts suggests that U.S. disputants talk about power early to try to gain dominance in the negotiation and again later when the structure of an agreement has appeared and they are trying to claim distributive gains.

The real question is not so much disputants' intent but how the information about power is received. My experience suggests that in the U.S. culture, information about power is either discounted as a negotiation ploy or taken as a serious threat. Even when the information is new to the other party, it is likely to be put in one category or the other. When we were studying union organizing campaigns in the United States, we would ask employees what the company spokesman had said in a meeting. We had transcripts of those meetings because the National Labor Relations Board in the United States regulates what can and cannot be said in such meetings, and companies and unions want to protect themselves.[40] The law prohibits direct threats—for example, to move the production facility to Mexico if the union wins the election. Companies are careful not to make threats. Instead companies say things like, "Remember the employer who used to be down the street? When his plant voted union, he shut his doors and moved production to Mexico." When we asked employees what was said in the meeting, they would tell us, "He said that if we vote union, he's going to move production to Mexico." It seems that it may be difficult to talk about power in a purely informational way in cultures such as the United States, where there is less emphasis on power than on interests and rights as dispute resolution strategies. Discussion of power in cultures such as Japan, where we have seen that such discussion is normative, may not be as easily discounted or quickly taken as a threat.

Here is some advice for using power strategically:

- Use power when all attempts to get the other party to the negotiating table have failed.
- Use power when negotiations have reached a deadlock.
- Use power very carefully if you are certain there is a zone of agreement and you want to claim as much value as possible. The better strategy in this situation is to trade off issues, just like in deal-making negotiations.

How to Change the Focus from Rights or Power to Interests

It is easy to shift the focus from interests to rights or power because negotiators reciprocate rights and power communications. What about shifting from power or rights to interests? Some of our research with U.S. negotiators suggests several ways that negotiations can be refocused from rights or power to interests.[41]

- *Do not reciprocate.* Disputants who refuse to echo or reciprocate the other party's rights or power communications significantly increase the likelihood that the other party will be deterred from continuing with this strategy. With some insensitive disputants, it may be necessary to redirect negotiations from rights or power several times before the point is made.
- *Declare the process ineffective.* Disputants who recognize that they are engaged in a rights or power contest or one that is

spiraling away from a true interpretation of the facts can label the process as counterproductive. For example, when disputing over what was promised, one party might suggest, "Let's agree to disagree and move on; this isn't getting us anywhere."

- *Combine reciprocity with a change of focus.* Some negotiators may fear that not reciprocating rights or power signals weakness. They may feel compelled to reciprocate to maintain their power position in the negotiations. Interestingly, among U.S. negotiators, combining a counterthreat with a change of focus to interests or a proposal for settlement is almost as effective as the "do not reciprocate" strategy in refocusing negotiations away from rights or power.

Excellent Dispute Resolvers

Conflict and disputes are inevitable within and between organizations. Cultural differences add misunderstandings, miscommunications, and misattributions to the disputing environment. Thus cross-cultural managers must be well prepared to resolve disputes. Preparation requires understanding cultural differences in why and how claims are made and rejected and how disputes are resolved across cultures. Resolving disputes requires respecting preferences for direct versus indirect confrontation and facility with direct and indirect interests, rights, and power procedures. Excellent dispute resolvers in a global environment understand how interests, rights, and power are construed in different cultures. They know when to focus on interests, rights, or power and how to change the focus and to deal with emotion.

The next chapter looks in more depth at the use of third parties in settling disputes. As we shall see, excellent dispute resolvers know when and how to involve third parties in disputes that cannot be settled via negotiation. They know how to make third-party dispute resolution easily available. And they shed any illusions that third parties are truly neutral and unaffected by role and culture.

Chapter Six

Third Parties and Dispute Resolution

In many cultures third parties facilitate the resolution of disputes. Disputants do not always have the option of choosing whether to involve third parties. Third parties may be imposed on disputants by cultural norms or the action of the other disputant. Third parties may also take it upon themselves to intervene, perhaps motivated by a feeling of responsibility to preserve communal harmony. Whether you choose to or are compelled to involve a third party in your dispute, it is useful to have a systematic way of thinking about the implications for dispute resolution of different third-party roles.

The major difference between third-party roles is whether the role gives or does not give the third party the authority to impose a resolution on the disputants. Bosses typically have such authority, as do judges and arbitrators. Peers (such as the other managers whom the Hong Kong Chinese involved in the Summer Interns dispute) and mediators typically do not have authority to impose a resolution on the dispute. They can only influence outcomes by advising, framing, managing the process, or contributing their stature or expertise to one settlement proposal or another. As we shall see, this distinction of roles (having versus not having authority to impose a resolution on disputants) makes a difference in whether the third-party process is rights-based or interests-based. It also has important implications for choosing a third party, because whether the third-party process is rights- or interests-based has an impact on how disputants and third parties act.

The chapter begins by looking closely at these two options. It describes arbitration (third-party roles with authority) and mediation (third-party roles without authority) and advises on how to select a third-party arbitrator or mediator. It then turns to culture, which may affect which third-party roles are available to disputants and the third party's inclination to focus on interests, rights, or power. Culture may also affect how early in the dispute's history third parties become involved.

Third Parties with Authority to Resolve Disputes

Litigation, arbitration, and organizational hierarchy are three widely used dispute resolution procedures that give third parties authority to resolve disputes. These are all rights-based procedures. That is, the third party resolves the dispute by deciding which disputant is right or wrong, usually under some standard of contract, law, or organizational precedent.

Litigation is a public judicial procedure in which disputants or their agents argue their claim and a third party or occasionally a jury makes a final and binding decision. Disputants often prefer not to litigate disputes. When Mitsubishi Electric rejected Fusion's claim that Mitsubishi had violated Fusion's Japanese patent rights, Fusion had the option of litigating the claim in the Japanese court system. It chose not to.[1] Litigation in the other party's legal system is seldom a very appealing choice for a number of reasons, including concerns about bias, the time and cost to litigate in another country, and the effect of litigation on future relationships.

Arbitration is a private adjudicative procedure. If privacy is important to disputants, arbitration is a better choice than litigation. Disputants who lose at arbitration do not have to be concerned about losing face publicly. The arbitrator, like the judge, is charged with interpreting contract or law in the context of the dispute. When parties agree to arbitrate disputes, they name the commercial code under which arbitration will occur. This gets around the problem that commercial codes in many developing countries are rudimentary. The parties may also specify a source of neutral arbitrators and a process for picking one. This alleviates the problem that judges in some countries are not experienced in handling complex civil litigation. Parties can pick an experienced arbitrator, a retired judge, or a lawyer from a third country.

The arbitrator has authority to impose an outcome on the disputants, and legal systems generally enforce arbitrators' decisions within their own jurisdiction. Of course, disputants from different national cultures do not share legal systems, which is one reason for choosing arbitration in the first place. However, there is potential legal recourse for enforcement of an arbitrator's award in local courts, if the country is one of the 132 nations that are signatories to the 1958 United Nations Convention on the Recognition and Enforcement of Foreign Arbitral Awards.[2]

Exhibit 6.1 provides a brief description of the arbitration process. Note that although commercial arbitration in the United States typically requires only the decision, not the reasoning underlying the decision, this is less true in international commercial arbitration.

How to Choose an Arbitrator

There are many international organizations that maintain lists of arbitrators.[3] It is useful to decide on a source of arbitrators when finalizing a contract with an arbitration clause, so that when an arbitrator is needed, there is no conflict over the source of the arbitrator. Ask the source for the résumés of several arbitrators with documented experience in your industry or in the area of law that your dispute involves. Ask for a list of cases in which the arbitrators have served. Find out the names and addresses of parties and lawyers representing both sides of the disputes this person has arbitrated. Interview them about the arbitrator. Here are some questions to ask:

- Was the arbitrator a good listener?
- Did the arbitrator treat your side fairly?
- Did the arbitrator treat the other side fairly?

Exhibit 6.1. How Arbitration Works.

Arbitration has been an alternative to litigation for hundreds of years. It was used as early as the thirteenth century by English merchants who preferred to have their disputes resolved according to their own customs (a legal system known as the Law Merchant) rather than by public law. Commercial arbitration in the United States antedated the American Revolution in New York and several other colonies and is widely used today. Labor arbitration became widespread during the 1940s, and now more than 95 percent of all collective bargaining contracts contain a provision for final and binding arbitration. Additionally, arbitration is used to resolve disputes in the construction industry, disputes between consumers and manufacturers, family disputes, medical malpractice claims, securities disputes, attorney's fee disputes, and civil rights disputes. It is even used to resolve disputes about salaries to be paid to major league baseball players. . . .

Because arbitration is a private dispute resolution procedure, designed by the parties to serve their particular needs, it cannot be defined or described in a manner that will encompass all arbitration systems. Still, arbitration typically contains the essential elements of court adjudication, in that unless the parties agree otherwise, the only pretrial discovery will be that mandated by the arbitrator.

Additionally, the hearing is usually more informal than a court hearing, and the rules of evidence are not strictly applied. Finally, commercial arbitration awards typically contain only the arbitrator's award; commercial arbitrators do not provide reasons for their decisions. This practice is not followed in the labor context or in international commercial arbitration, where arbitrators, like judges, issue reasoned decisions. Most private arbitration systems provide the following:

- Joint selection and payment of the arbitrator
- Objective standards on which the arbitrator's decision is to be based (typically the terms of agreement between parties, the customs of the trade in which they conduct business, the applicable law, or some combination of these)
- Procedural rules to be applied by the arbitrator

Source: S. B. Goldberg, F.E.A. Sander, N. H. Rogers, and S. R. Cole, Dispute Resolution: Negotiation, Mediation, and Other Processes, 4th ed. (Gaithersburg, Md.: Aspen, 2003), pp. 209–210. Reprinted with permission.

- Was the arbitrator knowledgeable in the [relevant] area of law?
- Was the decision handed down in a timely fashion?[4]
- Was the decision written in language that the claimant could understand? (This is especially important for employee disputes.)
- Did your side win or lose?
- Would you use the same arbitrator again? Why or why not?

You will receive more information that is directly relevant to your decision if you ask questions beyond whether your informant would use that third party again. If you can find a party who receives praise from people on both sides of the dispute, chances are that person will be a good choice for you.

Arbitrators and Culture

Although arbitrators are presumably neutral in the sense of not having an a priori preference for one or the other disputant, they are not unbiased. Culture matters. A recent study gave Chinese and American commercial arbitrators three different versions of an arbitration scenario. The scenario described a dispute between a wool supply company and a clothes company. The wool company was supposed to ship a certain amount of wool to a clothes company every day, but for two weeks it failed to do so. The dispute focused on whether the wool supply company was responsible for the failure of the shipment. The arbitrators were told that there had been problems with the electricity supply during the two weeks in question.

Chinese arbitrators made higher awards to the clothing company than American arbitrators. The reason was associated with the way they interpreted the information about the shut-off of electricity. The Chinese arbitrators attributed the failure to deliver to the wool supply company's actions (or lack thereof). The American arbitrators attributed the failure to deliver to the electricity problem, over which the wool company had no control. The arbitrators' decisions in this study are consistent with prior research that finds that Chinese and Americans make different attributions to explain failure when the actor is a company rather than an individual. In this study cultural biases strongly affected arbitrators' decisions.[5]

Third Parties Without Authority to Resolve Disputes

Why bother with a third-party procedure if the third party does not have the authority to resolve the dispute? In short, because third parties without authority are nevertheless frequently able to help disputants find acceptable settlements using procedures that are perceived to be much more fair than procedures in which third parties impose resolutions.[6]

Mediation Resolves Disputes!

In the U.S. commercial context, mediation practiced by the four major U.S. mediation companies resulted in a 78 percent settlement rate.[7] Whether the case went to mediation voluntarily or because of a contract clause or a judge's action did not affect the settlement rate. Mediation was equally successful in settling personal injury disputes, contract disputes, and construction disputes. Cases that did not settle were likely to be characterized by lawyers as "a party in search of a jackpot" or as "a situation in which it was not in the financial interest of one party to settle." These judgments were made after the fact and may be biased by the natural desire to attribute cause for failure to settle. However, if this bias were very strong, it would seem likely that many different characteristics would define the cases that did not settle. We questioned lawyers about twenty-one different characteristics. In their judgment, these were the only two characteristics that had a significant impact on the likelihood that a case would settle at mediation.[8]

There are no comparable data for intercultural disputes. Intercultural mediation settlement rates might be somewhat lower if mediators have difficulty understanding one or the other party's interests, due to cultural or communication biases. A solution is to have co-mediators, one from each of the cultures involved in the dispute.

How Mediators Get Disputants to Settle

Mediators have lots of ways to help disputants resolve their conflicts. Mediators control emotional outbursts and keep disputants focused on resolution instead of retribution. They have excellent negotiation skills. They know all the types of integrative agreements to resolve disputes that were listed in Exhibit 5.2. They know how to look for and integrate interests; how to construct proposals that link a future relationship to the resolution of the past dispute; and how to expand the scope of the dispute and get to the underlying issue or contract the scope and construct a non-precedent-setting agreement. Mediators get agreements by engaging in reality testing with disputants, by making them focus hard and rationally on their BATNAs. This problem-solving approach to mediation is described in Exhibit 6.2. (See also "Being Effective in Mediation When You Are the Disputant" and "The Mediation Process" on the CD-ROM.)

Mediators may also try to transform the relationship between the parties. This approach does not seek an immediate resolution of the dispute, but resolution is a secondary effect of the process. Transformative mediation focuses on empowering parties to define the problem in their own terms and to recognize each other's positions and interests.[9] This approach is most often used in interpersonal conflicts—conflicts within families, between neighbors, between coworkers, or within communities.[10] Although the mediation tactics listed in Exhibit 6.2 do not constitute an ordered sequence, mediation itself, like negotiation, is a highly ordered process. Mediators usually open with a statement about what the parties can expect in

Exhibit 6.2. How Mediation Works.

Mediation is negotiation carried out with the assistance of a third party. The mediator, in contrast to the arbitrator or judge, has no power to impose an outcome on disputing parties.

Despite the lack of "teeth" in the mediation process, the involvement of a mediator alters the dynamics of negotiations. Depending on what seems to be impeding agreement . . . the mediator may attempt to:

- Encourage exchanges of information
- Provide new information
- Help the parties understand each other's views
- Let them know that their concerns are understood
- Promote a productive level of emotional expression
- Deal with differences in perceptions and interests between negotiators and constituents (including lawyer and client)
- Help negotiators realistically assess alternatives to settlement
- Encourage flexibility
- Shift the focus from past to future
- Stimulate the parties to suggest creative settlements
- Learn (often in separate sessions with each party) about those interests the parties are reluctant to disclose to each other
- Invent solutions that meet the fundamental interests of all parties

Mediators' strategies vary widely. Some mediators attempt to focus the negotiations on satisfying the vital interests of each party; others focus on legal rights, sometimes providing a neutral assessment of the outcome in court or arbitration. Some encourage the active participation of both lawyers and clients; others exclude either clients or lawyers from the sessions. Some mediators endeavor to maintain neutrality; others deliberately become advocates of a particular outcome or protectors of non-parties' interests.

Source: S. B. Goldberg, F.E.A. Sander, N. H. Rogers, and S. R. Cole, Dispute Resolution: Negotiation, Mediation, and Other Processes, 4th ed. (Gaithersburg, Md.: Aspen, 2003), pp. 111–112. Reprinted with permission.

terms of sharing information about the causes of the dispute, ground rules for doing so (for example, no interruptions), the possibility of private caucuses with the mediator, and responsibilities regarding suggesting and considering alternative settlements. They then focus on learning about the dispute and helping each side hear the other side's concerns. When no more new information is forthcoming, the mediator then has to turn the discussion toward settlement, perhaps by asking for offers, or floating his or her own suggestions. Sometimes when one or the other or both parties are reluctant to seriously consider a settlement proposal, the mediator may engage in some reality testing in private, by talking with a party about his or her BATNA in the event of a failed mediation.[11]

How to Find a Mediator

It is wise to have a contract clause calling for mediation and indicating the source of potential mediators. This minimizes disputes over where to go to find a mediator. Most of the same services that keep lists of arbitrators keep lists of mediators. Ask the service or other source for the résumés of several potential mediators. Mediation is a very private dispute resolution procedure, but it is still normal for mediators to give references to lawyers with whom they have mediated. Interview people who have experience with the mediator. It is also more and more common to interview potential mediators themselves about their preferred style of mediation. The Website mentioned in note 10 during the discussion of transformative mediation suggests questions to ask when seeking a transformative mediator. Some questions to ask about problem-solving mediators are

- Was the mediator a good listener?
- Did the mediator treat your side fairly?
- Did the mediator treat the other side fairly?

- Did the mediator come to understand your side's interests?
- Did the mediator help you to better understand the other side's interests?
- Did the mediator involve both sides in generating options for agreement?
- Did the mediator provide an interpretation of the law or contract relevant to the case? Was that interpretation requested by the parties? Did it help the resolution of the case?
- Was the mediator able to put the appropriate amount of pressure on the disputants to settle?
- Did the case settle?
- Would you use the same mediator again? Why or why not?

Culture and Third-Party Roles in Disputes

In third-party dispute resolution, culture may affect which roles are available; how early third parties intervene; and whether they focus on interests, rights, or power. Across cultures, third parties are viewed as effective when they facilitate an environment of respect, regardless of whether they have authority to impose a settlement or not; how early they intervene; and how much they focus on interests, rights, or power.[12]

Making Third Parties Available

Disputes are inevitable in cross-cultural relationships, and the costs may be significant. When there is hierarchy in a relationship, there is a system for resolving disputes (go to the boss), although it does not necessarily encourage integrative agreements. When there is no hierarchy in a relationship, there is no system beyond negotiations for resolving disputes. When negotiations break down, parties may be too engaged in disputing to be able to think clearly about alternatives to litigation.

Dispute resolution systems are widely used in egalitarian societies such as the United States. Such systems often involve a contractual or normative agreement to negotiate in good faith, and, if unsuccessful, go to mediation, and, if still unsuccessful, go to arbitration.[13] Their purpose is to direct disputes to low-cost procedures (usually involving a third party) that also preserve the possibility of integrative outcomes.

A dispute resolution system needs to be in place before disputes occur. Once disputes have broken out, parties are often too emotionally involved to choose resolution procedures wisely. Yet negotiating a system to resolve disputes at the same time as negotiating the deal may be difficult. It is rather like telling your fiancé right before the wedding that you want a prenuptial agreement to govern the dispensation of assets in the event of a divorce! Negotiators from collectivist cultures that value harmony, interpersonal relationships, and trust are not likely to be very open to negotiating a system for resolving disputes before any business has been transacted. Such a proposal is also very direct. Yet the effort may be worthwhile. A dispute resolution system sets up norms unique to your relationship about how you plan to deal with each other if disputes do occur. Such a system might have kept the dispute over data between the U.S. and Chinese managers from expanding from task conflict to procedural and interpersonal conflict. The U.S. manager would have known the appropriate way to make a claim, and the Chinese manager would have known the appropriate way to reject the claim according to the norms of the joint venture's dispute resolution system.

Exhibit 6.3 provides contract language that was created by the CPR: International Institute of Conflict Prevention & Resolution (see also "Additional CPR Model Clauses" on the CD-ROM).[14] Its structure of negotiation, mediation, and arbitration can easily be adapted to relationships that involve parties from different cultures. Whether face-to-face negotiation is part of the system may depend on the parties' preferences for direct versus indirect confrontation. Mediation in some form should be part of the system so that there

Exhibit 6.3. A Three-Tiered Dispute Resolution System: Model Contract Clauses from the CPR.

CPR Model Dispute Resolution Clauses

This section offers a detailed multi-step clause and a variety of drafting options for domestic agreements. (*See* International ADR for International Models.) If no binding resolution clause is included, litigation, by default, would remain the means of dispute resolution.

Preamble

"Any dispute arising out of or relating to this Agreement shall be resolved in accordance with the procedures specified in this Article 00, which shall be the sole and exclusive procedures for the resolution of any such disputes."

CPR Model Multi-Step Dispute Resolution Clause

Negotiation

Negotiation Between Executives

"(A) The parties shall attempt [in good faith] to resolve any dispute arising out of or relating to this [Agreement] [Contract] promptly by negotiation between executives who have authority to settle the controversy and who are at a higher level of management than the persons with direct responsibility for administration of this contract. Any person may give the other party written notice of any dispute not resolved in the normal course of business. Within [15] days after delivery of the notice, the receiving party shall submit to the other a written response. The notice and response shall include (a) a statement of that party's position and a summary of arguments supporting that position, and (b) the name and title of the executive who will represent that party and of any other person who will accompany the executive. Within [30] days after delivery of the initial notice, the executives of both parties shall meet at a mutually acceptable time and place, and thereafter as often as they reasonably deem necessary, to attempt to resolve the dispute. [All reasonable requests for information made by one party to the other will be honored.]

All negotiations pursuant to this clause are confidential and shall be treated as compromise and settlement negotiations for purposes of applicable rules of evidence."

Mediation

"(B) If the dispute has not been resolved by negotiation as provided herein within [45] days after delivery of the initial notice of negotiation, [or if the parties failed to meet within [30] days after delivery], the parties shall endeavor to settle the dispute by mediation under the CPR Mediation

Exhibit 6.3.   A Three-Tiered Dispute Resolution System: Model Contract Clauses from the CPR, Cont'd.

Procedure [then currently in effect OR in effect on the date of this Agreement], [provided, however, that if one party fails to participate in the negotiation as provided herein, the other party can initiate mediation prior to the expiration of the [45] days.] Unless otherwise agreed, the parties will select a mediator from the CPR Panels of Distinguished Neutrals."

Arbitration

"(C) Any dispute arising out of or relating to this [Agreement] [Contract], including the breach, termination or validity thereof, which has not been resolved by mediation as provided herein [within [45] days after initiation of the mediation procedure] [within [30] days after appointment of a mediator], shall be finally resolved by arbitration in accordance with the CPR Rules for Non-Administered Arbitration [then currently in effect OR in effect on the date of this Agreement], by [a sole arbitrator] [three independent and impartial arbitrators, of whom each party shall designate one] [three arbitrators of whom each party shall appoint one in accordance with the 'screened' appointment procedure provided in Rule 5.4] [three independent and impartial arbitrators, none of whom shall be appointed by either party]; [provided, however, that if one party fails to participate in either the negotiation or mediation as agreed herein, the other party can commence arbitration prior to the expiration of the time periods set forth above.] The arbitration shall be governed by the Federal Arbitration Act, 9 U.S.C. §§1 et seq., and judgment upon the award rendered by the arbitrator(s) may be entered by any court having jurisdiction thereof. The place of arbitration shall be [city, state]."

—or—

Litigation Clause

(C) "If the dispute has not been resolved by nonbinding means as provided herein within [90] days of the initiation of such procedure, this Agreement does not preclude either party from initiating litigation [upon 00 days written notice to the other party]; provided, however, that if one party has requested the other to participate in a nonbinding procedure and the other has failed to participate, the requesting party may initiate litigation before expiration of the above period."

is a procedure beyond negotiation that preserves the possibility of an integrative agreement.[15]

Culture, Preferences for Third-Party Involvement, and Timing of Third-Party Involvement

There may be cultural differences in willingness to turn control over the outcome to a third party.[16] Disputants from collectivist, hierarchical, and high-context cultures may be more accepting of third-party authority than those from individualistic and egalitarian cultures. They may assume that third parties will keep the interests of the collective in mind and will protect the weak from exploitation by the powerful. They may also want the third party to maintain harmony and save face. Disputants from individualist, egalitarian, and low-context cultures probably neither make nor want to make such assumptions. They are concerned with furthering their self-interests and preserving their right to pursue those interests. Thus they may be less accepting of third-party dispute resolution and then only when their best efforts at negotiating for themselves have failed.

These cultural differences in preferences for direct involvement in dispute resolution lead to differences in the timing of when third parties get involved in disputes. Sometimes third parties, such as the Chinese boss in the joint-venture example, get involved very early in disputes, often at the behest of one party. Other third parties (for example, mediators who try to help parties reach agreement or arbitrators who are hired to make a binding decision) enter a dispute only after the disputants or their agents have failed to negotiate an agreement.

There seems to be a tendency for early third-party involvement in disputes in hierarchical cultures, in cultures with strong values for harmony, and in cultures that prefer indirect confrontation. Involving a third party is normative in these settings because it is seen as a face-saving, harmony-preserving way to resolve the dispute. The Chinese boss told both the U.S. and the Chinese managers that the report would not be amended to provide the requested data. The boss's decision took saying no out of the lower-level Chinese manager's hands, allowing her to save face, and the U.S. manager did not have to experience rejection by a peer. In Chinese culture, being told no by a superior is more acceptable than being told no by a peer. But of course, the incident did not occur just within the Chinese culture. The U.S. manager evaluating the procedure through the lens of his own culture judged neither the process nor the outcome as face-saving, harmony-preserving, or just. From his cultural perspective, the boss should not have been involved at all, and there was greater loss of face being told no by the boss than by a peer. From his egalitarian, direct cultural background, you only involve the boss after negotiations have failed. From his perspective, negotiations never started.

The decision to involve third parties early in the dispute may also be motivated by a desire to develop political power. Many of the Hong Kong Chinese managers in the Summer Interns dispute decided to involve peers and higher-level managers in resolving how the program would be run in the future. They may have been motivated not only by collectivist interests but also by the desire to generate political support for their positions.

The major concern about the timing of third-party involvement is that linked BATNAs enable a disputant to involve a third party before the other disputant is ready for third-party intervention. If the third party's role conveys authority to resolve the dispute, as soon as a third party is involved, disputants more or less give up control over the procedure and the outcome.

How Culture Affects What Third Parties Do

Culture and role generate different dispute resolution behaviors on the part of third parties. In one of our studies U.S., Chinese, and Japanese managers engaged in third-party dispute resolution simulation. We assigned them to play the part of a disputant (a design manager and a project manager) or a third-party manager. We indicated that even before the current dispute, there had been a series of incidents between the two disputants, and trust between them was low. The dispute itself centers on the specifications for a product: The project manager had signed a contract with an important customer for one set of product specifications, but the design manager came up with improvements and changed the product's specifications without checking with the project manager. The project manager told the design manager to change back to the old specifications, the design manager refused and threatened to leave with the job half finished. Time is of the essence to avoid delivery penalties, but it is not clear that even the product with the new specifications will be ready for delivery on time. Moreover, changing back to the old specifications will not only take time, it will also cost money—and more of both if the design manager quits. The negotiation occurs at the behest of the third-party manager, whose status (as peer or superior), relative to the disputing managers, was randomly varied across participants.

In this simulation we found that third-party intervention into conflict varied systematically with the culture and the status of the third party. Third parties who were *superiors* (especially in China and Japan) took charge of the process and outcome. They typically investigated the dispute, took a companywide perspective, and imposed the resolution that they thought was best, given the circumstances. Their decision was often to go back to the old specifications. Chinese and Japanese managers told us they went along with the decision because it was made by the boss. But third parties who were *peers* (especially in China and the United States) involved the disputants in the process and outcome. They focused on the disputants' interests as the primary concern. Often they negotiated integrative resolutions of the dispute that took into account those different interests. When Japanese third parties were peers they acted more like Japanese third parties who were superiors. When U.S. third parties were superiors they acted more like third parties who were peers.[17]

Respect, Neutrality, and Control Over Process and Outcome

Disputants tend to respect third parties who are neutral. They also tend to respect third parties who allow them to feel that they are still partly in control of and active in the resolution process.

Respect and Neutrality. To be neutral is to not favor one or the other disputant. But even neutral third parties bring their own interests to the dispute resolution settings they preside over. When acting as a mediator, the third party is primarily interested in resolving the dispute, and not so much in the nature of the agreement, its affect on the relationship between the parties, or its impact on a broader community of interests. Other third parties, such as judges and arbitrators, are interested only in resolving the dispute within the guidelines of contract or law. But bosses, community officials, and government agents acting as third parties are usually interested in the substance of the resolution and its impact on the community. They may bring their own interests to the table, which can transform the dispute resolution procedure into a three-way negotiation.

Third parties who receive the highest evaluations for fairness are those who treat disputants in a neutral and unbiased fashion (even when they have their own biased opinions), who convince disputants that they are trustworthy, and who respect disputants' positions and interests.[18] High ratings on these three criteria have less to do with the third party's role (does or doesn't have ultimate authority to impose a settlement) as with how the third party enacts the role. Even third parties such as bosses (who have authority to impose settlements and also have interests of their own and therefore lack neutrality) can promote an environment of fairness by paying attention to issues of neutral behavior, trust, and respect.[19]

Respect and Control Over Process and Outcomes. Disputants are concerned about the way third parties enact their roles because third parties' involvement in disputes comes at the expense of the disputants' control over the process and outcome. *Control over outcome* is what we have been discussing so far throughout this chapter. It refers to whether the disputants ultimately get to decide to settle or not, or whether a settlement is imposed by the third party. *Control over process* refers to how much involvement disputants have in the procedure. When procedures are adversarial, involvement is greater because disputants or their agents investigate the facts and present their own arguments to the judge (as happens in the adversarial U.S. court system). In inquisitorial procedures, involvement is less because an agent of the court investigates the facts and presents an opinion to the judge (as happens in the inquisitorial French court system, with its heavy reliance on experts). In mediation, disputants typically participate fully in presenting facts, arguing their positions, and revealing their interests (often in confidence with the mediator).

There do not seem to be cultural differences in preferences for control over process. Studies in many cultures indicate that when third parties have the authority to impose outcomes, disputants prefer the process of adversarial procedures to the process of inquisitorial procedures.[20] Negotiators' preference for the adversarial over the inquisitorial process appears to be due to the contrasting relationship that tends to develop between the disputants and the third party in adversarial versus inquisitorial systems. Disputants who participate actively in resolving their dispute feel they are respected.[21] Their involvement may also lead to a sense of influence over the outcome.[22] Adversarial procedures seem to involve disputants more than inquisitorial procedures. It is the difference between "It's my word against his" (adversarial) and "It's my word against his word against the expert's word" (inquisitorial).

Further substantial evidence indicates that people whose claim has been mediated are more satisfied with the dispute resolution process than are people whose claim has been arbitrated.[23] Disputants who have been to mediation generally rate their procedure as more open and involving than do disputants who have been to arbitration. One reason may be that arbitration is usually governed by judicial rules of evidence and turn taking but mediation is much more informal. But another important reason why disputants are more satisfied with mediation than arbitration is that they retain control over the outcome of the dispute. Ultimately, they decide to resolve or not to resolve their dispute. In contrast, in arbitration the third party imposes a resolution.

Respect and control are concerns of people involved in disputes throughout the world.[24] Third-party procedures vary in how much control over process and outcome the disputants have relative to the third party. Third parties themselves can also influence disputants' perceptions of respect and control by the way they act in the arbitration hearing or mediation conference. Why care about disputants' perceptions of respect and control? In short, because these perceptions can affect whether the dispute gets resolved and whether the settlement gets implemented without further disputing.

Effective Dispute Resolution in a Third-Party Context

Excellent dispute resolvers understand the different roles that third parties can play in dispute resolution. They know when to involve a third party with authority to impose a settlement and when to involve a third party without that kind of authority. They know how to choose a third party of each type. They know to make third-party dispute resolution easily available, by building dispute resolution systems into their contracts and relationships. They also have no illusions about neutrality. They know that third parties have their own interests and biases that are affected by culture. Finally, they know that third parties who show respect and give disputants opportunity to exert control over the process and the outcome will be those who in turn will be the most highly respected themselves.

The next chapter moves us from three parties to multiple parties. With multiple parties at the negotiating table, there are opportunities to use deal-making, dispute resolution, and especially third-party skills.

Chapter Seven

Negotiating Decisions and Managing Conflict in Multicultural Teams

Multicultural teams—groups of three or more people with diverse cultural backgrounds who must make decisions—are everywhere. Such teams run the European Union (EU) and the United Nations. They manage international peacekeeping, relief, and development efforts. They coordinate the global airline alliances, such as One World and Star. They develop software on a twenty-four-hour, seven-day-a-week schedule. They merge companies and then run them. For example, a group of multicultural teams will attempt to transform the communications services' companies Alcatel and Lucent Technologies into a merged entity, with Serge Tchuruk from Alcatel as non-executive chairman and Patricia Russo from Lucent as CEO.[1]

The proliferation of multicultural teams is not the result of the latest fad in management but of the complexity and the challenge of living and working together in an increasingly interdependent world. Individuals simply do not have the breadth of knowledge and skills to accomplish multifaceted tasks, the time to complete big tasks, or the relationships to ensure that such tasks get done.

Teams bring essential resources to big, complex tasks. Teams can produce creative ideas, meet deadlines with quality products, and negotiate decisions that generate corporate growth and prosperity. Research shows that when team minorities dissent, majorities are more likely to generate original and novel solutions to problems.[2] Organizations grow faster when top-management teams engage in constructive debate.[3] Companies with top-management teams that engage in debate have a higher return on investment.[4] Cross-functional, new-product teams are more innovative when

175

they have a lot of disagreement about task design if they have a norm for open expression of doubts or if they engage in collaborative problem solving.[5] Constructive controversy, the open-minded discussion of opposing views for mutual benefit, appears to be the key to creating value during multicultural team decision making.[6]

Researchers think that when teams are engaged in a routine or repetitive task, conflict is detrimental to performance.[7] It is only when the task is nonroutine (for example, making decisions under conditions of uncertainty) that conflict of ideas appears to enhance team performance. A close look at the research on successful teams suggests that if task conflict is going to enhance rather than diminish team performance, teams need norms for open expression of differences and procedures for resolving those differences.[8] Two procedures for resolving differences are by now familiar as they are the two major elements of integrative negotiation: information sharing and using that information to negotiate an integrative agreement. Thus effective multicultural team members need all the deal-making and dispute resolution negotiation skills (including third-party skills) that so far have been the focus of this book.

This chapter is about applying negotiation and third-party skills in a multicultural team setting. We begin with a discussion of three types of conflict—task or issue-related, procedural, and interpersonal—emphasizing the different team work procedures that team members from different cultures bring to the team. We then turn to managing and preventing these types of conflict. Last, we offer advice on how to set up a multicultural team to be effective, including members' skills and motivations, and the type of environment that makes such teams effective.

Three Types of Conflict in Multicultural Teams

Multicultural teams do not necessarily succeed at complex tasks. There are three reasons why they have difficulty achieving their goals. The first is that they must negotiate agreements in the context of difficult tasks and issues over which team members differ (*task conflict*). The second reason is that they must resolve disputes about *how* to do the task (*procedural conflict*). The third reason is that task and procedural conflict often transform into *interpersonal conflict* (emotional outbursts, attributions of bad intentions, withdrawal). Although there is good reason to believe that differences that manifest in terms of task conflict may be very important to multicultural teams' success, there is also good reason to believe that procedural and interpersonal conflict in any team is a recipe for disaster. Task conflict *may* interfere with the performance of multicultural teams, but procedural and interpersonal conflicts surely do.

Task Conflict

Complex tasks seemingly pit team members against each other on one issue after another. Yet multicultural teams can negotiate high-quality decisions in this task environment if team members prioritize their interests across issues and trade off concessions on low-priority issues for either immediate or future concessions from other team members on high-priority issues.

Task conflict occurs in multicultural teams when team members deal with the task as though only a single issue were at stake and seek a distributive outcome. A European pharmaceutical company expanding globally experienced this problem.[9] The company wanted to capitalize on efficiencies in getting the same drugs approved in the European Union, the United States, and Japan. It formed a multicultural team to identify duplicated efforts and to transfer learning from one national approval team to another. The first snag occurred because the team framed its task as deciding whose standards would be used. Studies run to EU standards did not, according to the American team members, meet the standards of the Food and Drug Administration in the United States. Trying to use European studies in the U.S. approval process generated frustration and irritation between U.S. and EU team members. At first, not fully understanding the differences in standards, the U.S. team members concluded that the Europeans were unable to do good research.

The Europeans, also not understanding the differences in standards, were suspicious of why the U.S. members' standards were so strict.

Task conflict in the drug approval team was legitimate and cultural. Team members' different perspectives were grounded in the different regulatory environments they faced. In putting the team together, top management knew of these differences but charged the team with creating an integrative solution that would realize synergies for the company as a whole. Synergies could be efficiencies realized by sharing resources or by transferring knowledge from one effort to the other. Think about the natural conflict of interests in this situation that needs to be overcome to find synergies. The European team members describe their system; the U.S. members react, "That would never be acceptable in the United States." The U.S. team members describe their system, and the Europeans see the approach as cumbersome and overburdened by minutiae. The solution, easier suggested than realized, is one we described in Chapter One—transforming the single-issue task into a multiple-issue task in which decisions across issues can be negotiated taking both sides' interests into account.

Procedural Conflict

Culture confounds multicultural teams' decision making because team members from different cultures often have very different ideas about teamwork. In a recent study Kristin Behfar, Mary Kern, and I identified a number of different multicultural teamwork challenges that generated procedural conflict and threatened team performance.[10] Among these challenges were what constituted a reasonable work day, deference to hierarchy, communication (especially degree of directness), and problem solving. (See "Identifying Effective Strategies for Multicultural Teams" and "The Problems" on the CD-ROM.)

What Is a Reasonable Work Day? "In Latin America, they just don't work during certain parts of the day. There's a siesta. And it's hard to make American clients or bosses understand why work is not getting done" [a Cuban-American attorney interfacing between U.S. clients and Latin American ones].[11]

"He was willing to come in and work hard when he was there, but he didn't want to come in outside of the normal business hours" [an American working in Great Britain talking about a British member of an audit team].[12]

"There were times when we would go for dinner or another team activity and there would be basically a division of three groups. One group definitely didn't want to hang out after work hours. One group would not mind whether we did one way or the other. The other group definitely wanted the team to hang out together. So even during dinnertime or social time there would be a lot of exchange of information. So people just felt that it was still social and you were not charging time, it was highly valuable for the client and also the job itself. There was always this sort of conflict" [an Asian describing a multicultural audit team offsite in Panama;[13] it was the Americans on the team who wanted to "hang out" together after work—the Asians and Latin Americans were less enthusiastic].

In these incidents team members came into conflict over their very different assumptions about what constituted a work day. Team members' beliefs of what is expected in terms of a work day are deeply embedded in local customs. After joining the workforce and learning local norms about work, people take for granted what constitutes a work day, until they join a team in which some members' norms are different. Although conflict over what constitutes a work day may seem mundane, when not dealt with, it risks transforming into interpersonal conflict, because some team members feel they are doing more work than others.

Deference to Hierarchy. "Anybody from the States is higher up the ladder than [the employees in India] are . . . so they [the Indians] really don't want to disagree" [an American talking about a corporate multicultural team of Indians, Germans, and Americans working on consolidating a process across geographical sites].[14]

"Hierarchy isn't really a big issue in the U.S. and even in the English language—it doesn't have that kind of way to show respect.

Korea, there's about four or five kinds of ways to show respect depending upon who you are talking to. Is he lower? Is he upper management?" [a Korean working for a Korean bank on an acquisition of Korean assets by a U.S. company].[15]

"In Mexican culture, you're always supposed to be humble. So whether you understand something or not, you're still supposed to ask it in the form of a question. You have to keep it open ended . . . out of respect. I think that actually worked against me because they [Americans] thought I really didn't know what I was talking about . . . so it made me feel like they thought I was wavering on my answer" [an American of Mexican heritage working on a credit and underwriting project with an American and a Russian].[16]

In some teams, cultural differences in the degree to which members defer to hierarchy mean that disagreement never surfaces. In other teams, members are offended when their status is not acknowledged. And in still other teams, members feel their deference is equated with lack of knowledge or expertise. As we saw in Chapter Two, people in hierarchical cultures may be reluctant to confront higher-status people out of a concern for maintaining and using social hierarchies. Team members from egalitarian cultures may not understand this deference. They think because they are willing to confront, they run all the interpersonal risks. It's not fair! And, if there is not a strong confrontation of ideas about the task, the team risks negotiating a mediocre decision at best.

Communication. "I definitely noticed some cultural differences between the British and Americans. The first one being Americans are far more direct than [the British] are. So sometimes I kind of felt as though people were, not really offended, but that I was much more to the point in my conversations, both within the team and with the client, than they were. I was getting a little frustrated by how indirect they could be, kind of beating around the bush. So they might have interpreted that as being kind of confrontational on my part" [an American working with British team members on an audit in Great Britain].[17]

"One guy who is half Filipino and half Thai, he even said that he tends to be a little . . . passive-aggressive at times. He equated that to his Filipino culture and his Filipino upbringing . . ., he kind of expected you to understand that. And a lot of the times we don't [sic] understand how he's feeling so it gets to almost like a tipping point to where he's kind of had enough and it'll escalate almost into an argument at times" [an American working on a twelve-person technical sales team].[18]

"They never came out in the open or they never came forward with what exactly their viewpoints were. In the conference room, they would say 'yes we believe in this, we agree' . . . but they would come back on the phone and say this is not really what is working" [an Indian manager based in Singapore working for a multinational company talking about the Japanese members of his team].[19]

There were several major problems with communication, but directness was most vexing. Some team members were too direct, others not direct enough. Until team members got used to each other's communication style there were great risks of interpersonal conflict. Team members who were too direct risked causing others to lose face; those who were not direct enough lost face (respect) in relation to their more direct teammates. One of the major learning points for multicultural team members was what other team members meant when they said "yes." *Yes* sometimes means "yes, I'll do it" but sometimes means "yes, I'd like to do it"; sometimes means "yes, I'm listening"; and sometimes means "no."

Problem Solving. A challenge we heard a lot about in our interviews had to do with differing approaches to the team's overall task.

"The lady from Greece would say 'Here's the way I think we should do it.' It would be something that she would be in control of. The guy from Poland would say 'I think we should actually do it in this way instead.' The lady would kind of turn red in the face, upset, and be like, 'I just don't think that's the right way of doing it.' It would definitely kind of switch from just professional differences to kind of personal [differences]" [an American on a consulting team].[20]

The experience of French and U.S. engineers working for Bull, an international information technology consulting organization, thoroughly illustrates cultural differences in problem solving that foreshadow the challenges that Alcatel and Lucent Technologies are likely to have over the next few years putting their French and U.S. engineers together.

A U.S. Bull engineer says of the French, "They use a sort of Cartesian logic when approaching problems. It is important to them that they analyze the problem correctly, that they get the right conception of the problem." A French engineer responds, "The Americans are much less concerned with having the proper intellectual approach to a problem or developing a clear logical structure. Their priority is getting quickly to the action even to the point of being partly wrong." One U.S. engineer describes the French approach to problem solving as "analysis paralysis." She says that so much analysis and attention to detail slows the process down. A French engineer describes the U.S. approach as start, realize after three months it's not working, stop, change approach, and start over.[21]

These cultural differences in problem solving described by Bull employees are the result of differences in the way engineers and technicians were trained in school and were expected to perform at work before the merger that brought together the U.S. Zenith Data Systems and French Groupe Bull. Both French and U.S. employees describe the French approach as focusing on the negative—what is wrong with the suggested approach—and the U.S. approach as focusing on the positive—what is right.

These differences in approach to problem solving are neither trivial nor easy to bridge. The Alcatel-Lucent merger needs to integrate the best of the French and American problem-solving systems. But even if Alcatel Lucent develops its own corporate culture of problem solving, the differences in orientation between French and U.S. employees are going to continue. These companies are not going to change either the U.S. or the French school systems for training engineers. Both companies are going to continue to hire employees from the U.S. and France. These companies need not only a corporate approach to problem solving but also a system for resolving conflict when slower French and faster U.S. cultural approaches collide.

Interpersonal Conflict

Interpersonal conflict occurs when team members feel insulted or affronted when they are denied an opportunity to express their ideas or when their ideas are rejected. In Chapter Five I pointed out that people feel affronted when their social identity (*face*) is threatened.[22] Social identity is our sense of our own reputation, the impression we think we have made on others. People generally want to maintain a positive social identity, to be accepted and respected members of social groups to which they wish to belong or in which they must work.

Multicultural teams provide many opportunities for public confirmation and disconfirmation of social identity. Team members who look like us, talk like us, and agree with our views about the task or procedures reinforce our sense of who we are and what we know. They confirm our social identity. Their behavior *gives us face*. But multicultural teams are by definition heterogeneous. Team members who look different, talk differently, or disagree with our views may cause us to lose face and therefore threaten our social identity.

My colleague Maddy Janssens and I observed a meeting of a multicultural team charged with coordinating human resources policy across a global business. One member of the team, an Asian woman, said little the first day of the meeting. She was new to the team; previously her boss had attended. The second day the team turned to an agenda item on which she had clearly been briefed. The approach the team was planning to take was going to be a problem for her geographical area. The team listened attentively while she described the problems and suggested an alternative. Then the subgroup that dominated the team moved on, ignoring her input. She withdrew and did not say anything more for the rest of the meeting. Her action was not an emotional outburst, but it was emotional nonetheless. Whereas before the incident she had been slowly increasing her participation, afterward she stopped participating altogether. She had lost face in the interchange and been shown that she was not a powerful player in the group.

One common response to affronts to one's social identity is to hold others personally responsible and strike back. A team member may strike back immediately and push the team into open conflict, or hold back, waiting for an opportunity to extract revenge. Whether the response is immediate or delayed, when team members engage in revenge, the team is not engaged in its task.

In multicultural teams, another common response to threats to social identity is retreating into *ethnocentrism*. When team members engage in ethnocentric thinking, they focus on the superiority of their in-group (team members with whom they share characteristics or interests) and the inferiority of the out-group (team members with whom they do not share characteristics or interests). When French and U.S. managers at Bull realized how differently they approached problem solving, each group engaged in ethnocentric thinking. French managers argued, "Our way is best because we do it right and we get the right answer." The U.S. managers argued, "Our way is best because there is no single right answer and we don't waste time looking for it."

French and U.S. employees of Bull were differentiating themselves in order to maintain a positive social identity.[23] Unfortunately, this only increases social distance and competition between the two warring groups. Increasing social distance is the same psychological phenomenon that occurs when two countries go to war. Each country's press emphasizes the rightness of that country's values and the wrongness of the other country's values, resulting in in-group cohesion and a strong competitive orientation toward the out-group. Protecting social identity in multicultural teams by engaging in ethnocentric thinking only exacerbates social distance and hinders the team's ability to use different cultural perspectives.

Ethnocentric thinking does not create synergistic integrative agreements. Ethnocentric thinking can bring the team to a halt; if neither cultural group will accept the other's approach, no decisions get made, no problems get solved, and no integrative value gets discovered. According to the interviews we did with multicultural team members, when multicultural teams founder in ethnocentrism, higher-level managers step in and impose a solution that no one on the team especially likes.[24] The other undesirable effect of this action is that the team has not learned to manage its cultural differences and is likely to need management intervention again.

Yet another response to a threat against social identity (another way to save face and maintain a positive identity) is decreasing social distance between in-groups and out-groups by exerting pressure for social conformity. European and U.S. managers on the drug certification team mentioned earlier took this approach. Each cultural group tried to convince the other to adopt its protocols, arguing that its way was the right way. Of course, both groups were right: their way was right for their own environment. But the team's task was to identify synergies that could emerge from both cultures' environments.

Social conformity pressure can bring the team to a halt if neither side gives in to the pressure. If one side capitulates and the other side imposes its approach, as occurred in the team Maddy Janssens and I observed, the differences out of which synergies and integrative value could be constructed are lost to the group. This loss is important because task conflict and procedural conflict are the resources from which teams construct innovative solutions to complex problems. There has to be a better way.

Negotiating High-Quality Decisions and Managing Conflict in Multicultural Teams

Groups naturally jump into their tasks.[25] Members rely on norms imported from other group experiences for procedures[26] and use stereotypes and categorization (who looks like me, who talks like me) to make judgments about likely friends and foes. This approach may work reasonably well even for complex, multi-issue tasks when there is little or no conflict over procedures and when cultural and individual differences are few. Unfortunately, multicultural teams must anticipate complex tasks, for which different team members will have different interests (task conflict), different approaches (procedural conflict), and prejudices and stereotypes about each other's culture.

Multicultural teams set themselves up for failure unless they start out by creating procedures to neutralize procedural conflict, to negotiate and resolve task conflict, to prevent gratuitous interpersonal conflict, and to deal with interpersonal conflict when it inevitably arises.

Three Approaches to Neutralizing Procedural Conflict

Teams need procedures—norms or rules to follow when engaged in teamwork. Conflict over procedures is endemic to multicultural teams because teamwork procedures are functional solutions to managing social interaction, and different cultures come up with different procedures. It is not that one culture's procedures are right and another culture's procedures are wrong. It is just that the procedures are different avenues to solving the same problem of social interaction. In the previous section we discussed procedural conflict over norms for what constitutes a work day, issues about deference to hierarchy and status, directness of communications, and problem solving.

To neutralize procedural conflict, teams need procedures for each of these areas of conflict. However, to set up such procedures a priori would be an enormous task that would distract the team from its purpose. The solution is to have a collaboration model—a meta-model for how the team will manage conflict over procedures. Research and theorizing have identified three rather different collaboration models: subgroup dominance, hybrid, and fusion (as in fusion cooking—a cultural mix of ingredients and cooking techniques).[27]

Subgroup-Dominant Collaboration. In subgroup-dominant collaboration a coalition of team members imposes its procedures on the team. The coalition may be a majority of the team, or it may be a small group, or even a single member. It does not take much to form a dominant subgroup.[28] There are several related and consistent theoretical explanations for why subgroups form spontaneously in teams. One says that subgroups form on the basis of members' similarity to each other, and people seek to distinguish their in- and out-groups.[29] Another says people establish relative social roles on the basis of status.[30] A third explanation says that demographic faultlines appear in teams based on team members' similarities and differences. Which characteristics generate the faultlines depends on social, cultural, and personal background.[31]

Subgroups can be composed of team members from a single national culture; team members from corporate headquarters; team members from low-context, direct-communication cultures; or team members with the greatest facility with the team's common language.

In this form of collaboration the subgroup's process norms will prevail. Team members who are not part of the dominant subgroup will receive social reinforcement for following procedural rules and social ostracism for not doing so. When there is conflict over what procedures should be, the subgroup will impose order, or try to.

The subgroup-dominant model is expedient. There should be little procedural conflict. At the same time, this collaboration model may suppress different perspectives about the task that may be necessary for negotiating an integrative decision or implementing new procedures across geographical areas. The manager of one multicultural team we studied had a problem with three subgroup "tribes" (U.K., U.S., and European Continent members) of his financial research team. When he would talk, the "tribes" would quit contributing. In response, he hired a consultant to act as a meeting facilitator.[32]

Hybrid Collaboration. Hybrid collaboration is a consistent coherent-collaboration model that relies on a mix of different cultural procedures for teamwork, cherry-picked from different members' cultural models. It may therefore take some time to develop. However, once in place it provides a simplified but explicit set of rules, norms, expectations, and roles that team members share and enact. In order to work, once the hybrid model is in place, hybrid collaboration requires team members to sublimate their own cultural collaboration models (while working on the team) and conform to the team model.[33] Thus once developed, a hybrid collaboration model is not likely to change much.

Research suggests that when multicultural teams' members are culturally highly heterogeneous they are most likely to form hybrid collaborations.[34] The reason is that members of culturally heterogeneous teams cannot help but observe their differences, and out of concern for getting their work done, they actively try to understand each other and construct a collaboration that will help accomplish that. Thus a requirement for hybrid collaboration seems to be an overarching concern for accomplishment of the team's task. This group-level concern provides a justification for sublimating individual concerns. It also may serve as a standard against which members can evaluate whether their teamwork behavior is or is not appropriate. Procedural conflict, if it occurs, is managed by asking the question that evokes the teams' overarching goal: "What is best for the team as a whole?"

The research does not show that team members from different national cultural subgroups can reliably reach productive hybrid collaboration. The challenge is whether they can overcome the inherent differences in their collaboration models and surface and integrate a diversity of insights.[35] Subgroups may enable teams to extract information from team members who as individuals hesitate to speak up. However, recall the example from Chapter One of the peacekeeping team. National cultural differences blocked that team until the leader restructured the subgroups to cross national boundaries.

The financial research team, according to the member we interviewed, took about three years of twice-yearly face-to-face meetings to develop its collaboration model. The first step was to work with an outside facilitator to generate a set of team values, which included integrity, teamwork, creativity, and innovation. The values served as a set of overarching team goals, gave the team identity, and gave the team and its manager a set of criteria for evaluating performance.

When we asked in the interview what happened when a team member was not performing or participating, we received this response:

> And—and my boss has communicated that to that person [in private] . . ., you know, he's [the boss] got nice reference points. . . . Because he can go . . . " This is the value that [it] seems like you're not living." And he always puts it in that context. It's not that like, you know, you are being unethical or you are being something. It's like "look this is a value that you're not living and it's not carrying down to your group."[36]

Fusion. In fusion collaboration, different cultural-collaboration models coexist. Team members with different norms for teamwork have to figure out how to make their differences compatible. The core idea of compatibility is respect for and tolerance of cultural differences.[37] The idea underlying fusion collaboration is that the best multicultural teams find a way to agree that different members can operate under different norms.[38] Fusion refers to three means of achieving coexistence. One means is replacing one cultural-collaboration norm with another (for example, substitute the practice of formal voting with polling team members at coffee breaks). Another means is introducing the unexpected (for example, using visual images rather than PowerPoint outlines to make a point). A third means is mixing norms from different cultures (for example, giving team members sufficient information in advance so that those from collective and hierarchical cultures can consult peers and superiors, or make team decisions contingent on the consultation with constituencies, or both).

A team may develop fusion collaboration because it just does not want to spend the time to develop a hybrid model. More likely, different team members' cultural-collaboration models are sufficiently strong that the team is unable to reach a hybrid model that requires sublimation of one's own culture.

There is some evidence that teams are more likely to generate fusion collaboration if their members score high on cultural cognition.[39] Cultural cognition is a dimension of cultural intelligence. *Cultural intelligence* refers to an individual's ability to deal effectively in situations of cultural diversity.[40] Those with high cultural intelligence should be able to develop and sustain positive working relationships with those who have different cultural backgrounds, work effectively on multinational task forces, adjust successfully to short- and longer-term assignments overseas, and function effectively in jobs with international contacts and responsibilities.[41] The cultural-cognition dimension is the individual's level of cultural consciousness and awareness during social interaction.[42] (See "Cultural Metacognition Questions" and "Normative Sample for Cultural Metacognitions" on the CD-ROM.)

Fusion collaboration is both more and less than hybrid collaboration. It is more in the sense of being more flexible. Coexistence implies that the team will have an array of procedures to choose among, or to enact simultaneously. But while flexibility makes fusion collaboration more than hybrid collaboration, flexibility also makes it less. With a hybrid model or a subgroup-dominant model, team members know what the collaboration model is. With fusion, the collaboration model is always in flux.

This means that fusion collaboration takes a lot of time. It is a continual process of recognizing, respecting, tolerating, and working to make different collaboration models compatible.

The financial research team's collaboration model had some elements of fusion. As our interviewee said:

> The three individuals that are in Continental Europe, it's not blatant, but in observing them it's obvious that they're much more communal in the way that they express themselves. . . . if one of them starts to get put on the spot . . . in terms of . . . being questioned or what can we do about that or how can you [do] better, the other two will jump in and

help them. Whereas in the case of those in the U.K., and especially in the United States, we're much more individualistic. . . . So . . . for the first time [after three years], we actually called them out on it. And I think that's a huge step in terms of progress because we said okay now wait, now wait, don't start defending him . . . just let him finish, . . . we have questions for him. . . . I think if you would have tried to do that three years ago, they just would have shut it down. Everybody would have been like okay you're just picking on me. . . So a big part . . . is getting to the point of where you can acknowledge it [cultural differences] because you can't make it go away and you shouldn't make it go away. . . . You know it literally took three to four years to get to the point of where we are now. And it's nice because different cultures, it brings in nice checks and balances. . . . Americans will just forge ahead and start trying to rip apart things and let's do this and that and . . . the British take a much more pragmatic approach, let's not hurry up, you know, let's think about this. So I mean it really—I think that the group is really stronger than it's probably ever been because they are able to work together. . . . It's not like we have to work through our boss to go talk to another person or another region.[43]

The Collaboration Models in Practice. We have described the three collaboration models rather distinctly, but in practice, as with the financial research team, a team may use more than one. With effort teams may generate either a hybrid or a fusion collaboration that should minimize the problems of some parties not participating—the Achilles heel of the subgroup-dominant model. In the next section we emphasize the importance of meaningful participation in multicultural teams in order to capture differences and generate integrative decisions that team members can deliver to their constituencies.

Negotiating to Resolve Task Conflict

For multicultural teams, there are two negotiating challenges involved in resolving task conflict: generating information across multiple parties and multiple issues, and integrating that information into decisions that capture synergies and can be implemented.

Before exploring those challenges, it is worth revisiting the two criteria discussed in Chapter Three for evaluating good deals and bad deals: transaction costs, and relationships and long-term gains. Both criteria are highly relevant to multicultural teams. By their very nature multicultural teams generate high transaction costs. These costs need to be defrayed by very high-quality outcomes. A team product or decision that is innovative, captures synergies, and so on is only so good as its acceptability to the teams' constituencies. Multicultural teams need to be attentive not just to the integrative, synergistic beauty of their decisions, but also to whether those decisions can reasonably be implemented.

Generating Information—Meaningful Participation. Multicultural teams are likely to be dealing with multiple issues. They have multiple members whose interests are unlikely to be perfectly aligned and, as we have just seen, who will have different culturally based collaboration models. The challenge then is to get team members to share information. All the techniques suggested in Chapter Four for eliciting information from people from high- and low-context cultures apply in the team environment. In addition, there is one more technique: establishing a norm of meaningful participation.

Meaningful participation means a team member enters the dialogue when he or she has unique information to contribute.[44] One of the problems with teams is that a few people do all the talking.[45] A second problem is that teams tend to spend the bulk of their time talking about commonly held information rather than unique information.[46] A norm of meaningful participation is intended to counter both of these tendencies. The norm is not a panacea, it will not make these problems go away, but it will allow team members and leaders to keep the team focused on generating new, unique information and involving team members with access to it. Meaningful participation focuses on two obligations of information sharing:

- Group members should enter the discussion as their knowledge, expertise, or contacts become relevant to defining or acting on the group's task.

- Group members should enter the discussion when they harbor doubts about the direction the group is taking or the feasibility of the group's plan.

Meaningful participation was originally conceived to encourage individuals to participate in team deliberations. However, dividing the team into subgroups may be another way to encourage meaningful participation. Recall the peacekeeping team in Bosnia mentioned in Chapter One. When it became clear that the group was too culturally segmented to work together effectively as whole, the leader set up multicultural subgroups with one Russian, one Turk, one German, and one American officer in each. Meaningful participation took place in the small subgroups. Of course, the subgroups still had to present their recommendations to the group as a whole for decisions to be negotiated, but the subgroup structure used the expertise of all the team members to generate those recommendations.

Team members may be a little less reluctant to share information about priorities and interests than are deal makers or dispute resolvers because the team's task provides a common goal. Common goals encourage cooperation. Cooperation encourages information sharing. Making group goals salient encourages information sharing. Still, there may be language, cultural, structural, and psychological barriers to meaningful participation that need to be addressed.

Language Barriers. Language can be a powerful tool to exclude or include certain group members and thereby reduce meaningful participation. Examples of such language-based power practices include making personal remarks in a language some members do not understand or refusing to attend a meeting that will be conducted in another language. One of our interviewees told a pretty funny story. His team was in Korea to buy product for Latin American customers. During the negotiation, the Korea side would caucus at the table speaking Korean. This annoyed the buyers, but knowing that Korea is a high-context culture, the buyers did not complain about the caucuses, they just began to have caucuses of their own in Spanish. Members of the buyer's team who did not speak Spanish pretended to, much to the Spanish-speaking team members' amusement and to the Korean team's bewilderment. By common, implicit consent, the caucuses diminished.[47]

Language can also be a source of misunderstanding. English was the working language of the pharmaceutical team, but not all team members were equally fluent. A French team member who addressed a U.S. team member by saying "I demand . . ." was perceived as rude until both members realized that the French member was using a direct but erroneous translation of *je demande*, a perfectly polite way of saying "I am asking . . ."

Language also can be a source of frustration and anger. French and U.S. employees of Bull discussed the frustration of trying to work in a second language. One manager said, "You feel like you've lost half of your body, you feel intellectually hampered, you get frustrated, and your emotion blocks your facility with the language; you get angry."

Teams need to confront their language problems. Failing to get information from group members because they are not fluent in the team's lingua franca threatens the viability of the team's project. Here are some ideas that might help:

- Discourage jargon and make available glossaries with translations of key terms.
- Use visual aids when collecting information from group members. Expand the Negotiation Planning Document (Exhibit 1.1) by adding a column for every group member, and fill the chart in as the team discusses issues and interests. When presenting information to the team, use simple slides (lots of white space, main points, minimum of text), and make copies for all group members. When trying to reach agreement, write multi-issue proposals on a chalkboard or flip chart.
- Arrange for frequent breaks to let team members discuss what was going on in the meeting in their own language. Follow breaks with a question-and-answer session.

- Consider using an electronically networked meeting room with one or two central screens and a conference table with a small screen and keyboard at each place. These electronically supported meeting rooms are especially helpful when teams are brainstorming, working on documents, or coming up with multi-issue proposals for agreement.

- Adopt a team-endorsed way to stop a meeting and ask for clarification. For example, some teams give members flags to wave when they do not understand.

Regarding this last point, one European manager on the drug certification team described an incident in which humor eased misunderstanding and led to a clarification norm:

> I was in a meeting with both French- and English-speaking colleagues, and we listened to a presentation by an American colleague. She's a very bright woman, and when she got into her story, she started talking very fast. My other colleagues and I were starting to have difficulty in following her when suddenly she started to regularly use "LOE." Now I was completely lost. I raised my hand, "What does that mean, 'LOE'?" "Oh," she said, "lack of efficiency." A few minutes later, I was lost again. I raised my hand again, saying, "LOU." "LOU?" she asked. "Yes," I said, "lack of understanding." We started to laugh. From then on, LOU became "ell-o-you," "hello you," our way of expressing ourselves when we don't understand anymore.[48]

If this European manager had not intervened and asked for an explanation, the team would have de facto developed a norm that tolerated misunderstanding. Instead this manager promoted a norm of understanding. His first polite intervention communicated "I respect you, but I need to understand you." His second humorous intervention communicated "We need a way to alert each other when we don't understand." "Ell-o-you" or "hello you" became the group's norm.

Cultural Barriers. Another barrier to meaningful participation is cultural differences over what is appropriate behavior for teamwork. Collectivism's emphasis on harmony and hierarchy's emphasis on deference to status do not encourage people with dissenting opinions to contribute their ideas. Team members from cultures in which these values are strong may have difficulty participating in face-to-face open discussion, especially if their contribution is to dissent. Their culture's normative approach would not be to confront directly when face might be lost. Both high- and low-context communication norms can also be barriers. Direct communication may be offensive to group members from high-context cultures. Group members from low-context cultures may not understand indirect communication.

Multicultural teams need to develop a norm of meaningful participation, but realistically, cultural reasons will make some group members be more reluctant than others to share information. Here are some ideas that may help:

- Charge someone in the group with monitoring meaningful participation. The team leader can do this, but the team leader is also trying to get the team to move ahead with its task. Someone else might be better, both because the team leader will be occupied with other matters and because the team leader may need to be reminded not to dominate the dialogue. The monitor can remind the group as a whole of its norms or take individuals aside and encourage them to participate.
- Have the whole team brainstorm about not only the positive implications of an idea or approach but also the negative implications. This makes dissenting opinions the responsibility of the whole group, not just a few members.
- Gather information by e-mail.[49] E-mail has important limitations, but it also has benefits. An e-mail environment minimizes differences in power. People are less inhibited by social

norms when they communicate by e-mail.[50] Although this can be a problem, it can also encourage unrestrained participation of team members from cultures that greatly value harmony and are greatly concerned about face.[51] In cultures in which it is difficult to say no face-to-face, e-mail may actually facilitate communication about interests.

Another barrier that culture imposes on information sharing is misunderstanding and misattribution. People process meaning through the lens of their own culture. Direct eye contact implies honesty in U.S. culture but is impolite in Japanese culture. U.S. team members may distrust Japanese team members whose eyes are averted during conversation. Japanese team members may interpret the U.S. members' directness as rude and offensive. Either way, not only is meaning lost, but feelings are engaged and trust is challenged. French and U.S. members of a Bull team were exasperated with one another when the French, in keeping with their cultural norms, focused on the negative and the Americans focused on the positive. Here is some advice that may help deal with cultural misunderstanding:

- Find out if the annoying behavior is truly cultural, meaning that it is a group rather than an individual characteristic. Then find out what it means in the other culture.

Structural Barriers: Distance and Time. In multicultural teams, distance and time differences are the primary structural barriers to meaningful participation. The team will need to experiment with alternative electronic communication media, learning when and how to use e-mail, computer conferencing, and teleconferencing effectively and when to insist on face-to-face interaction. A case in point: the members of the top-management team of a high-tech company hated their weekly meetings and loved e-mail, so they decided to make most of their decisions via e-mail, meeting face-to-face only to confront tough problems.[52] The result was that face-to-face meetings became like hand-to-hand combat. E-mail had eliminated the easy issues as well as the social manners that had made face-to-face meetings tolerable, if not enjoyable.

The major problem with electronic communication is that it increases social alienation. People working electronically do not identify with their groups as strongly as people working face-to-face.[53] When we had students from Canada, Mexico, and the United States working by e-mail on a joint North American Free Trade Agreement (NAFTA) project, instructors in all three cultures received frequent complaints that team members from the other cultures were not motivated, were holding up the project, and were therefore responsible for poor quality.[54] When we do not get regular communications from remote team members, we tend to assume that they are not working. When our e-mail is not answered promptly, we conclude that they just don't care enough about the project or, even worse, that people from their culture are lazy. We tend to attribute inactivity to willful negligence, not to environmental factors, such as time zone differences or access to e-mail, that are beyond the others' immediate control.

By attributing inaction to willful activity rather than to environmental factors, we exacerbate interpersonal animosity. Teams that produced the best NAFTA projects were the ones that developed norms relating to electronic communication. They recognized the potential pitfalls of e-mail and developed proactive strategies for dealing with coordination and logistical problems. Successful teams not only alerted each other about deadlines but also consistently confirmed receipt of material, keeping everyone up to date.

Here is some advice for overcoming the barriers to information exchange due to electronic communication:

- Set norms for use of e-mail. For example, decide if receipt of correspondence needs to be acknowledged, even when no substantive answer is necessary. Decide if all correspondence should go though the team leader or whether team members are expected to copy the whole team. Decide within what time frame e-mail should be acknowledged. Set up means for alerting others when a team member is unavailable.

- Minimize having the same team members participate in conference calls in the middle of their night. One multicultural team rotates its monthly conference by time zone, not by how many people on the team are in a time zone.

Psychological Barriers. A major psychological barrier to efficient information sharing is that team members, especially those who are friends, tend to discuss common rather than unique knowledge.[55] Yet it is the knowledge that team members hold uniquely that gives the team leverage to do its task well. Meaningful participation does not imply that all team members participate equally at all times.[56] Focusing team members with relevant knowledge on the task while others are listening or doing something else is an efficient use of team resources.[57] It is also challenging to do. Here is some advice:

- The team leader and at least some team members need to have transactive memory. *Transactive memory* is knowledge of who on the team knows what.[58] For example, the member of the drug approval team who knows the most about EU standards may not be the same person who knows the most about setting up clinical trials in EU countries. When one or more team members have transactive memory, they can encourage the participation of the expert at the right time. When no one knows who is the expert, and the expert for whatever reason is unwilling to speak up, expertise is lost.

Another psychological barrier to information sharing is the tendency to focus on achieving group consensus or groupthink rather than on reaching a solution that integrates information. The Kennedy cabinet's management of the Bay of Pigs military operation to invade Cuba in 1961 is a widely cited example of groupthink. Members of the Kennedy cabinet had serious doubts about the wisdom of this invasion and the planning that went into it. Yet concerns about being accepted by other more hawkish members of the cabinet led them to keep their doubts to themselves. The invasion was a fiasco.

Teams that are overly concerned with the political repercussions of their decision can end up in this psychological trap. Groupthink leads to poor-quality decisions because groups tend to focus on a single objective when other objectives are also important. They fail to generate a full array of alternatives, fail to reassess alternatives in the light of new information, fail to examine the pros and cons of preferred alternatives, and fail to create contingency plans.[59]

The advice given earlier for avoiding cultural barriers to information sharing should also be helpful in avoiding groupthink. In addition, team members may need to be assured of confidentiality and even protection:

- Have a norm of confidentiality. Some team members may be worried that their opinions will be broadcast beyond the group and therefore do not express them, fearing harmful repercussions from outside the team.

- Protect team members from social ostracism. Some members may be worried that they will be shunned for expressing dissenting opinions. Team members should be assured that team membership is protected.

Integrative Negotiation in Teams: A Collaboration Model for Making Decisions in Multicultural Teams.

People do not always think about group decision making as a negotiation. They may think that once the information has been generated the team leader should make the decision, or the dominant subgroup, or that the group should vote or engage in dialogue until they reach a consensus. But different group decision-making norms exist in different parts of the world, in different organizations, and even within organizations, and teams need a model for decision making. I suggest integrative negotiation.

I suggest an integrative negotiation model for group decision making not just because this is a book about negotiation. Integrative negotiation fits well with meaningful participation for sharing information. It is also a better fit with hybrid or fusion collaboration models that are most likely to use the diverse knowledge inherent in a multicultural team than with a subgroup-dominant model that is not. Integrative negotiation focuses team members on interests. When interests are integrated, the decision sweeps up all the potential value from team members' diverse information and interests. Also, because their interests have been addressed, team members should be motivated to work together to implement the decision.

Getting parties to reach integrative agreements is difficult in any circumstances. In deal making it is difficult because parties assume that the resource pie is fixed and that sharing information will be detrimental to their interests. In dispute resolving it is difficult because parties are usually emotional and distrust not only each other's motives but also the information provided. In teams it is difficult because of the multiplicity of issues and interests. However, there are some ways to structure team decision making to encourage integrative decisions. The first is to make sure that the group is set up to engage in meaningful participation. The second is to apply all the integrative negotiation strategies discussed in previous chapters. What follows is specific advice on structuring issues, making multi-issue proposals, decision rules, BATNAs, and second agreements in multicultural teams.

Structuring the Issues for Integration. When multiple issues and alternatives exist and team members' priorities are spread across issues, reaching an integrative decision is usually possible. When issues or alternatives are few or team members' priorities are focused on just a few alternatives, reaching an integrative decision may not be possible, even if the team fully shares information about interests and priorities. If an integrative decision does not seem feasible because of the structure of the task and the distribution of interests, here is one option to consider before giving up entirely on integration:

- Add issues or subdivide issues. Do whatever it takes to get more elements of the task on the table to work with simultaneously.

Making Multi-Issue Offers. Teams have a tendency to follow agendas, and if they negotiate they tend to do so one issue at a time. Such practices are unlikely to produce integrative agreements. In fact they may produce no agreement at all. In one of our studies we created four-person teams and asked each team to negotiate five issues that affected all team members. Half of the teams were composed of four people whose social motivation was cooperative. (See Chapter One for a discussion of social motivation.) The other half of the teams were composed of four people whose social motivation was individualistic. Half of the cooperative teams were given an agenda to follow that required deciding one issue before moving on to the next of the five. The remaining cooperative teams were told to vote on a multi-issue offer three times during their deliberations. The individualistic teams were similarly divided and instructed.

Exhibit 7.1 shows the rate of agreement. Note that in the multi-issue offer condition, both individualistic and cooperative groups reached agreement. In the agenda condition, not even all the cooperative groups reached agreement and the individualistic groups struggled. Following an agenda inhibits trade-offs, so we wondered how the cooperative groups were getting around that problem. Videotapes of their discussions revealed that they were reciprocating each other's concessions: if A conceded to B when working on an issue that was important to B, when an issue came up that was important to A, A expected B to help out. But B was not necessarily in a position to help A on that issue. C was the problem. But because C owed something to B, B was able to help A by calling in C's debt to B. Sound complicated? Actually, it is not when team members are all cooperatively motivated. The problem is when all or even some team members are individualistic. They do not trust each other sufficiently to help out on a later issue that is important, and so they fail to make prior concessions.

Exhibit 7.1. Agreement Percentages of Individualistic and Cooperative Groups Using Agenda and Offer Decision Processes.

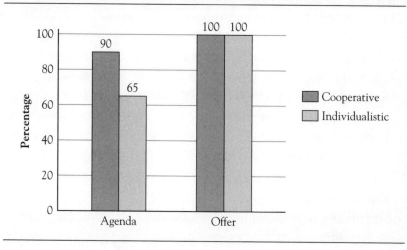

One option in teams is to try to get a commitment to generalized reciprocity as a team norm or value, much like the values that the financial research team developed to guide their collaboration. Generalized reciprocity takes advantage not only of the fact that team members have different priorities but also that some priorities are stronger than others. Teams whose members are cooperative, concerned for both their own and others' interests, operate with the implicit understanding that members whose interests are least affected by the decision should concede when they can. In return for their concession on a less important decision these team members can expect to prevail on a subsequent issue more important to them.[60] Here is some advice:

- Get a commitment to long-term reciprocity.

Another option is to set a norm to discuss all the issues before deciding or put an offer on the table that incorporates all the issues. The proposals in Exhibit 5.2 for resolving disputes are also useful for making decisions in multicultural teams. The obvious way to integrate is to agree to a set of complex trade-offs that take into account all team members' interests. Proposals to experiment for a limited period and then evaluate give those team members who have reservations about a decision an important role in monitoring its progress. Non-precedent-setting decisions preserve future flexibility and let teams take into account unique circumstances. Decisions to minimize costs to team members who are going to suffer losses build widespread commitment even among those who will bear the costs.

Decision Rules. *Decision rules* prescribe what proportion of the team must agree before a decision can be made. Such rules affect whether the team considers the opinions of minority and dissenting members. There are many choices for group decision rules.

Subgroup dominance imposes the interests of the dominant subgroup on the team. This decision rule discourages minority input and is not likely to lead to an integrative agreement.

A *majority* decision rule may have almost the same affect as subgroup dominance. This rule implies that a decision can be reached if more than half of the group's members agree. Often large factions or coalitions exist before the start of the information-sharing phase of group decision making. These a priori majorities discourage the expression of minority views. Why bother to speak up, thinks the minority member, our faction does not have the strength to prevail. Yet the research is clear that attention to minority views causes majority views to diversify.[61] Teams that let the majority rule are less likely to integrate than are teams that must reach a unanimous agreement.[62]

Achieving a *two-thirds majority* usually requires that an a priori majority gain members to control the group's decision. This often forces the dominant team members to pay attention to the views of minority members.

Consensus, too, should force the dominant subgroup or the majority to pay attention to minority views. *Consensus* is a form of majority rule in which the team continues to talk until no team member still actively opposes a decision. Team members with doubts about the merits of a decision agree that the team should make that decision despite those doubts. A consensus decision rule that is not accompanied by a norm of meaningful participation risks leading the group into a false consensus in which team members with doubts do not agree that the team should move ahead, but are unwilling to speak up.

A truly integrative, negotiation decision-making model for teams requires unanimity. This may be difficult to achieve in teams because, with multiple issues and multiple parties, some team members are likely to have some doubts about some aspects of the team's decision.

When unanimity cannot be achieved, voting may be a better alternative than consensus.[63] The reason is that voting preserves differences, gives differences legitimacy, and gets decisions made. After the vote, although some team members are on the wining side and others are on the losing side, the concerns of the losing side have increased legitimacy and may be able to be incorporated into a second agreement (see section further on).

Voting, of course, has its own pitfalls.[64] When the decision rule requires a simple majority, the order in which alternatives are voted on can affect the outcome. This is why it may be preferable to rank alternatives rather than vote on them according to some sequence. Ranking has problems, too. Team members may engage in strategic manipulation to make sure that some undesirable option will lose.

Other decision rules reduce the likelihood of integration. When one party has the authority to make a decision, that member is usually expected to act in a self-interested way. As a result, other team members may hide information. The same is true when a dominant subgroup has the authority to impose a decision on the team. Factions are not motivated to learn about others' interests because integrating the interests of nonfaction members is likely to dilute the gains available to distribute among faction members.

BATNAs. Like deal makers and dispute resolvers, teams also have BATNAs. A team's collective BATNA is whatever will happen if the team cannot reach agreement. This collective BATNA, like deal makers' BATNAs, may have vastly different implications for different team members. Reaching no agreement may be a better outcome for some team members than for other team members. Team members whose interests will be hurt the most by no agreement will be the most motivated to reach agreement and likely the most cooperative and flexible. Team members whose interests will be hurt the least by no agreement are likely to be the least cooperative and make the most demands on the group. This means that any decision will need to be better than no agreement for the team as a whole and for each individual member individually, unless the group is prepared to sacrifice a member. Trying to satisfy everyone motivates the search for an integrative agreement.

Consider the pharmaceutical team in the example early in this chapter. Japanese, European, and U.S. team members all want to maintain their own separate drug trial programs, but the parent company wants to reduce costs and duplication. The team's BATNA, no agreement, is not the status quo of three separate drug trial programs; its BATNA is an integrated program imposed by top management. Because Japanese regulations require separate drug trials on Japanese nationals due to genetic differences between Japanese and North Americans and Northern Europeans, the Japanese team members have less to lose if no agreement is reached. This means the U.S. and European team members should be strongly motivated to negotiate a synergistic agreement, and the Japanese team members should be sufficiently powerful to be sure that that agreement meets their interests.

Second Agreements. There are two different ways to search for an integrative agreement: either brainstorm about multiple alternatives and identify the best in terms of meeting parties' diverse interests, or engage in *second agreement* negotiations: agree to seek a minimum agreement and to then try to improve it.

After the team has shared information, it can use brainstorming to come up with multiple alternatives. Brainstorming rules should apply: generate as many alternatives as possible; the more unusual the idea, the better; aim for quantity of ideas without worrying about quality; do not criticize options during brainstorming; and feel free to elaborate on and extend others' ideas.[65] It may help to give the team the list of types of agreements in Exhibit 5.2. During brainstorming, alternatives should be displayed visually so as to minimize misunderstanding. Ranking should be used rather than voting because it preserves options and forces the team to make its judgments in the context of realistic alternatives. The French employees at Bull might like this approach because it results in a single "best" decision. The Americans should like that many alternatives are generated, not just one, and that this approach identifies a fallback alternative if something goes wrong with the first choice. Of course, this procedure takes time, and there is no guarantee that it will generate an integrative decision.

The second agreement requires reaching a first agreement and then trying to improve on it. After completing a Negotiation Planning Document like that in Exhibit 1.1, teams might fill in another chart documenting the least each member would agree to on the issues. If this process generates an alternative that all members can agree to, then that alternative serves as the first agreement. The next step is to move the elements of the first agreement around to see if there is a second agreement that is as good or better for all team members.[66]

Second-agreement deliberations may not stimulate much in the way of creativity, because the structure of the first agreement may constrain creative thinking about alternatives. But second-agreement deliberations do force team members to deal with issues simultaneously and so encourage integration. Of course, there are integrative agreements that generate a great deal of value and others that generate less.

Preventing Gratuitous and Unnecessary Interpersonal Conflict. Interpersonal conflict can and should be avoided. A team with a clear collaboration model that encourages sharing information and negotiating integrative decisions will still have task conflict that can spill over into interpersonal conflict, but it should have relatively little procedural conflict. Thus the first step in avoiding unnecessary interpersonal conflict is to have a collaboration model to govern team deliberations and decision making. There are a few other things that can be done as well. Task clarity helps prevent unnecessary conflict. So do respect and tolerance for social and cultural differences and creativity in the face of those differences; task-based trust; and norms for interpersonal interaction. Teambuilding, as it is typically practiced, does not necessarily build respect, tolerance, and trust that are sustainable when task conflict erupts.

Task Clarity. When team members know what is expected of them, and their expectations are consistent, they should be able to avoid conflict about the team's mission. It is management's responsibility to define the team's task, if possible. However, global management, to whom the team ultimately reports, and local management, to whom individual team members report, may have different perspectives on just what the team's task is. Part of a multicultural team's ongoing responsibility is to manage its relationships with global and local management. Consistent communications are essential to keep global and local management and the team itself focused on the same task.

Often multicultural teams have ill-defined tasks, not because management has foresworn its responsibility, but because there would be no need for a team if the task were clear. A multicultural team given no mission statement needs to define its mission and sell that mission to global and local management, from which it will need to acquire resources and cooperation to implement its projects. To develop and sell a mission, the team needs a collaboration model for making decisions. This is what the U.S.-U.K.-European financial research team accomplished; it took them three years!

Respect, Tolerance, and Creativity. There is a fine line between tolerating differences and confronting them. Used selectively, freely, and especially creatively, toleration can be a very effective way to reduce conflict.[67] Multicultural team members we interviewed had lots to say on this subject. Recall the earlier example of the Indian manager talking about the Japanese members of his team who were not willing to say no openly, but also were not cooperating? This is what the manager told us he did:

> We realized that there must be certain cultural reasons why they were not very willing to say no in our face. . . . we took some short-term action . . . to try and . . . build consensus . . . in the whole Japan IT team rather than just addressing those two people [assigned to our team]. Our idea was to do [an] eBusiness road show every time we would go to Japan. We would pull all the eBusiness team . . . into a cafeteria . . . where we would buy lunch for everybody, and my colleague and I would actually walk through success stories for the business when they had aligned with the larger business priorities. . . . We thought about just going and addressing this [the problem with the two Japanese team members] as an escalation with the Japan IT leader, but thought that would not be a great idea because the Japan IT leader would again go back to his team and seek a consensus. So we thought just going in . . . across the team would be a better idea. And we did not see any resistance in terms of the team coming in and attending a road show because the way we positioned it was just bringing everybody on the same page in terms of what successes we were achieving. It was rather subtle, not directly going and addressing the issues that we had with the two individuals. . . .[68]

Trust. Trust reduces conflict in several ways. People who trust expect trusted others to honor commitments, even commitments that are hard to define or hard to monitor.[69] With social pressure to honor commitments, people are more likely to follow through, and fewer missed commitments mean fewer recriminations over fault and less conflict. Trust also reduces conflict in a more subtle way. When we trust someone, we expect benevolent behavior and tend to interpret what we see through the lens of that expectation. That same behavior exhibited by someone we distrust is easily attributed to malicious intent. So trust reduces conflict because it increases tolerance. One of our interviewees told us about the process of building trust on a U.S. –Japanese multicultural team. The team worked in Japan for several months to evaluate whether a retail chain should expand to Japan. A U.S. team member said:

> We were very interested in immersing ourselves in the culture. . . . the Japanese associates invited us into their world. Typically it's very rare in a business environment to get invited to the home of Japanese. . . . we actually got invited to someone's home, which was a great honor. One [Japanese] associate was taking tea ceremony lessons. . . . so we actually got to go on a Saturday morning for several hours and observe, and we didn't participate, but observed her training in the Japanese tea ceremony. I think the fact that we were willing to engage her . . . helped her [be patient with us] when we didn't understand what she was trying to convey to us.[70]

Norms for Interaction. Teams' norms for interpersonal interaction develop quickly as members start working together. Although team members import interpersonal interaction norms from prior experience just as they import decision-making norms, a lot of modeling also goes on. The way team members treat each other is very visible behavior; so are team members' reactions. Either disrespectful or respectful treatment of others can rather quickly become the group norm. Recall the example of the multicultural audit team working in Panama with some members who did and others who didn't want to hang out together after work. Ultimately, the team confronted this conflict and set some rules:

> I think we had to sit down and say, hey, I understand that some people don't want to hang out together and some people do, so let's do half and half. When we say this is going to be [a] team event, then everybody has to show up. Then if you want to do something separate, either do it afterwards or do it on the days that we're not going to have a team event.[71]

Here is some advice for preventing gratuitous and unnecessary interpersonal conflict:

- Develop a common understanding of the team's task.
- Accept that all team members have legitimate interests.
- Recognize that no team member's approach is necessarily superior to any other.
- Treat all team members with dignity and respect.
- Build trust.
- Set norms of interaction.

This advice promotes a team environment that is similar to the environment fostered by well-regarded third parties in dispute resolution. Such norms of interaction reduce gratuitous and unnecessary conflict because they recognize the inevitability of differences and encourage toleration. They also provide a basis for trust that is depersonalized or group-based rather than individually based. Finally, norms such as these channel conflict toward an interest-based resolution.

The drug certification team developed the following set of interaction norms:

Don't

- Don't assume that the best ideas come from your own country or organization.
- Don't reject ideas that come from another place in the organization.
- Don't treat people from other parts of the company as second-class citizens.

Do (willingly!)

- Listen to others' ideas.
- Share your own ideas.
- Change opinions.

- Consider alternatives.
- Admit there may be more than one right way.
- Admit uncertainty.
- Work together to reduce uncertainty.
- Compromise (split the difference).
- Reciprocate (your way this time, my way a future time).
- Confront and talk through differences.

I would encourage them to add:

- Make trade-offs.

Teambuilding. Teambuilding is supposed to transform a disparate set of individuals into a cohesive, coordinated team by breaking down social and cultural barriers and building trust. Teambuilding can be physically challenging, as teams trek through wilderness, build rope bridges, or sail tall ships under the distant but attentive supervision of experts who are being paid to ensure the safety of all parties. It can be fun and constructive when teams renovate community centers or parks. Pride in team accomplishment can also generate team identity—"we did this together."

What teambuilding typically does not do is replace cultural stereotypes with transactive memory that is relevant to the task. The team member who is awfully good at tying knots for the rope bridge may not be very good at solving the knotty problems associated with the team's task. The survival television programs represent the conflicting individual and group interests of multicultural teams even better than teambuilding simulations in one important respect: in teambuilding simulations, team members' interests are aligned, whereas in real multicultural teams, members have individual and group interests that may conflict.

Trust and tolerance acquired in the context of doing the task should help multicultural teams avoid unnecessary task and procedural conflict. It cannot hurt to get to know other team members as individuals in a fun setting. But there are also risks. Distrust generated in a physically challenging teambuilding setting may carry over into the intellectually challenging task setting, even though the two settings require very different skill sets. Multicultural teams need more than teambuilding as it is typically practiced to learn to work together effectively without gratuitous conflict. Developing a hybrid or fusion collaboration model should help teams build and maintain trust and tolerance. Building the collaboration model generates expectations, using it confirms expectations, and monitoring and adjusting it builds trust.

Constructive Ways to Confront Dysfunctional Conflict. Shouting matches are not the only form of dysfunctional conflict. Conflict is also dysfunctional when team members withdraw from meaningful participation, causing decisions to be made without their input.

What to do when dysfunctional conflict erupts? There are many options. The member charged with monitoring meaningful participation could intervene in private with the withdrawn member or with the group as a whole in the case of an outburst. The monitor also might be authorized to mediate between group members or between the disgruntled member and the group. The group might have a norm that members are expected to talk to each other when their tolerance is stretched to the point that an emotional outburst or withdrawal is imminent.

It is possible to intervene in groups experiencing dysfunctional conflict and get them working together effectively, but it is not easy.[72] It is better to have conflict confrontation norms in place before conflict erupts. If the team Maddy Janssens and I were observing (earlier in this chapter) had had a conflict monitor, the woman who withdrew would have had a legitimate channel for expressing her feelings. She might have talked to the monitor instead of withdrawing. Or the monitor, sensing the woman's urge to withdraw, might have called a recess, taken the woman aside, confronted the situation, and possibly even engaged the group in a discussion of the underlying problem that this episode uncovered.

Conflict, even when associated with strong negative emotion, is not always bad for groups. Conflict lays bare important differences of opinion, and emotion conveys the strength of feelings. Just as in disputing when there is not much alternative but to threaten the other party with your BATNA, so also in teams, members sometimes have to reach an emotional stalemate before they are motivated to generate a new collaboration model.

Emotional conflict can be extremely dysfunctional for a group, but talking about emotions can be a powerful conflict management technique. As discussed in Chapter Five, apology is often helpful, especially when it is directed toward emotions ("I'm sorry you are upset"). Sometimes an apology is sufficient to resolve an interpersonal conflict. At other times, at least it reduces the tension between parties so that they can return to their task. Used in the team setting, an apology focused on feelings may be very effective in reducing interpersonal tension.

Effective Multicultural Teams

To be effective, multicultural teams need collaboration models that encourage information sharing and integrative decision making. Yet just having the collaboration model is often not enough. Team members need the skills and the motivation to use the model. They also need support from the larger organizational environment.

Skills

The skills that multicultural team members need are the deal-making skills discussed in Chapters Three and Four, the dispute resolution skills addressed in Chapters Five and Six, and a cultural consciousness and awareness during social interaction (cultural cognition)—the theme of Chapter Two. A good way for team members to acquire those skills is training the team as a whole. Team training avoids singling out particular team members who for cultural or other reasons may not come to the group with much facility in one of areas of negotiation or cultural sensitivity. Team training also helps build interaction norms that can carry over into the workplace.

Motivation

Acquiring skills is one hurdle; using them is another. Team members have to be motivated to use their skills to participate meaningfully and seek high-quality integrative decisions. Culture complicates motivation because what is motivating in one culture may not be in another. Consider the following two incidents that occurred in two executive programs on different continents in the space of a week. A U.S. manager asked me for some advice. He said that his team was using his ideas but he was not getting any recognition. He was tired of "doing all the work and not getting any of the credit." He described a team that typically generated multiple alternatives, considered their pros and cons, and then selected the alternative that had the most team support. "By the time the team members reach a decision, they all own my alternative," he complained.

That the group appeared to be using a pretty good process was not what this man wanted to hear. He wanted me to tell him how to get the team to recognize his contribution. I suggested that he start recognizing others' contributions, assuring him that the team would soon begin to model his behavior by giving him credit when credit was due. The point is not what advice I gave but rather the contrast with this next story. I sent materials for a four-day course in decision making to China two months in advance so that they could be translated. The young woman who was assigned to assist me had done a great job by any standard in organizing all the materials. Yet when I praised her in front of other staff members, I could tell that she felt very uncomfortable. "I'm just doing my job, Professor," she said. The public recognition that was so embarrassing to my Chinese assistant was exactly what the U.S. manager required to maintain his meaningful participation in his team.

Structuring financial incentives for multicultural teams is at least as challenging as determining how to use nonfinancial incentives.

Advice about team performance evaluation and pay structures suggests basic principles—establish target performance levels, quantify the criteria used to determine payout, balance individual and team-based pay, determine timing of evaluation, and so on.[73] When teams are multicultural, this advice may be too pat. Performance and financial incentives need to be sensitive to cultural differences. For example, some team members may come from affiliates or organizations where pay is performance-based and others from affiliates where it is not. An incentive system that is normative and motivating to team members from some cultural backgrounds may be foreign and even offensive to others. Even the advice to involve the team members in devising their own incentive system[74] may be anathema to team members from hierarchical cultures in which such decisions would normally be a responsibility of upper management.

It is impossible to give specific advice about motivating team members beyond two generalizations: pay attention to motivation, and pay attention to cultural differences in what is motivating.

Environments and Managing Effective Multicultural Teams

Multicultural teams are embedded in organizations or, in the case of joint ventures and alliances, in interorganizational relationships. Most discussions of teams and their organizational contexts focus on acquiring team resources, such as members' time, team space, and capital and assets. There is no question that these are important resources if a team is to be successful.

A more subtle resource is organizational support for the team's mission and collaboration model. Organizations tend to use and reinforce the use of particular collaboration models. One of the reasons multicultural teams may experience procedural conflict is that members from different parts of the organization or different organizations in the alliance have learned and are importing different ways to collaborate. A multicultural team using a hybrid or fusion model to negotiate integrative decisions may find it difficult to sustain its approach when embedded in an organization or alliance that relies heavily on subgroup-dominant collaboration.

Powerful organizational actors need to buffer multicultural teams from inhospitable environments. Ideally, these are managers whose subordinates are team members and whose areas of responsibility are likely to be affected by team decisions. These managers need to be kept apprised of the team's progress, both its successes and its failures. The purpose of keeping powerful actors in the information loop is not to prepare them to intervene if the team has difficulties but rather to build their trust in and support for team activities. The rule of no surprises works well for multicultural teams managing multifaceted interfaces with their environments.

Requirements for Effective Multicultural Teams

Multicultural teams cannot be left alone to deal with task, procedural, and interpersonal conflict as best they can. These teams need guidance in using collaboration models that neutralize procedural conflict. They need to negotiate task conflict by sharing information and making integrative decisions. They also need to know how to prevent gratuitous and unnecessary interpersonal conflict and to have norms for dealing with interpersonal conflict when it occurs. Finally, team members need the skills, motivation, environmental resources, and protection to use their collaboration model.

Managing multicultural teams is extremely challenging. Culture increases the challenge because culture affects team members' interests, the procedures that they know and feel comfortable using, and their motivation. When a multicultural team encounters a serious internal problem, its manager needs to avoid the trap of expediency—simply telling the team what to do.[75] While this may solve the immediate problem it does not allow for team learning or insight into why the problem occurred in the first place. Smart multicultural team managers, like the one responsible for the financial research team, intervene early and help the team set norms, and then encourage the team to find creative solutions to their cultural problems, much as the Indian IT manager did to get the Japanese IT division working cooperatively with the company's eBusiness strategy.

In the next two chapters we begin to focus on the broader environment in which global negotiations are embedded. Chapter Eight takes up the problem of social dilemmas—multiparty situations that require negotiation skills to manage incentives to compete and cooperate. Chapter Nine discusses the role of government in global negotiations.

Chapter Eight

Social Dilemmas

When the fishing trawler *South Tomi*, Spanish-owned but registered in Togo, West Africa, was challenged for illegal fishing by an unarmed Australian fisheries inspection ship, the trawler fled westward four thousand miles before being picked up by the South African Navy and a detail of Australian soldiers. The ninety tons of Patagonian toothfish in her hold was worth about $800,000. Since becoming the "sweetheart" dining fish when introduced to American menus in the mid-1990s, the toothfish, sold as mero in Japan and Korea and Chilean sea bass in North America and Europe, has become a symbol of the struggle to save fisheries and other natural resources. Its stocks, like those of other fisheries, have been overexploited such that reproduction cannot keep up with harvesting. It has been the focus of an unusual cooperative effort by chefs who refuse to serve this endangered species. Its fishing has been heavily monitored by governments whose agencies, like the Australian team that caught the *South Tomi*, try to distinguish between legally caught and pirated fish.[1]

The struggle to save the Patagonian toothfish is a social dilemma—a situation in which a party's pursuit of self-interest conflicts with the common good of a collective to which the party belongs.[2] The self-interest of owner-operators such as that of the *South Tomi* is to spend as little as possible to catch as much fish as possible. The collective interest of the world population that relies on fish as a major source of protein—which includes the *South Tomi*'s owner—is to maintain the fish stock.

219

This challenge of balancing self-interests with collective interests was described by Hardin as the "tragedy of the commons."[3] Hardin described a group of herdsmen grazing their cattle on a common pasture. Each herdsman has the incentive to maximize profits by increasing the size of his herd, but if all do so, the pasture will deteriorate and be unable to sustain any of the herds. If one herdsman increases his herd, others will follow, so as not to be exploited, and this will cause the pasture to deteriorate even faster, leading to the tragic destruction of the common.

If our global society is to preserve critical common resources—clean air and water, animal populations, energy, fisheries—decision makers from many different nations must negotiate resource use that places global common interests ahead of local self-interests. In service of that aim, the theme of this chapter is negotiating cooperation in multiparty social dilemmas. The chapter begins by discussing the two-party concept of a prisoner's dilemma and then turns to an overview of different types of social dilemmas. Although the public interest in many social dilemmas is for parties to cooperate, there are some instances, for example, price fixing, when the public interest is for parties to compete. The chapter discusses power-, rights-, and interests-based approaches to negotiating cooperation in social dilemmas. It includes examples of how people in different parts of the world negotiate social dilemmas.

Social Dilemmas and Prisoner's Dilemmas

Social dilemmas are multiparty prisoner's dilemmas, a concept familiar from economics. In a prisoner's dilemma two parties get locked in a competition, pitting self-interests against collective interests. A typical prisoner's dilemma example involves two suspects (let's call them Joe and Ed) who are picked up by the police on charges, say, of breaking and entering. The police would like to make a felony charge against them, but do not have enough evidence to do so unless one of them gives evidence (squeals) on the other. To encourage squealing, the police separate the two suspects and make to each the offer in Exhibit 8.1.

Looking at Exhibit 8.1 we see that if neither Joe nor Ed confesses (cell A) they each get two years on the breaking and entering charge. However if both confess (cell D), each gets the longer five-year sentence. The incentive comes in cells B and C. In cell B if Ed does not confess and Joe confesses (essentially gives evidence against Ed), Ed gets ten years and Joe gets off. In cell C it is the opposite. Rational self-interest is to confess, hoping that the other

Exhibit 8.1. A Prisoner's Dilemma.

		Joe's Choices	
		Do Not Confess	Confess
Ed's Choices	Do Not Confess	A Joe = 2 years Ed = 2 years	B Joe = 0 years Ed = 10 years
	Confess	C Joe = 10 years Ed = 0 years	D Joe = 5 years Ed = 5 years

party will not confess, and so get no prison term. But if confessing is in Joe's self-interest, then it is also in Ed's self-interest, meaning that rational self-interest leads to the worst collective outcome—both go to prison for five years. The best solution is to trust the other party not to confess and not to confess yourself, but then if you trust the other party not to confess, the rational choice is to confess yourself and get out of jail free!

If you think this dilemma is difficult for two parties to resolve, consider how much more difficult it is in the multiparty situation. In May 2002 the seventy members of the International Whaling Commission thought they had reached a compromise by doubling to four the annual take of whales by the Caribbean country of St. Vincent and the Grenadines in return for Japan and its Caribbean allies' votes the following day to renew the aboriginal subsistence quotas of Arctic native peoples. But the day after the St. Vincent-Grenadine vote, Japan and its allies voted against the Arctic peoples' subsistence quotas.[4] In a multiparty dilemma the risks of exploitation are multiplied by the size of the group, and even a small coalition can defect and upset the world order.

Types of Social Dilemmas

One important distinction among types of social dilemmas is whether the public interest is for the parties to compete or cooperate. Then, within the type of social dilemma for which the public interest is cooperation, there are two further subtypes based on whether parties are taking from the common resource pool or contributing to it. Although each type of dilemma has some unique characteristics, all have in common the tension between self-interests and collective interests.

Competitive Dilemmas

Competitive social dilemmas are situations in which it is in parties' self-interest to cooperate but in the broader public interest for parties to compete. The competitive dilemma that affects most of us on a day-to-day basis as we turn on our lights, heat and cool our houses, and drive our cars for work or recreation concerns the price of oil. OPEC (the Organization of Petroleum Exporting Countries) is a small group of competitors trying to determine production quotas so that they can control the price of their product. OPEC can do so because it is a global organization and not restricted by national or international law. It is in the public interest for OPEC to pump sufficient oil that it is plentiful and cheap. But here is the competitive dilemma: it is in the self-interest of individual OPEC countries to pump oil, as the more they pump the more revenues they generate; but when all OPEC countries increase their supply, the price of oil drops faster than the excess supply is bought. Volume does not make up for lost margin, and all oil-producing countries lose. OPEC's collective interest is to restrict the supply of oil by self-imposing quotas and thereby increasing the price and OPEC members' revenues.

Consumers of OPEC oil have a public interest in cooperation that leads to a cooperative social dilemma of their own. The only sure way to encourage OPEC to pump more oil and so reduce the price of oil is to decrease the demand for oil. Negotiating a worldwide reduction in energy consumption is a cooperative social dilemma. Let the other guy drive a hybrid car, or make do with fans instead of air conditioning! So far, as we shall see a bit later in the chapter, there has been some progress in reducing emissions from burning fossil fuel to produce energy, but not much success in reducing basic energy use.[5]

Collusive pricing is a response to a competitive social dilemma. *Barrons* defines collusive price setting as a combination or conspiracy for the purpose and with the effect of raising, lowering, or stabilizing the price of a commodity in interstate commerce. This is what OPEC does. But collusion to set prices is illegal in the United States and the European Union. Yet despite illegality, there are many examples of collusive price setting that occur because of the underlying competitive dilemma. Colluders know that if they collude and set prices among themselves, they will share the market at higher margins. Among colluders receiving publicity recently are producers of vitamins, corn syrup, and memory chips.

Some of the largest multinational corporations, including Hoffman LaRoche of Switzerland, Rhone Poulenc of France, BASF of Germany, and two Japanese companies, Eisai and Daiichi, conspired to raise the price of vitamins over a ten-year period ending in 1999, when these companies admitted to the conspiracy. Representatives of these companies met secretly in hotels and homes around the world to agree on how much of each product each company would sell and how much they would charge for it. The FBI's hidden camera caught an executive at one of these meetings saying to another, "They [the consumer] are not my friend. And we gotta have 'em. Thank God we gotta have 'em, but they are not my friends. You're my friend. I wanna be closer to you than I am to any customer. 'Cause you can help me make money."[6]

The nature of the competitive dilemma makes involvement risky: someone is likely to tip off the regulators. It may be the consumers, angry because they get the same price quote no matter which supplier they contact, as was the case for memory chips.[7] It may be an outbreak of dissent among conspirators, since defecting from the price arrangement is in the self-interest of the colluders.[8] It may be senior executives who know the activity is illegal and want to save their own careers, as was the case in one of the companies producing the sweetener known as high-fructose corn syrup.[9]

Involvement in a competitive dilemma is also risky because in the United States convicted price fixers go to jail and their companies pay huge fines. Michael D. Andreas, the former vice chairman of Archer Daniels Midland, served a prison term for price fixing associated with the lysine market. The same company paid $400 million to settle the corn sweetener lawsuit. It is rare for executives caught in a price fixing scheme to serve jail time in the European Union, because EU regulators do not have the legal rights to go after individuals in the same way U.S. regulators do. But the European Union does impose substantial fines, up to 10 percent of overall worldwide sales. For example, the Swedish-Swiss engineering company ABB paid €70 million, or approximately 20 percent of its pipe sales. The German cartel office billed Heidelberg Cement €702 million, and the French office collected €534 million from a group of mobile phone companies.[10]

Explicit collusion such as that engaged in by the vitamin price fixers is in violation of antitrust laws. However, companies do cooperate implicitly by publicly signaling the choices that they make. Airfares and frequent flyer awards are good examples of this. Airline executives do not engage in collusive decision making like the vitamin price fixers did. They do something more indirect. They announce a new fare increase a few days ahead of the date the fare will be implemented and wait to see what their competitors do. If the competitors match the increased fare, all share the market with higher margins. If the competitors do not match the increase, the initiator can roll it back and continue competing for market share at lower margins.[11]

Competitive dilemmas are pervasive and complex because there are two sets of collective interests: the collective interests of the competitors and the collective interests of the public—consumers of the competitors' products. When OPEC nations make decisions about production quotas, there is no representative of the oil-consuming countries at the table. OPEC has to judge how much it can restrict production and increase prices before oil-consuming countries and consumers react, for example, by buying low-fuel-consumption cars or by releasing oil reserves. Consumers are not without power vis-à-vis a competitive cartel, but they have to coordinate their actions, and that may be difficult and take time. Meanwhile, if the cartel holds, it reaps windfall profits.

Here is some advice about managing competitive dilemmas when collusion is a violation of anti-trust:

- Signal your strategy into the market place.
- Keep your strategy simple. You want your competitors to understand it!

- Do not be the first to defect; signal your willingness to cooperate.

- Focus on your own payoffs, not your payoffs relative to others. This is a strategy to gain margin, not market share.

- Consult your lawyer to make sure you are not crossing the line of illegal collusion.

Cooperative Dilemmas

As we noted earlier, there are two subtypes of cooperative dilemma, depending on whether parties are taking from or contributing to the common resource pool.

Taking Dilemmas. Taking dilemmas are social dilemmas like that of the tragedy of the commons. People in industries that extract or use resources—fishing, forestry, agriculture, energy—have to make decisions in the context of a social dilemma. If they extract too much, the resource will be depleted, but while they are depleting the resource, they are profiting greatly. This is OPEC's long-term problem. OPEC nations are extracting a resource that cannot be replenished. How much should they extract to serve current interests versus conserve for future generations? In contrast, the fishery and forestry industries are extracting resources that can be replenished, if self-interests can be sublimated to collective interests. Since the Patagonian toothfish was introduced to American menus in the mid-1990s, stocks have been depleted by 50 percent.[12] Given the fish's slow rate of reproduction in the cold waters of the Antarctic, and its remote natural habitat, making the way it is caught and sold difficult to regulate, you should order this fish now. That way, when the fish becomes extinct (you of course helped make it so), you can boast that you tasted it once!

Taking dilemmas pose particular problems because surveillance of extraction and harvesting is often difficult and expensive, due to the remote locations of the resource. Resource consumers are also often spread across the globe and have no social identity as a group that might be used to control consumption.

Contributing Dilemmas. A free rider is a person who does not personally contribute but benefits from the contributions of others. Free-rider dilemmas are social dilemmas about the decision to contribute to a public good. Tax evaders, despite paying no taxes, benefit from public services: they are free riders. Public radio and television in the United States are beset by the free-rider problem: a great many people listen or watch but do not make financial contributions during membership drives. The same can be said of teams. Free-rider team members who do not contribute nevertheless share in the team's rewards along with team members who do contribute. If the team is unsuccessful, the free rider, unlike other members of the team who contributed, will not feel exploited. The first challenge in managing free riders is identifying who they are. The second challenge is instilling in them a sense of responsibility to contribute to the public good.

Using Negotiation Skills to Manage Social Dilemmas

Social dilemmas are all around us. They may be local, involving the use of water in an area beset by drought, free riding on a grade school history fair project, or competition between gas stations or fast-food restaurants on facing street corners. They may also be global, involving emissions that deplete the ozone level, free riding as a member of a global airline alliance team, or competing for international market share of laundry detergent. Regardless of whether the dilemma is local or global, managing it requires negotiating the balance between self-interests and collective interests.

A good standard for determining whether a social dilemma is under control is whether there is a balance or equilibrium between self- and collective interests, such that the public interest is being met by the availability of the collective good: clean air and adequate water, or public entertainment or the arts. When the public interest is not being met, self- and collective interests are in disequilibrium. This section addresses the question of how to use what we have learned about negotiations to turn a social dilemma in which self- and collective interests are in disequilibrium into one in which the collective interest is being met.

Chapter Five introduced three ways to resolve disputes: interest-based approaches, rights-based approaches, and power-based approaches. This framework also provides a way of determining how to intervene in social dilemmas to protect the public interest. Just as we saw that interests, rights, and power approaches were not all equally acceptable across cultures, in managing social dilemmas some approaches may be more acceptable to parties from some cultures than from others.

Power-Based Approaches to Negotiating Social Dilemmas

Not all parties to a social dilemma are equal. Some parties are more powerful than others, and they can lead the way to cooperation in social dilemmas, if they only will. Chefs from Chicago's most famous restaurants (such as Charlie Trotter's, Frontera Grill, and so on) signed a pledge in March 2002 to keep Chilean sea bass off their menus as part of a nationwide boycott to preserve this endangered species. Yet at the same time there was little pressure on Chicago caterers to join the boycott, since the fish is a staple of their business. (It does not taste fishy; can be served baked, grilled, broiled, or sautéed; and is difficult to overcook.) Still, said Frank Mendoza, at the time executive chef at Ristorante We in the W Hotel in Chicago, "if you put something on the menu, people are more likely to cook it at home." Mendoza's logic argues that if the celebrity chefs take it off the menu, people will be less likely to cook it at home or order it in a noncomplying restaurant.[13]

There are many examples of powerful parties taking the lead in negotiating a cooperative equilibrium in social dilemmas. Wal-Mart's chief executive announced in March 2006 that the company planned to spend $500 million a year to reduce greenhouse gases, build more energy efficient stores, and reduce packaging waste. No matter Wal-Mart's motivation, it is investing money that it could be using for other purposes. And just like the Chicago celebrity chefs, green initiatives of a company such as Wal-Mart, which controls so much of the retail market and has such an impact on its suppliers, are likely to have a huge ripple effect.[14] McDonald's is another powerful party that is taking a somewhat different leadership role in maintaining biodiversity of agriculture. In 2002 McDonald's joined with an NGO, Conservation International, to see what its food suppliers could do to reduce environmental impact at no or low cost. McDonald's met with its key suppliers and "negotiated" a set of guidelines for what McDonald's calls a "socially responsible food supply." Irrespective of whether these guidelines were negotiated or dictated or whether their costs are affecting McDonald's margins, along with those of its suppliers' margins, when McDonald's speaks to its suppliers, many listen and cooperate.[15] There is another somewhat counterintuitive but very important effect of being a powerful party in a social dilemma. Even when a powerful party will not cooperate, there are incentives for weaker parties to cooperate among themselves. A good example of this is the fact that 164 countries have signed the Kyoto Protocol to the United Nations Framework Convention on Climate Control. Among the signatories are Canada, China, Russia, the European Union, and all countries in Latin America. The United States and Australia are notably not on the list.[16] Why sign if you know that the United States, the world's largest producer of greenhouse gas, will not cooperate? Well, some cooperation is better than none, and politics are dynamic. Ironically, in 2000 President Clinton was prepared to sign a protocol that had many of the features of the current one, but the European Union was not yet ready for it. Once George W. Bush became president, the United States pulled out of the Kyoto Protocol negotiations.

Although you may never be called upon to represent your country in international negotiations like the ones to generate a plan to implement the Kyoto Protocol, you may lead your company in negotiations such as occurred between McDonald's and its suppliers. The principles for leading such a negotiation are the same as those for deal making, discussed in Chapters Three and Four, for dispute resolution, discussed in Chapters Five and Six, and for negotiating in multiparty situations, discussed in Chapter Seven.

- It is essential to understand parties' interests.
- It is important that parties know the issues and options in advance and have time to negotiate with their constituencies.
- It is important to put multi-issue proposals on the negotiating table that build in trade-offs that capture differences in interests. (There will be more about how to do this when we discuss tradable permits.)

The first set of negotiations to generate a plan to implement the Kyoto Protocol failed at the last minute in November 2000 because of strong political differences between the European Union, whose green constituency wanted overall greenhouse gas reductions and top-down regulation, and the United States, whose industrial and agricultural constituency wanted carbon sequestration (credit for trees and managed farmland acting as "sinks" to absorb greenhouse gas), market mechanisms (tradable permits), and minimal regulation. One of the negotiation errors at this stage was that the idea of "sinks" had only been introduced to some negotiators at the meeting, far too late to be viewed by the EU countries as anything other than the United States trying to get something for nothing. A year later, this time without U.S. participation (the newly elected George W. Bush administration in the United States was not interested in participating in negotiating global regulation on environmental issues) an agreement was reached on a set of trade-offs. One of those insisted upon by Russia, Canada, and Japan was credit for carbon sinks. Another was unfettered trading of greenhouse-gas emissions. In return, the European Union got what it wanted in terms of definitions of what was an infraction, how to decide a case, and what the penalties would be, as well as an overall goal of cutting emissions to levels about 5 percent below emissions levels in 1990.

Rights-Based Approaches to Negotiating Social Dilemmas

Rights-based approaches to negotiating equilibrium in social dilemmas involve either generating social norms for cooperation or legal regulation to allow monitoring and enforcement of cooperation.

Generating Social Norms. A norm, as we learned in Chapter Two, is a rule of appropriate social interaction—what one ought to do in a given situation. Norms are useful in regulating peoples' behavior in social dilemmas because they provide a means of self-regulation and do not require infrastructure for monitoring and enforcement. Research has identified three norms that seem to regulate behavior in social dilemmas: commitment, reciprocity, and equity.[17] In addition, in local environments unique and elaborate norms can emerge to regulate social dilemmas.

Norms of Commitment. When we make public commitments, we signal our intentions. This gives others a basis for forming expectations of us and for acting according to those expectations. This allows for coordinated action, assuming we follow through on our intention. If we fail to do so, we not only disrupt social equilibrium but also generate distrust, loss of face, and other social sanctions. For all these reasons, the norm of commitment works to generate cooperation in social dilemmas.

Our research indicates that in all cultures it is very important to communicate commitment to cooperate in order to get a group to cooperate in a social dilemma. We frequently run a social dilemma exercise concerning fish harvesting (SHARC) in executive programs on negotiation. SHARC involves four parties who are harvesting different amounts of shark from the Atlantic Ocean: the most powerful party in economic terms, the large commercial fishers (big boats); the small commercial fishers (smaller boats that fish closer to shore); and two economically less powerful parties, namely, recreational competition fishers ("Compete in how big a shark can you catch") and recreational tour fishers ("Come out with us and catch a shark to mount on your family room wall").[18] To maintain the resource these fishers have to reduce the overall harvest by one half, from 5000 to 2500 metric tons of shark per year. How to do so is the social dilemma. We assign participants to one of the four roles, give them time to prepare, and ask them to make a decision about how much they will reduce harvesting and how much they expect others to reduce their harvesting. Then we put them in a group with three other fishers, allow them to discuss the problem for thirty minutes, and bring them back to once again make separate decisions.

Exhibit 8.2 shows that communication (the thirty-minute discussion) significantly reduced the overall level of fishing, regardless of whether the parties involved were American, Korean, Japanese, or Chinese managers. The biggest reduction was in the American data, since prior to discussion American managers were not very willing to reduce their harvesting. Post-discussion fishing levels are

Exhibit 8.2. Differences in Group-Level Harvest Pre- and Post-Discussion, by Culture.

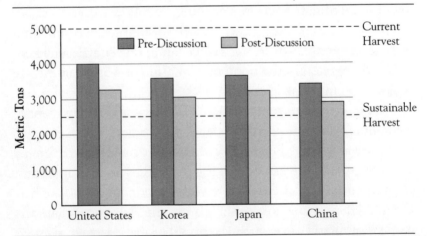

not significantly different across cultures. A few groups in all cultures do reach the 2500 metric ton level, which is sustainable.[19]

We use commitment norms almost unconsciously in many situations. For example, when working in teams at the end of the meeting, we go around the table and get everyone to openly commit to what he or she is going to do. They work, too!

Norms of Reciprocity. The norm of reciprocity is the social imperative to give benefits to others equivalent to the benefits they give you.[20] As we saw in the example of team decision making using agendas in Chapter Seven, generalized reciprocity of cooperation allows a multiparty team to develop integrative agreements.

Reciprocity works in a similar way in social dilemmas, so long as trust is not violated. Of course, trust is sometimes violated, as in the International Whaling Commission example earlier in this chapter, in which Caribbean countries and Japan failed to reciprocate following a vote to double the St. Vincent-Grenadines catch. Recall from Chapter Seven that agenda voting only works when all parties' social motives are cooperative, which turned out not to be the case among members of the Whaling Commission.

Norms of Equity and Equality. An equity norm distributes resources according to some standard of fairness, usually in proportion to contributions, inputs, or costs.[21] The problem with the equity norm in the context of social dilemmas in which parties are from different cultures is that what is perceived to be fair in one culture may not be fair in another. For example, in the SHARC fish-harvesting dilemma exercise, the large commercial fishers are more powerful economically than the others. This party has the capacity to harvest more fish than the others, and makes a large profit from doing so. We found that the powerful party seems to be using a different equity norm in U.S. and Chinese groups than in Korean or Japanese groups.

Exhibit 8.3 shows the difference between what the powerful party (large commercial fishers) in the SHARC dilemma harvested

Exhibit 8.3. Perceptions of the Powerful Party:
What Is Fair for the Powerful Party to Harvest Minus
What Is Fair for the Two Weak Parties to Harvest, by Culture.

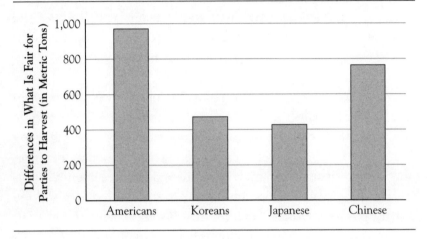

and what that party thought the two weakest parties should harvest. (Note that the vertical scale is not the same as the one in Exhibit 8.2.) The difference in these allotments is almost a thousand metric tons when Americans take the powerful party's role and almost eight hundred metric tons when Chinese take this role. Their behavior exhibits an equity norm. It is fair for the powerful party to harvest more and the weaker parties to harvest less fish. In contrast, the Japanese and Koreans' decisions illustrate an equality norm: it is appropriate for the more powerful party to make a bigger reduction and the weaker parties to make a smaller reduction in harvesting. The differences between the powerful party and the weaker parties in these two cultures are five hundred metric tons or less.

This contrast in the response of the powerful party when the dilemma is negotiated in the United States versus in an East Asian country appears to be due to cultural differences in the value for hierarchy in East Asian cultures and egalitarianism in the United States.[22] Recall from Chapter Two that in hierarchical cultures there is a social imperative for powerful parties to take care of weaker parties. This may explain why the powerful-party role players from

Korea and Japan—both hierarchical cultures—perceive a fair distribution of resources as needing to be more equal across participants than do the U.S. managers in a powerful-party role. They seemed to be using an equality norm. Are you wondering about the Chinese? In Exhibit 8.3 they look more like the Americans than like the other Asian groups. In a follow-up study, the Chinese managers in the powerful role still harvested according to an equity norm (meaning they harvested like the Americans), but they admitted at the same time to feeling responsible for the welfare of the weaker parties.

Emergent Local Norms. So far we have been discussing norms of commitment, reciprocity, equity, and equality that are general and can be observed directing and controlling people's behavior in many different cultures. In addition to these general norms, very specific norms emerge in local communities for the purpose of resource conservation and management.

These emergent local norms have two characteristics. First, allocations are based on local cultural definitions of fairness. Second, the sustainability of the norm is based on the ability and willingness to bar outsiders.[23] Examples range from forest and meadow management in Japan and Switzerland to irrigation of farmland through the use of common water canals in Spain; the Philippines; and Bali, Indonesia.

Bali's unique system of water management combines Hindu religious values dictating equal sharing with elaborate social structures and complex engineering.[24] Balinese rice farmers belong to community organizations called *Subak*. All *Subak* members have the same right to irrigation water in return for free communal work on *Subak* activities. The water is allocated by dividing the total amount of water available by the number of *Subak* members. Work obligations are directly proportional to the amount of water farmers receive. Members can participate in the manual labor necessary to maintain the complex irrigation system or provide financial compensation in lieu of manual labor. Upstream and downstream participants cooperate in this system because the flow of water also affects the population dynamics of rice pests. If downstream fields are not sown because of lack of water, pests will move upstream!

An important factor in developing and maintaining local norms is keeping control of the resource out of the hands of outsiders. The *Subak* system in Bali has successfully done so for over a thousand years. So long as the need for water in Bali was primarily agricultural, the *Subak* system worked extremely well. However with increasing demands for nonagricultural use of water, the *Subak* system is being challenged.[25]

Advice for Using Norms to Regulate Behavior in Social Dilemmas. There are two problems with relying on norms to regulate behavior in social dilemmas: different cultures use different norms to allocate resources, and those engaged in the dilemma may not adhere to the norms.

The cultural problem means that when a social dilemma involves people from different cultures, the norms that they think are fair are not likely to be the same. Recall that in the first round of Kyoto Protocol negotiations, the European Union thought emission reduction and regulation were fair and the United States thought that credits and trading were fair—cultural differences that are consistent with differences in political, economic, and social ideology between the United States and the European Union.

Adherence to norms works on several levels. Commitment and reciprocity norms align self- and collective interests. Equity norms provide a basis for one's own and others' behavior, and so minimize disruptive surprises that otherwise can be viewed as defection from cooperation. Barring local area norms from incursions from the outside sustains the norm and reduces defection. Here is some advice for using norms to generate cooperation in social dilemmas:

- Make commitments that you are willing to follow through on.
- Ask for others to make similar commitments.
- Ask for generalized reciprocity and indicate when you are willing to engage in it.

- Find out whether equity or equality dominates social interaction in the cultures with which you are interacting.
- When local norms are working to generate equilibrium, try to buffer those local areas from incursions by outsiders.

However, in this increasingly global world, it is increasingly difficult to buffer local norms from external pressures and social change. It is at this point that more formal, rights-based solutions are needed in the form of government regulation.

Legal Regulation. Regulatory solutions to social dilemmas range from privatizing commons to capping use to setting up tradeable permits programs. Each of these different approaches to regulating behavior in social dilemmas has strengths and weaknesses. They also appeal differently and at different times to people from different cultures.

Privatization of Commons to Regulate Behavior in Social Dilemmas. Privatization works by defining boundaries within which an entity—person, organization, or community—has the sole rights to use the resource. For example, each *Subak* in Bali has total control over allocation of water within its own watershed area. While this area is not private property, it is treated as such. Privatization works to conserve resources (the public interest) because it aligns self-interests with the public interest. Resource users who control their resource (like the Balinese *Subaks*) conserve the resource.

Privatization is appropriate for managing resources such as meadows and forests that do not move. But many natural resources move in unpredictable paths through air, water, and soil. Managing these resources requires negotiating harvesting caps and monitoring and enforcement.

Caps, Goals, and Incentives to Regulate Behavior in Social Dilemmas. Goals motivate performance. Resources are conserved when governments set goals for reduction of greenhouse gas emissions and provide positive incentives (for example, tax reductions) to parties who meet those goals and negative incentives (for example, fines) to those who do not. British Prime Minister Tony Blair has called on Britain to reduce carbon emissions to 60 percent of its 1990 levels by 2050.[26] California Governor Arnold Schwarzenegger has called on his state, which is twelfth in the world in generating greenhouse gases, to cut emissions to 2000 levels by the year 2010. Together Britain and California are planning a joint market for trading permits for greenhouse gas emissions.

Tradable Permits. Tradable permits work along with caps and goals to regulate behavior in social dilemmas. This is the mechanism of the market-based system set up by the 1990 amendments to the U.S. Clean Air Act. The U.S. Congress set up a trading system in which power companies can buy and sell permits to emit sulfur dioxide. Each year the number of allowances drops, with the goal of halving emissions by 2012. First the government gave power companies emission allowances or permits based on historical patterns and required power generators to put monitors on their smokestacks. Then the power companies had a choice: buy permits and keep polluting up to their limit or else install expensive scrubbers on smokestacks. For a company such as Duke Power that was burning low-sulfur coal and whose emissions were already pretty clean, scrubbing a ton of sulfur out of their emissions might be extremely expensive, for example $300 a ton. For a company like Illinois Power that was burning high-sulfur coal and whose emissions were pretty dirty, scrubbing a ton of sulfur out of their emissions might be cheaper, for example, $100. So if Illinois power would sell Duke Power a permit for $200, Illinois power would make $100 and Duke would save $100. However, possessing one less permit and Duke Power's $100, Illinois Power would have to install a scrubber to remove the ton of sulfur dioxide that it no longer was permitted to emit.

Although not without its critics, because some "hot spots" remain across the eastern United States, the U.S. system has been quite successful in emissions reduction. The latest data from 2004 show a 40 percent reduction of emissions compared to 1980 levels. The goal for 2010 is to reduce emissions to 50 percent of 1980 levels. And compliance is close to 100 percent.[27] Not only have the costs of eliminating the emission of ten million tons of sulfur dioxide been substantially less than U.S. government or power industry estimates, but also the cost of monitoring the system has been five to ten times less expensive than expected.[28]

The success of the U.S. tradable permits system provided a model for carbon trading within the Kyoto Protocol. The EU program began in January 2005 to help members meet their Protocol commitments. European Union members negotiate with Brussels to receive permits and then divide permits among companies located in their nations. These companies then buy or sell allowances according to the same market mechanisms as for the Duke and Illinois Power companies in the earlier example. Emissions contracts are being traded in Amsterdam, Paris, Oslo, and Leipzig as well as in markets in Austria and Spain.[29]

Advice on Using Regulation. Regulation and markets have had a remarkable effect on reducing greenhouse gases in the past few years. The U.S. system that coupled goals with tradable permits demonstrated that this combination of regulation and free market could be successful within a nation-state. The European Union's new system, assuming it too is effective (at this writing in summer 2006, it is suffering some two-year-old growing pains), should demonstrate that the combination of goals and free market also can work across national boundaries.

Interest-Based Approaches to Social Dilemmas

An interest-based approach to managing a social dilemma involves realigning self-interests so that they are consistent with collective interests. This requires either a reframing of the situation or a shift in social identity from the self to the group coping with the social dilemma.

Reframing the Situation. Give different people the same social dilemma situation, such as the fish-harvesting problem, and you will be surprised at the variation in their behavior. For example, the powerful party in our SHARC dilemma exercise can harvest between four hundred and two thousand metric tons of fish. American managers playing this role use the full range; and 50 percent of them harvest less than sixteen hundred metric tons, which leaves them with a loss of profits no matter what other parties do. Why do they do so? In class discussions they take the moral high ground: "It was the right thing to do." Several different research studies suggest that framing a social dilemma as a moral or ethical problem is more likely to engender cooperation than framing it as a business or economic problem.[30] Framing a social dilemma as a moral or ethical problem versus an economic or business problem seems to work because the "frame" focuses parties on the context[31] and stimulates those context-dependent knowledge structures we talked about in Chapter Two. The moral or ethical frame stimulates a cooperative and possibly even an altruistic knowledge structure. The economic or business frame stimulates a competitive and defensive structure.

Shifting Social Identity from the Self to the Collective. The way to shift social identity from the self to the collective is to make group membership salient.[32] Consider OPEC again. OPEC member nations have national self-identities. When OPEC nations are ignoring OPEC quotas, their self-identity is as a nation, not as a member of OPEC, whose standard they are ignoring. When OPEC nations are maintaining the group's quotas, their self-identity is aligned with the group—how else can they explain their compliance? Certainly not by self-interest.

There are three techniques for making social identity salient. The first is setting collective goals. A *collective goal* is a goal that all group members agree to. A collective goal may help parties recognize that their self-interests can be promoted by cooperating with others. A major factor motivating OPEC members to renegotiate quotas and stick to them in 1999 was their individual economic problems caused by low oil prices. OPEC members' collective goal of improving their individual economic situations was aligned with their self-interests. (See "OPEC Negotiations" on the CD-ROM.)

A second technique for making social identity salient is increasing contact. *Contact* places dispersed parties to a social dilemma in touch with one another. Contact works if it generates respect for differing interests and leads to trust that cooperation will be reciprocated and commitments to quotas will be kept. The hierarchical structure that links the Balinese *Subaks* provides contact among *Subaks* responsible for different watershed areas. Without something like the thousand-year history of the Balinese *Subaks*, it is sometimes necessary to build trust between parties who are interdependent but who previously have had little contact. The way to do this is to signal cooperation, much the same way the airlines engaged in competitive dilemmas do when raising prices: one or all parties take small cooperative steps that are easily monitored. Once there is an initial basis for trust, larger cooperative steps may be possible.

A third technique for making social identity salient is recategorization. *Recategorization* involves encouraging parties to a social dilemma to see themselves not as separate entities but as a single group confronting a common problem. This often involves invoking a superordinate category. For example, in dealing with oil-consuming nations, Saudi Arabia might represent itself as Saudi Arabia, the largest oil-producing country in the world, or as OPEC member Saudi Arabia. The distinction is subtle but important because the difference signals the priority of collective interests over self-interests.

Cultural Differences and Making Social Identity Salient. The three techniques for making social identity salient may work somewhat differently for people from collective and individualist cultures. In collective cultures, as we discussed in Chapter Two, the unit of social perception is the group, the self is viewed as interdependent with social identity groups, in-group goals have primacy over personal goals, and in-group harmony is valued. In contrast, in individualist cultures the unit of social perception is the individual; the self is viewed as an independent rather than a socially interdependent entity; personal goals are primary, in-group goals are secondary; and in-group confrontation is acceptable.[33]

The implication of these differences between collective and individualist cultures is that members of collective cultures should find it easier to align self- and collective interests than should members of individualist cultures. Our studies comparing U.S., Korean, Japanese, and Chinese managers participating in the SHARC social dilemma confirm this prediction. Exhibit 8.2 shows that U.S. managers confronted with a decision to reduce harvesting from the current rate of 5,000 metric tons of fish to the sustainable 2,500 metric tons reduced their harvesting only from 5000 to 3988 metric tons when simply confronted with the problem, whereas Korean (3581), Japanese (3637), and Chinese (3416) managers reduced significantly more. But given the opportunity for discussion—when commitments can be made to harvesting levels—the overall level of harvesting evened out.

How then to manage a social dilemma when parties are from individualist cultures? Exhibit 8.2 shows that communication helps managers from all cultures, but especially managers from the United States. One effect of discussion that leads to cooperation in social dilemmas is the opportunity to make and extract commitments from others.[34] Cooperation also may result from hearing others articulate the logic for harvesting patterns that are different from one's own self-serving interests. This may lead parties to reassess their judgments of fairness. It is also possible that just meeting as a group enhances group identity, leading to recategorization and cooperation, regardless of what parties talk about![35]

In-Groups and Out-Groups: Risks in Making Social Identity Salient. Increasing social identity using collective goals, contact, or recategorization works by redefining the in-group—those with whom cooperation will result in a sustainable social dilemma in equilibrium. Doing so entails risks that can be somewhat mitigated by understanding and managing the distinctions between in-groups and out-groups.

One of the most effective ways to use recategorization is to increase the salience of the in-group by creating a contrast with an out-group. Group members making decisions in social dilemmas are twice as likely to cooperate with other in-group members when there is an out-group to compete against than when there is no out-group.[36] This is the very familiar situation that causes the formation of alliances among nations with seemingly disparate interests against other nations or alliances. Strategists frequently use out-groups to increase cooperation among in-group members.

There are also culture-related risks in trying to increase social identity. First, culture may differently affect the boundaries parties draw between in-groups and out-groups.[37] Second, members of collectivist cultures tend to make sharper distinctions between in-groups and out-groups than do members of individualist cultures.[38] Third, members of collectivist cultures tend to cooperate more with members of their in-groups and compete more strenuously with members of out-groups than do members of individualist cultures.[39]

Here is some advice for avoiding risks when making social identity salient:

- Identify potential in-groups and out-groups. Be sure to build in sufficient buffers between them (such as the geographical buffers between Balinese *Subaks*) so as to minimize out-group competition when you increase in-group salience and cooperation.

- If you cannot build in buffers, consider contact or recategorization to enlarge the size of the in-group.

Negotiating Individual and Collective Interests in Social Dilemmas

The first step in becoming more effective in negotiating cooperation in social dilemmas is to recognize that all dilemmas are a balance between self-interests and collective interests. The requirement to balance those interests will not disappear no matter how effectively the dilemma is managed. The challenge is to negotiate solutions that keep self-interests and collective interests in balance. Regulation may be the obvious approach, but there are more subtle and more psychological approaches, using norms and interests, that may limit the need for regulation and work effectively when regulation and enforcement are not practical. If regulation is necessary, then experience with caps, goals, and tradable permits suggests that negotiating a combination of government regulation and free markets is an effective way to manage social dilemmas, even across national boundaries.

In this chapter we have begun to see the role of governments in negotiating global solutions to social dilemmas. In the next chapter we delve into the role of government in negotiating foreign investment.

Chapter Nine

Government At
and Around the Table

Companies operating in the global marketplace encounter some nasty surprises. Rock and roll musicians rally around Mike Matthews because someone is trying to steal his Russian factory that makes vacuum tubes for guitar amplifiers. Wal-Mart, citing losses, pulls out of Korea and Germany. The Chinese company Lenovo successfully buys IBM's personal computer business, but the Chinese National Offshore Oil Company is stymied when trying to acquire Unocal. China Mobile passes at the last minute on acquiring Millicom International Cellular, causing the latter's stock to plunge 25 percent. The French prime minister creates a policy of "economic patriotism" to help French dairy giant Danone fend off a bid by Pepsi. Half of the $1.05 billion Mobil (now ExxonMobil) paid for 25 percent of the Tengiz oil field in the Caspian Sea never makes it into Kazakhstan government accounts.[1]

Foreign direct investment (FDI) is a major engine of globalization, but not all such investments are successful. One of the reasons is that companies fail to understand how to take foreign governments into account in order to make their investments succeed.

Even if government is not actually at the table in negotiations that cross national boundaries, it is close by. Government provides the political and legal context for negotiations. In domestic negotiations, this context is essentially neutral and fixed, affecting both parties similarly unless a dispute arises over the application of a law. When negotiations cross national boundaries, they enter a context of political and legal pluralism. This makes cross-national negotiations much more complex than same-culture negotiations. Governments scrutinize

245

and interfere with foreign investments in order to align their interests with those of their foreign investors.

In this chapter we analyze the interests of governments, foreign investors, and publics in global negotiations. We look at challenges associated with foreign investment related to governments' instability, bureaucracy, and corruption. We also touch on the problems of ensuring the safety of employees overseas and avoiding complicity in violations of human rights.

Government Interests in Foreign Investment

Governments' primary interest in negotiations regarding FDI is to stay in power. Any investment that jeopardizes a government's political longevity is likely to be turned away. Secondary to, but associated with, governments' interests in staying in power are concerns about economic development and control over it; about security; and sometimes about personal enrichment of government officials and private operatives.

Governments Want to Stay in Power

Having the government at the table raises a number of special issues for the cross-cultural negotiator. Governments' principal goals may not be related to cost, since many of the costs of infrastructure development are borne by international agencies such as the International Monetary Fund (IMF) or the World Bank. Although loans either must be paid back or forgiven, politicians and bureaucrats (not unlike others with incentives to focus on short-term gains) are frequently willing to sacrifice the future for immediate gains. Nor are governments' principal goals the investor's profitability. Some governments are satisfied if foreign investors just break even after taxes (although governments do realize that the prospect of breaking even would not likely lure foreign investment in the first place). Governments' interests surely will be political, economic, and social, and probably in that order. In general, officials in power prefer to remain in power. It is not unreasonable to assume that political survival is a major underlying interest.

A striking example of governments' concern with political longevity is the deal struck between Libya and the United States that culminated in the announcement of full diplomatic ties between the two countries in May 2006. Libya, ruled by Moammar Gadafi since 1969, directly implicated in the destruction of at least two civilian airplanes, and listed by Freedom House in 2006 as one of the five worst countries in the world in terms of free flow of information, gave up its fledgling nuclear program in 2003 in return for tacit assurances that the U.S. government would not seek to oust Gadafi from power, as the United States had done to Saddam Hussein.[2]

The positive economic repercussions for Libya have been significant in the hydrocarbon sector, though not necessarily in other sectors. The U.S. economic embargo had kept new technology and equipment out of Libya and driven down production in this country that possesses the world's eighth largest oil reserves. Since 2004, when the United States lifted the embargo, at least six U.S. oil companies have resumed drilling and exploration that was suspended in 1986. However, Libya is still a state-run economy. Although the government has partially liberalized rules on FDI in some sectors, according to The Economist Libya's "bumbling, grasping, erratic bureaucracy discourages investors."[3]

Governments Want Economic Development

All governments are interested in economic development, though not equally interested in FDI. Countries high on the World Economic Forum's list of competitiveness (such as Singapore, the United States, and the United Kingdom) view private investment as a social good. Economic incentives associated with private ownership generate efficiencies, profits to be reinvested, and economic growth that in turn generates jobs and increases the standard of living. Government negotiators from other nations may not look so favorably on foreign investment, especially when that investment is private and threatens to challenge valued ways of life.

How Governments Signal Interest in Development Through Foreign Direct Investment. Governments interested in economic development via FDI are willing to engage in some surprising activities to signal that they will be a good partner. One way to signal is by resolving disputes with former investment partners. Two very interesting recent examples illustrate how far governments will go in this regard.

The first example concerns the Turkish government's dealings with Motorola and Nokia. The two companies had engaged in what is called vendor financing with a Turkish cellular phone operator, Telsim. Essentially, Motorola and Nokia lent Telsim money to buy telecommunications equipment (from them) with the loan to be paid back out of future earnings. In July 2001, Motorola announced that Telsim had defaulted. Motorola and Nokia won legal rulings against Telsim in 2004, but were unable to collect. Telsim's offshore assets were not sufficient to cover the money owed, and several members of the Uzan family, owners of Telsim, had gone underground. Motorola and Nokia were rescued by the Turkish Savings and Deposit Insurance Fund (TMSF), which conducted a sale of Telsim's assets, earmarking 20 percent to Motorola and 7.5 percent to Nokia, which had made a smaller investment.

Why did the Turkish government essentially bail out Motorola and Nokia from poor investments in Telsim? Certainly one factor was Turkey's pending bid to join the European Union. And following the agreement, Motorola made this public statement: "The Turkish government's cooperation and diligent efforts to find a solution to allow Motorola to collect on its debt while preserving the business operations of Telsim, instills confidence in Turkey's strong economic and investment climate."[4] (See "Nokia and Motorola Versus Telsim" on the CD-ROM.)

The second example of signaling is the negotiations in 2004–2005 leading to the scheduled reopening of the Dabhol power plant. In the early 1990s, Enron set up a wholly owned subsidiary called Dabhol Power Company (DPC) in the state of Maharashtra, India. In 1999, DPC began generating power but charged such exorbitant rates for it that the government of Maharashtra terminated its contract to buy the power, and the plant was shut down in May 2001. In 2004, GE and Bechtel (the two surviving parties with a major interest in Dabhol Power Plant; Enron no longer existed as a company at this time) wanted to liquidate their investments or start the plant selling power again, so they filed a Rs 260 billion claim in arbitration. The government of the national state of Maharashtra, the government of India and the main Indian financial institutions that were lenders to this project came to the negotiating table. A year later a deal was struck: GE received $145 million and would stay on as consultant to the project; and Bechtel received $160 million.[5] (See "The Checkered Negotiation History of the Dabhol Power Project" on the CD-ROM.)

Why did these Indian governments and financial institutions facilitate this settlement? Their reasons were social, economic, and political. By May of 2005 the government of Maharashtra faced severe criticism for not producing sufficient electrical power. Some of its industrial cities were experiencing power cuts up to eight hours a day. These power outages led to riots. Social unrest and unreliable infrastructure do not endear a government to its electorate. They also discourage foreign investment by other potential foreign investors. In this instance the local and national governments' interests converged. The dispute was settled and the plant reopened.

Governments Want Control Over Development. Governments want FDI, but at the same time they also want to maintain control of economic development so that locals gain needed technology and management skills, labor displacement and social unrest are minimized, and profits are reinvested. Recall the example in Chapter Two of Lafarge investing in cement companies in Yunnan Province in China. The Chinese government wanted technology and management skills from Lafarge, but it also wanted to maintain Chinese control over this important segment of the booming construction sector and avoid labor and social displacement.

It is not just governments in the developing world that get involved in controlling foreign direct investment. Concerns about takeovers are rampant throughout the developed world. As noted earlier, French Prime Minister Dominique Villepin created a policy of "economic patriotism" in response to Pepsi's bid to take over French-owned Danone.[6] In contrast, the Russian minister of energy and industry accused European governments of "double standards" for pressuring Russia to be more open to foreign investment but then encouraging the European steel company, Arcelor, to accept Mittal Steel's bid and turn down the bid from the Russian company, Severstal. The Russians claimed "Russophobia," a bias against Russian businesses and businessmen.[7]

Governments Want Security

Governments get involved in deals because of security concerns. Any business deal involving a U.S. company and national security issues must be approved by the Congressional Committee on Foreign Investments in the United States (CFIUS). That committee has been busy recently. For example, when Chinese Lenovo bought IBM's PC business, key concerns of the committee were that U.S. government contracts not be filled by the Chinese government and the Chinese government not have access to IBM technology used by the U.S. government. The structure of the deal (especially IBM's retention of sensitive technology) assuaged the committee's concerns.

However, no assurances were acceptable to the U.S. government engaged in a war on terrorism when DP World (owned by the United Emirates) bought British shipper P & O, as long as the deal would put DP World in control of operations at six U.S. ports then controlled by P & O. To assuage U.S. government interests DP World agreed to divest the U.S. ports.[8] The DP World negotiations with the CFIUS congressional committee are particularly worth noting because the U.S. interests lead back to political viability. Regardless of the economics of the deal (which President George Bush favored), the politics were a disaster to Congressional representatives facing a mid-term election.

Governments Are Concerned About Personal Enrichment

Personal enrichment is another major concern of some government (and private) officials. In the fall of 1995, Mobil (now ExxonMobil) wanted a stake in the Tengiz oil field in the area of the Caspian Sea that is controlled by Kazakhstan. At a meeting in Nassau between Mobil officials and Kazakh president Nazarbayev (at this writing Nazarbayev is still president), the Kazakhs' alleged demands for entry included a new Gulfstream jet for the president, funds for a tennis court at his home, and four trucks with satellite dishes to be used by his daughter's TV network. It is pretty clear Mobil was asked; it is less clear what if anything Mobil provided. In May 1996 Mobil concluded its negotiations for the Tengiz oil field, paying over a billion U.S. dollars for a 25 percent stake. The cases regarding personal enrichment that are still winding their way through the U.S. court system are not aimed at Mobil.[9] The personal enrichment at issue is payments that went to James Giffen, the middleman who put this deal together. Mobil allegedly paid Giffen $51 million, and the Kazakhs allegedly paid him $78 million. Being paid by both sides is a potential violation of Federal Corrupt Practices Act. At this writing Giffen's trial has once again been postponed due to an investigation of claims made by Giffen's defense that he was a superspy for the U.S. government.[10]

Handling issues of corruption and bribery isn't trivial. We address them near the end of the chapter.

Identifying Governments' Vulnerabilities and Interests

In all negotiations, parties' interests make them vulnerable, and governments are no exception. Just as governments' interests are not necessarily the same as those of a private company, neither are governments' vulnerabilities. Private companies are vulnerable to the opinions of financial markets that normally value growth and change. Governments are vulnerable to the opinions of their political supporters: religious organizations, labor unions, and the military—all groups that frequently prefer the status quo and strenuously resist change.

When negotiating across national boundaries it is critical to understand the interests of the local and national governments concerning your plans. There are many Web-based resources, but you need to know what you are looking for. Here is some advice about what to look at:

- *Economic policy statements.* What is the government saying domestically? What is the government saying in world forums?
- *Economic development plans.* How controlled is the economy? How can you frame your investment as a contribution to the country's economic development plan?
- *Economic legislation.* What laws have been passed to encourage FDI? Are those laws enforced?
- *Recent history of foreign investment.* Who has and who has not been investing? How have they been treated?
- *The press.* A free press is powerful in generating economic transparency. Is there a free press in the country? What is it saying as opposed to the press that is the mouthpiece for the government? Are there Internet blogs that discuss the current economic, political, and social conditions?
- *Other sources.* What are information sources such as the World Heritage Foundation saying about the political, economic, and social conditions of the country?

Foreign Investor Interests, Risks, and Hedges

Foreign investors of course want to make money on their investments, but to do so they have to be willing to take some risks. In this section we discuss investors' interests and the risks of political instability, economic instability, and legal interests and risks. We also discuss how negotiation skills can be used to hedge some of the risks.

Political Instability

Where there is economic opportunity there is also risk. One major risk is political instability in the nation where an FDI is made. This is the key question underlying the major offshore investment choice today between China and India. Which should a foreign investor choose? Both countries have plenty of low-wage workers, highly educated engineers, and English speakers. Both have had about the same degree of experience with market economics. India opened its markets in 1991 after fifty years of socialism. China's move to a market economy started earlier with leader Deng Xiaoping's introduction of the socialist market economy in the late 1970s, but developed more slowly. On infrastructure China seems to be ahead inasmuch as multinational corporations in China buy electricity and water, whereas in India they supply their own! But what of political stability? India has been a democracy since 1947; China, as Thomas Friedman puts it, "has had a good run for the past twenty-five years, and may make the transition from communism to a more pluralistic system without the wheels coming off. But it may not."[11]

Most political change is less drastic than "wheels coming off," but there are investment risks associated even with peaceful local political change. A widely studied example involved Enron in India (the ultimate settlement that we discussed earlier in this chapter). In February 1995, Enron reached an agreement with the Congress Party to build a power plant at Dabhol in the Indian state of Maharashtra. One month later, the party lost its majority in the state's government to a coalition of two other parties, Shiv Sena and BJP.

The new state government set up a committee to investigate the agreement with Enron, and six months later, even though construction had begun, the state minister canceled the project.[12]

Investors currently are wary of Russia, because it is not clear what the government's role is in business or in protecting business. In the mid-1990s, during the early days of transition from the planned Soviet economy to a market economy, government authority collapsed and teams of armed thugs carried out takeovers. More recently, government agencies such as the tax police and special force units have enforced and facilitated the transfer of property. For example, the huge new Russian oil company Rosneft was formed largely with a transfer of assets to pay back taxes of the now bankrupt Yukos, an oil company formerly headed by Russian oligarch Mikhail Khodorkovsky, who is now serving a Siberian prison term for failure to pay personal taxes. The transfer of assets in Russia is still going on at this writing but has become a bit more white collar, with the mysterious "loss" of paper indicating titles and ownership. An Interior Ministry official investigating the theft of more than 346 enterprises commented that "the process is ever more frequently accompanied by gross violations of the law."[13]

All this suggests that global negotiators need to hedge their deals as much as possible against risks of political instability. They also need to be willing to renegotiate.

Hedging Against Political Risks. Financing revolution is probably not the intent of most foreign direct investment, yet foreign investors do get caught up in such political affairs. Since the twelfth century B.C., when Phoenician trade routes spanned the Middle-East, Asia, Africa, and Europe, commerce has mixed with politics. For centuries merchants have consorted with kings and would-be kings to change the political situation and further their economic interests. They still do. Guus van Kouwenhoven, a Dutch businessman and lumber trader, got mixed up with Charles Taylor, the former president of Liberia, during the period of revolution in that country, 2001 to 2003. Mr. van Kouwenhoven was found guilty in a Dutch court of violating the United Nations arms embargo by smuggling weapons into Liberia. According to the NGO Global Witness, "the barbaric regime of Charles Taylor was financed and maintained by the revenues generated from the timber trade in which Guus Kouwenhoven was the biggest player."[14]

Here is some advice for hedging political risks:

- Diversify foreign investments, if economics of scale and scope allow.

- Cultivate well-connected friends located at local and national levels. In India making well-connected friends means being open to relationships with politicians of multiple parties at local and national levels. In China it means having friends who have friends who can navigate the intricacies of the Chinese bureaucracy.

- Try to frame the investment in terms of the general interest of the citizens. Political parties find it easier to embrace arrangements with foreign investors that contribute to the general interest than arrangements that cater to the interests of a special group. But be careful of making the assumption that you know the local interests. For example, foreign investment usually means new jobs and so should be particularly appealing to regions where unemployment is high. The problem with this thinking is that many in high unemployment areas who have any work experience at all want jobs like their *old* jobs because they feel competent and capable in handling them or lack the skills and confidence for the new jobs. This was certainly Disney's experience during its rocky start in Marne La Valée outside of Paris.[15]

- Maintain those political relationships after negotiations conclude. You likely will need them again.

- Be willing to just say no or take other measures to avoid getting entangled in someone else's revolution. There is more about this later in the chapter, in the discussion about corruption and bribery.

Economic Instability

Economic conditions that made a global deal favorable can change. Changes can bring two closely related types of economic risk. The first has to do with the economic stability of the country in which the negotiated deal is to be enacted. The second has to do with the stability of its currency. When a country becomes economically unstable, its currency may collapse, leading to rampant inflation. However, even without economic instability, currency may lose value.

Economic stability means controlled growth, controlled inflation, and controlled unemployment. The Chinese government was juggling all three of these issues, and as we saw in the Lafarge example in Chapter Two, has tried to balance interests in foreign investment with other concerns like local employment, and transfer of technology and managerial expertise. Turkey, according to a series of summer 2006 articles in the *Turkish Daily News*, experienced a series of "sharp economic curves." Some of these curves were thrown by standard economic indicators: growth with accompanying inflation that reached 20 percent in June 2006. But at the same time Turkey was also experiencing pressures from both external sources (mainly the European Union, which Turkey wanted to join, and the IMF) and internal sources, such as the military, which is highly influential in Turkish politics.[16]

Hedging Against Economic Risks.   Hedging against the economic instability of a country requires having investments in other less risky markets.

How to hedge against currency fluctuations depends on whether the money is movable or immovable.[17] Movable money is currency that is easily converted (dollars, yen, euros). Immovable money is currency that is not easily converted. It's the money of governments that "regulate the entry to, possession in, and exit from their territories of both foreign and local currencies."[18]

Hedging Against Moveable Money.   Hedging against movable money currency fluctuations can be managed in the futures market, which essentially shifts the risk to a third party.[19] Hedging can also be part of the negotiated deal, and that's our focus here.

One negotiated hedging technique for currency fluctuations is to limit the term of a contract; another is to include a renegotiation clause that specifies the conditions under which the contract will be reopened. Either method prevents parties from being locked into prices that make no sense for either one party or the other, given changes in currency valuation. What can happen without such provisions? Consider the fate of a Thai company producing athletic shoes for a U.S. company. The agreement, negotiated in 1996, provided that the Thai company be paid entirely in baht at a rate that at the time provided it with profits over its costs, both of which were paid in baht. This was a reasonable deal for both companies when it was negotiated. However, when the baht lost its value in the summer of 1997, the U.S. company began making extraordinary excess profits. It was able to buy many more baht for the same amount of dollars. This made the shoes cost the U.S. company less, but it was still selling the shoes for the same price in dollars as before the baht decreased in value. Because of inflation that accompanied the drop in the baht, the Thai company was no longer making money on the shoe contract.

Why would negotiators, especially ones from countries whose currencies are stable, enter into a contract that essentially rules out excess profits due to currency fluctuations? The question itself is cultural, for negotiators from hierarchical cultures might not even consider it a question. It is the negotiator from the egalitarian-individualist culture (such as the United States), in which all parties look out for their own interests, who may find it difficult to contemplate a renegotiation clause. Recall the example in Chapter Two of negotiations between the U.S. companies Rubbermaid (now Newell-Rubbermaid) and Wal-Mart. Rubbermaid was the leading brand-name maker of common kitchenware and household items such as laundry baskets. But when the price for the resin component in its products more than tripled because of oil price fluctuations, Wal-Mart (Rubbermaid's biggest customer) balked at renegotiating the contract. When Rubbermaid insisted on raising its wholesale price to Wal-Mart, Wal-Mart relegated the manufacturer's items to undesirable shelf space and used its market power to promote a Rubbermaid rival.[20]

The negotiator from the hierarchical-collectivist culture is more likely to presume that risk must be shared and accept that unforeseen circumstances are legitimate reasons for reopening negotiations. When cultures value relationships, negotiators are more likely to think that windfall profits due to currency fluctuations are to be made in the currency markets, not at the cost of the viability of your business partner.

Hedging Against Immoveable Money. When money is immovable, it is more difficult to repatriate profits in a hard currency. After all, the reason the country has instituted currency controls is to reduce currency flight. In this situation, it is essential to negotiate a priori arrangements for payment. Creativity and expert advice are key. Many options have been used more or less successfully. Negotiating a foreign currency allotment from the country's central bank is one approach. Beware, however: central bank regulations can change abruptly, and new regulations can be applied retroactively. Structuring the transaction so that profits are withdrawn in ways other than cash is acceptable in some countries that restrict currencies. Two examples are royalties on technology and inflated prices for raw materials.

And there is always countertrade. Countertrade is a transaction that links imports and exports in addition to or in lieu of financial settlements. The timber-for-arms deal between van Kouwenhoven and Charles Taylor is an example of countertrade (albeit an illegal one according to United Nations sanctions). Countertrade occurs because of the need for imports and the difficulty in gaining access to hard currency to pay for them due to non-convertible currency, a lack of commercial credit, a shortage of foreign exchange, or, in the case of Liberia, international sanctions. It may be an excellent way for a developing country's raw materials to gain entry into new markets. Van Kouwenhoven, for example, sold Liberian hardwoods to European and Asian buyers.[21]

Be especially careful to find out prior to negotiating a price whether countertrade will be required, because the transaction costs of countertrade will change the cost structure of the deal. There are various forms of countertrade with different transaction cost structures. Pepsi for vodka, the countertrade arrangement with the Soviet Union, is an example of pure barter. Other countertrade examples are more indirect—for example, in exchange for supplying shoe manufacturing equipment to a Thai company, taking payment in shoes manufactured by that company, or agreeing to pay hard currency for products produced in the host country, or reinvesting profits in other host-country companies. Countertrade makes deals possible when otherwise there would be none. However, it is not without risks. In a well-known example the Soviets offered Pepsi vodka, Lada cars, or caviar. Pepsi wisely stuck close to its own business by limiting its countertrade to vodka. (Later Pepsi took payment in ships from Russia's mothballed navy, which Pepsi sold for their scrap steel.) Coke got second choice and took the much less attractive Lada deal, underestimating the cost of transporting these automobiles to the U.S. market and, even worse, U.S. consumers' aversion to buying them.[22]

Legal Interests and Risks

There is always a risk that the goodwill and good intentions generated at a negotiation table will fade when parties turn to implementation. After cross-cultural negotiations, so much can still go wrong: the central bank refuses to authorize the repatriation of profits in hard currency, the goods you were to receive in countertrade are not supplied, building permits are delayed, your technicians' visas are revoked.

Legal pluralism makes things harder. Because cross-cultural deals are captives of two or more tax systems, two or more legal systems, and two or more court systems, it's especially important to plan for dispute resolution while you are making the deal.

If you are reluctant to raise issues of potential implementation problems before a deal is finalized, fearing that doing so will taint the trust developed during negotiation, keep in mind that a sovereign state has the power to take property, cancel contracts, and halt business activity.[23] Any of those actions will cost you money. If you are not willing to cut your losses and leave, if you want to be compensated, who will make the decision? Without a dispute resolution clause that specifies judicial jurisdiction, the most you can hope for is hometown justice—decisions by local courts that may elevate national interests above those of foreign investors.

Hedging Against Legal Risks. Contracts that cross national boundaries should have explicit dispute resolution clauses. Among other things, these clauses should specify the jurisdiction to which the contract terms are subject. English common law dominates international business,[24] but any legal system that has a well-specified commercial code will do. The clause should state that in the event of a dispute, the parties should endeavor to negotiate a resolution. That dispute resolution clause also should provide for neutral third-party assistance, in the form of mediation and arbitration that is outside the influence of either of the disputing parties. In mediation, as described in Chapter Six, the third party tries to facilitate an agreement but does not have the authority to impose a settlement. When parties hope to continue their relationship, mediation is the preferred third-party procedure, as a mediator may be able to help the parties negotiate a settlement that preserves the relationship. When the relationship has ended and the claim is for damages, arbitration may be preferable because it is binding. Recall that this is the route Motorola and Nokia took after the Turkish telecommunications company, Telsim, reneged on loan payments. However, although these companies prevailed at arbitration, they could not collect until the Turkish government took matters into hand.

Challenges When Negotiating Globally

Bureaucracy and corruption are often sources of challenge.

Bureaucracy

In many countries the politicians come and go but the bureaucracy remains. It is the bureaucracy that implements political initiatives, and it is the bureaucracy with which foreign investors will have to negotiate for all permits, tax rates, and infrastructure access to power, water, sewage disposal, and other essentials.

There are three pitfalls in dealing with bureaucracy when negotiating globally: failure to understand the bureaucracy's interests, failure to understand its power, and failure to understand the fact that bureaucracy is not monolithic.

Understanding Bureaucracy's Interests. It is usually valid to assume that bureaucrats will resist change that might threaten their lifestyle. It is also usually valid to assume that there are competing factions within bureaucracies, either between ministries or between national and local agencies. Thus when negotiating globally, it is wise to learn about the bureaucracy at all levels of the government. What you are seeking is information that will help you discover bureaucratic interests relevant to negotiating the deal and implementing it. Find out about the country's bureaucratic structure.

- Are policy decisions made or only implemented by the bureaucracy?
- What decisions are implemented at what level of the bureaucracy?
- How do bureaucrats get their jobs? Are they elected, appointed, hired on merit? How well and regularly are they paid relative to private sector employees in the country?
- What are the relationships between various agencies and between national and local levels?
- Is there a climate of corruption and extortion?

Understanding Bureaucracy's Power. Bureaucracies are usually entrenched. Their BATNA is usually to keep operating as they

have always done, outlasting the pressures of elected parties and foreign investors. To get a bureaucracy to change requires helping the
bureaucracy understand that change will occur regardless of the bureaucracy's interests. Then smart bureaucrats, realizing they cannot
stop change, will likely participate in order to protect their interests, and smart foreign investors will let them do just that.

The best way to evaluate the power of a bureaucracy is to consider its BATNA, which may be simply to refuse approvals, permits,
or licenses that are required for foreign investment, or make the
wait for them interminable. In Chapter Five we discussed the power
tactic of threatening the interests of parties that are reluctant to
come to the table. This same general principle applies to getting reluctant bureaucracies to the table: threaten their interests. But this
can be a big challenge because a bureaucracy's major interest is to
remain in power. Even if the nation's political leadership changes,
the bureaucrats are likely to remain. The first step in appealing to a
bureaucracy's interests may be to help bureaucracies acquire new interests that you might be able to further. I am not advocating
bribery! I am advocating creativity! Try to find a way to frame what
you want from the bureaucracy in terms of giving it more power.

An Example of Bureaucratic Behavior in Global Negotiation.
The 2004 acquisition of Shenzhen Development Bank by Newbridge was a case of deal making turned into dispute resolution and
back into deal making. In the process, government bureaucracies
played a complex role. (See "Newbridge and Chinese Negotiations
Over Shenzhen Development Bank" on the CD-ROM.)

Newbridge is an American investment firm affiliate of Texas Pacific Group, one of the largest U.S. private-equity firms. Shenzhen
Development Bank (SDB) at the time was the smallest of China's
publicly listed banks, with $25 billion in assets, a nonperforming
loan ratio of 10 percent, and 72 percent of its shares publicly traded.
A small group of shareholders, including the Shenzhen city government, held 17.89 percent of the shares. Newbridge's acquisition
of these shares would have given it voting control (because other

shares were widely dispersed) without majority ownership, which was limited by government regulation to 15 percent for any single foreign investor when the negotiation began and, it is important to note, raised to 20 percent by the time it ended.

Foreign investment in the Chinese banking industry is highly regulated by several Chinese government agencies. Every proposal for foreign investment in an existing Chinese bank must be submitted to the China Banking Regulatory Commission (CBRC). Because shares in SDB were traded publicly, Newbridge had to file a disclosure form to the China Securities Regulatory Commission (CSRC). And because this acquisition was to effectively transform SDB into a foreign-invested enterprise, the approval of the Chinese Ministry of Commerce was also needed.

Cooperative initial negotiations between Newbridge and SDB shareholders (not current management) yielded a framework agreement that established a transition committee to run the bank for ninety days while negotiations continued. Negotiations broke down when the transition committee found out that the bank's nonperforming loan portfolio was significantly greater than 10 percent, and Newbridge reduced the price of the offer. A series of lawsuits were filed, and the CSRC (the securities commission), encouraged by incumbent bank management, challenged the legality of the framework committee. Newbridge countered by providing a statement to the international financial press indicating that it expected the Shenzhen city government (the lead Chinese shareholder) to honor its obligations under the framework agreement. This statement generated a response from CBRC (the banking commission), which announced that it had raised the ceiling for any single foreign investment in a Chinese bank from 15 percent to 20 percent. The timing of this announcement sent a strong signal to the SDB shareholders that the government wanted the deal done.

This example illustrates four points about the bureaucratic context in which deal making and dispute resolution negotiations occur. The first point is that multiple agencies can be involved with different and nonaligned interests. The banking commission's interests involved complying with the privatization of the financial services industry required by the Chinese government's commitments when it joined the World Trade Organization. It therefore was sensitive to China's image in the international financial press. By contrast, the securities commission's interests involved protecting shareholders by helping them claim the highest possible price for their shares. It was sensitive to shareholders' concerns. The lead shareholder, the Shenzhen city government, was also concerned with the employment implications of the deal for current management as well as the bank's four thousand employees.

The second point is that some bureaucracies are more powerful than others. The CBRC apparently was more powerful than the CSRC or the Shenzhen city government. The third point is that when bureaucracies' interests are engaged (CBRC's interests in compliance with WTO obligations), they will act. The fourth point is that, in a hierarchical and high-context-communication culture such as China, bureaucracies understand their power positions and signals.

Corruption

Corruption is behavior that departs from what is legally, ethically, or morally correct.[25] Thus to understand what is a corrupt practice you must first understand the laws and ethical and moral norms not only in your own nation but also in the nation in which you will be negotiating.

Illegal Acts. The U.S. Foreign Corrupt Practices Act makes it unlawful for any American to bribe a foreign official either directly or through an agent for the purposes of obtaining or retaining business.[26] The U.S. Department of Justice's Website provides an easy-to-read explanation of the act. It clarifies the definition of "any American" as an individual or a representative of a firm, including such a person authorizing or assisting a third party. It defines intent and points out that the act need not be consummated; an offer or a promise is sufficient to violate the act. It defines a foreign official as any public official and points out that the role of the foreign official is less important than the intent of the payment. The business purpose test is whether the act was intended to obtain or retain business.

U.S. companies routinely brief their negotiators not to pay bribes, give in to extortion, or accept personal gifts. Yet violations of the act do occur.[27] For example, in 2003 Halliburton, one of the world's largest oil services companies, disclosed to the Securities and Exchange Commission that it had dismissed several employees from its KBR subsidiary for their involvement in $2.4 million in improper payments to Nigerian officials to obtain favorable tax treatment. Halliburton paid the fine. It also stated that none of its senior officers had been involved, though a year later it severed ties with the chairman of KBR. Evidence indicated that he had enriched himself by as much as $5 million from an alleged bid-rigging scheme associated with a Nigerian oil project, which, while not a violation of the FCPA, may have been in violation of antitrust laws.[28]

The United States is not alone in regulating corrupt practices in global business. The 29 member countries of the Organization for Economic Cooperation and Development (OECD) have signed the OECD's Convention on Combating Bribery of Foreign Public Officials in International Business Transactions. The convention targets the offering side of the bribery transaction in an effort to eliminate the supply of bribes to foreign officials. Signatories take the responsibility for the activities of companies registered in their states by passing, implementing, and sanctioning tough legislation against bribery and corruption. OECD has recommendations against the tax deductibility of bribes, for combating corruption in aid-funded procurement, and for ending money laundering. Exhibit 9.1 lists the nations that have signed the convention. The World Bank, with 181 member countries, also has adopted guidelines stating that if a company is found to have engaged in corrupt or fraudulent practices in competing for or in executing a bank-financed contract, the company becomes ineligible to bid on future bank-financed contracts.[29]

Exhibit 9.1. Signers of the OECD Convention on Combating Bribery of Foreign Public Officials in International Business Transactions.

Australia	Hungary	Poland
Austria	Iceland	Portugal
Belgium	Italy	Slovak Republic
Canada	Japan	Spain
Czech Republic	Korea	Sweden
Denmark	Luxembourg	Switzerland
Finland	Mexico	Turkey
France	Netherlands	United Kingdom
Germany	New Zealand	United States
Greece	Norway	

Source: Organization for Economic Cooperation and Development, available at http://www.oecd.org/document/21/0,2340,en_2649_34859_2017813_1_1_1_1,00.html. Reprinted by permission.

Unethical or Immoral Acts. The definition of corruption does not stop with what is legally correct; corruption can also be failure to abide by what is ethically and morally correct. How do you know if a business activity is ethically or morally correct? There is guidance in corporate codes of business ethics, but ultimately you have to have your own internal code of ethics.

Companies such as Halliburton have their own internal code of ethics. Exhibit 9.2 is an excerpt from Halliburton's code that distinguishes between illegal and facilitating payments.

Facilitating payments deserve a little attention. Note in the language in Exhibit 9.2 that facilitating payments are public, entered into Halliburton's books, not secret. This is the key distinction between what is and what is not a violation of Halliburton's code. However, the recipient of such a payment is unlikely to be willing to accept a check or another financial instrument that can be traced, and such people do not give receipts.

Generating Your Own Ethical Standards. Negotiators who lack a legal or corporate standard on which to base ethical judgments must

Exhibit 9.2. An Excerpt from Halliburton's Code of Business Ethics Regarding Sensitive Transactions.

"Company policy prohibits its Directors, employees and agents from entering into sensitive transactions. If such a transaction occurs, the Company and its officers, Directors and employees directly involved may be subject to fines, imprisonment and civil litigation.

"The term *sensitive transactions* is commonly used to describe a broad range of business dealings generally considered to be either illegal, unethical, immoral or to reflect adversely on the integrity of the Company. These transactions are usually in the nature of kickbacks, gifts of significant value, bribes or payoffs made to favorably influence some decision affecting a company's business or for the personal gain of an individual. These transactions may result in violation of various laws, including the United States Foreign Corrupt Practices Act (the FCPA) and similar laws of other countries.

"This policy does not prohibit properly made and recorded facilitating payments. Sometimes the Company may be required to make facilitating or expediting payments to a low-level government official or employee in some countries other than the United States to expedite or secure the performance of routine governmental action by the government official or employee. Such facilitating payments may not be illegal under the FCPA and similar laws of other countries. Nevertheless, it may be difficult to distinguish a legal facilitating payment from an illegal bribe, kickback or payoff. Accordingly, facilitating payments must be strictly controlled and every effort must be made to eliminate or minimize such payments. Facilitating payments, if required, will be made only in accordance with the advance guidance of the Law Department. All facilitating payments must be recorded accurately as facilitating payments in the accounting records of the Company."

Source: cobc summary, Sensitive Transactions, available at http://www.halliburton.com/default.aspx?pageid=943&navid=.

determine their own ethical course, balancing profits and ethics to make ethical choices in a given situation. As the Halliburton code of ethics reveals, there is much more to making ethical decisions in global negotiations than merely conforming to the standards of the Foreign Corrupt Practices Act or the OECD convention.

To act unethically means to violate the legal, social, and or personal norms of conduct in your own culture. To act ethically you need a personal standard that gives you guidance.

Here is some advice for having a personal standard:

- *Have a personal standard that focuses on your reputation.* Would you want your act announced on the front page of your home-town newspaper? Would you want your proud parent or mentor to know you did this? This "reputation" standard rules out "game" standards such as "Everyone knows the rules," or "No one is being forced to play, so anything goes," or "Don't worry, there's no future anyway." The reputation standard recognizes that there is always a future and it is a small, global world. Your reputation will precede you.

- *In responding to another party's unethical act, be imaginative and restrained.* A high-context response using literature, metaphors, and stories should help the other understand he or she has violated your ethical standards without so much loss of face that the relationship is irreparably damaged.

- *Have some ideals.* Believe that an ethical basis for interaction is a fundamental structural imperative for a democratic society and a free economy. Act accordingly.

- *Know the limits of your standard.* There are situations of survival that can test anyone's ethical standards. Thankfully, these do not occur very often in global negotiations.

- *Have someone you respect that you can talk to outside your industry.* It is important that the respected someone be outside your industry. Organizations and even industries may slip into a phase of unethical and illegal behavior in which "everyone is doing it, and nobody is being questioned about it." Halliburton's KBR subsidiary may have had that culture. Enron certainly did. In court testimony the prosecutor asked Andrew Fastow, "Were you a hero to Enron when you stole?" Fastow replied, "Within the culture of corruption that Enron had, that valued financial reporting rather than economic value, I believed I was being a hero."[30]

What to Do When Confronted with Corruption. The decision whether to engage in or reject corrupt practices is ultimately a social dilemma. If all parties engage in corrupt practices, trust will be low, transaction costs will be high, and integrative potential will go unrealized. If all parties refuse to engage in corrupt practices, trust will be high, transaction costs will be low, and integrative potential will be realized.

The interesting case is when some parties reject corrupt practices and others engage in them. Research and theory suggest that in large groups in which some parties are ethical and others unethical, over time the ethical parties will choose to interact with each other, ultimately generating an environment for which unethical parties are unfit.[31]

Cooperation is ultimately a long-term utilitarian response. Utilitarianism judges the morality of an act by the consequences it produces, and those consequences are evaluated either against a "greatest good" criterion or against a set of principles.[32] In the short term, being ethical costs. "Just say no," the strategy suggested by a Mexican government official at a Latin American business conference at my school when questioned about corruption, satisfies your own ethical standards. However, it does nothing to change the practice of corruption and may mean that you will lose the business opportunity. (Caving in to extortion, of course, reinforces the practice and may cause it to escalate.)

Negotiators willing to apply moral imagination can sometimes generate strategies that may actually stymie an unscrupulous opponent. Corruption cannot sustain itself in the spotlight of publicity. Corruption thrives in environments in which information is controlled and withers in the light of public scrutiny. As part of its response to the Asian financial crisis in the late 1990s, the IMF pressed countries to publish more financial information, which is now available on its Website (www.imf.org). In assessing the same financial crisis, The World Bank concluded that a freer, more aggressive, and more critical news media would help reduce governmental corruption and crony capitalism (doing business with families of governmental officials). It began financing training for journalists from developing countries.[33] In Indonesia in 1999, the fact that the government was unable or unwilling to prosecute corruption did not stop the Indonesian Bank Restructuring Agency from resorting to a strategy of shaming. It began publishing the names of the country's one hundred worst debtors in local newspapers.[34]

Choosing to expose corruption and holding people accountable for actions that have inflicted harm on others is a negotiation strategy itself. Confronted with corruption and being unwilling to acquiesce, the global negotiator must consider the costs and benefits of whistle-blowing. Exposing corruption takes moral courage. It is much easier to simply cut your losses and walk away from corruption than to face it down. For these reasons, when confronting corruption, a collective response is likely to be stronger and more effective than an individual response. Parties who would not confront corruption on their own may be willing to engage in joint action. Joint action to confront corruption will be more powerful because it is difficult to ignore, and you will be more difficult to prosecute when you act in concert.

How far can a cross-cultural negotiator go in confronting a corrupt opponent? Current theorizing about business ethics draws the line at collaborating in the overthrow of governments. Besides, at the end of the twentieth century, the IMF seemed to have taken on this role. Its outgoing head, Michel Camdessus, acknowledged that the IMF "created the conditions that obliged President Suharto to leave his job" as president of Indonesia and that President Boris Yeltsin of Russia was warned by the IMF that the same forces could end his control in Russia.[35]

Companies that find themselves facing corruption in global negotiations have at least the following options:

- *Publicize the corruption.* Corruption thrives in the dark but has trouble sustaining itself in the public spotlight.
- *Unite with other firms to resist the corruption.* Joint action is more effective than working alone. It is also more difficult for a country to prosecute its major foreign investors for defying a country's law than to prosecute a single foreign investor acting alone.

- *Promote NGOs and other institutions that are fighting corruption in the regions where you are investing.*

- *Leave or choose not to invest at all, and make public your reason for doing so.* Operating in an environment of corruption significantly increases costs of doing business and protecting personnel.

Keeping Your Employees Safe in Global Assignments

In October 2000, ten engineers working at an oil exploration site in the Amazon basin in Ecuador were kidnapped. A team with members from the men's employers (Schlumberger, Helmerich & Payne, Erickson Air-Crane), insurers, experts from international security firms, and the FBI was formed to negotiate for their release. Notably there were no representatives of the kidnapped men's families. Eighteen days after the event, the kidnappers demanded $80 million. This demand was significantly higher than the experts on the team had previously encountered and led to a two-week, intrateam negotiation to come up with a counteroffer. Note the different interests represented on the team. Insurers wanted to pay as little as possible. Companies had conflicting interests; they wanted their employees back but they also wanted to minimize future insurance premiums. The experts and the FBI wanted to end the kidnapping in a way that would be viewed publicly as successful: quickly with no loss of life, at low cost. The counteroffer of $500,000 prompted a series of threats from the kidnappers, their blowing up a section of Ecuador's main oil pipeline, a two-month stalemate, and then an ultimatum that someone would die. Although the offer was increased to $1 million in response to the ultimatum, by the time it was delivered, it was too late: a hostage had already been executed. Over the next ten days pressure on the negotiating team from hostages' families and the media spurred a series of offers and a settlement for $13 million and a release of hostages.[36]

Keeping your employees safe while on global assignment is an important consideration in deciding to do business in a nation in which there is an environment of corruption and ineffective government. Weighing the risks themselves, along with the cost of private security and other measures to minimize the risks, against the anticipated gains from doing business in that nation may make you decide to stay out or leave.

If the decision is to initiate or continue activities in such an environment, it is essential to have a single point of contact within the company who is offsite but responsible for monitoring safety conditions for employees working in that country. Among this point person's responsibilities should be keeping in touch with on-site employees, monitoring outside reports of safety conditions, and making the call and arrangements to pull people out if necessary. This person should be positioned to coordinate the company's response to events like the kidnapping in the example. As such this person needs to have direct access to the CEO.

Some Advice About Negotiating with Hostage Takers

As in any negotiation, one starts analyzing a hostage or kidnap situation by understanding interests, your own and theirs. The example of the Ecuadorian kidnapping illustrates the competing interests on the company side that had to be balanced. The kidnappers' interests in this situation were financial and only indirectly political—they needed money to sustain their revolution. In other situations the motive for kidnapping may be primarily political. Negotiating a politically motivated hostage or kidnap situation is substantially more difficult than negotiating the financially motivated situation, because to address politically motivated hostage takers' interests requires involving an array of governments each with its own complex interests. Coordinating a response was difficult enough when the parties on the team were the companies, their insurers, their consultants, and the FBI. Consider the complexity of coordinating a response to the kidnapping of *Wall Street Journal* reporter Daniel Pearl, who was taken hostage in Pakistan and subsequently executed.

The second step is analyzing BATNAs on both sides. The hostage takers' BATNA is to kill or maim the hostages, which they will do one by one, but only reluctantly if their motive is money, and less reluctantly if their motive is political. The reason for reluctance to follow through on threats in a financial situation is that the other sides' response may not be to increase the offer but to call in a SWAT team. Remember from Chapter Five that if one party goes out to power the other is likely to reciprocate. The goal of using threats is not to have to follow through on them. On the corporate side, a SWAT-team-type response to the kidnapping of your employees in a foreign country is not a good BATNA. In the first place it's too risky; your employees might get killed. In the second place, you may not know where your employees are being held, and even if you do they may be moved. An analysis of your own and the other party's BATNA in hostage or kidnapping situations strongly implies that negotiations with a generous reservation price are in order.

Here is some negotiation advice:

- *Make contact as quickly as possible, to get a demand, make a counteroffer, and settle quickly.* Moving quickly helps prevent anchoring, and it keeps kidnappers' hopes alive that money will be forthcoming. The hostage is worth nothing to the kidnappers dead, and is usually not a threat alive and released, because the kidnappers are pros and cover their faces.

- *Understand the market.* Initial demands for cash are typically three to four times what the final settlements are. Overpaying is bad because it doesn't seem to reduce the number of incidents but rather raises the ante. The FBI and private consulting firms generally are quite good at helping to identify where the market is.

- *Keep understandably terrified family members off the negotiating team.* At the same time, the family needs a single point of contact into the negotiating team, who will keep them informed of events and strategy. Without such communication family members may try to initiate a second negotiation channel, use the media, or otherwise jeopardize the negotiation strategy.

The Ugly Side of Free Trade

One purpose of foreign investment is to produce goods and services more cheaply than can be produced in the developed world. By producing goods and services more cheaply, more people in developed and developing economies can participate in using those goods and services, generating a global economic boost. But there is a trap. Governments of developing countries may not have labor and work safety laws to protect workers, or they may not have the ability to enforce such laws, or they may simply turn a blind eye to worker exploitation and safety infractions. The conditions under which their low-cost goods have been produced have caused substantial negative publicity to foreign investors and contractors.

According to an investigation by *New York Times* reporters, more than a quarter of Jordanian garment factories producing clothing for J.C. Penny, Sears, Wal-Mart, Gap, and Target provide substandard conditions for mostly foreign workers. Gross charges range from human trafficking of workers from Pakistan and China to involuntary servitude in which workers' passports are taken so that they have no ID and if picked up by authorities can be imprisoned or deported. Local charges include forcing people to work eighteen-hour days seven days a week, paying less than minimum wage, not paying overtime, and so on.[37]

What can be done? As Wal-Mart points out, it neither owns nor manages any of these Jordanian factories. Has it then no moral or ethical obligation concerning working conditions? Wal-Mart and other retailers recognize an obligation, if only to avoid the kind of grassroots activism (stimulated by a CBS special report in March 1997) that has linked Nike's swoosh icon with slave labor. Retailers say they send inspectors around the world and will work with a factory to improve conditions rather than simply withdraw their business, recognizing that their business with the factory is their only leverage to negotiate improved working conditions. Nothing is said about who bears the cost of improved working conditions. Is Wal-Mart willing to pay higher prices for better working conditions? Are you?

The flip side of this debate deserves discussion. Should factories in developing countries (where workers making products for multinational firms are often paid more than workers in an economy's domestic sector) have the same safety and pay and working conditions as in factories in the industrialized world? Do lower safety and pay standards make them more competitive and attract work? Are news articles and anti-sweatshop protests merely a smokescreen for protectionism? There are always two sides to a debate. Offshore sourcing is here to stay. So are buyers' ethical and moral responsibilities to protect workers' rights. Developing countries need employment. However, they may not have legal protections for workers, especially foreign workers, and they are unlikely to have monitoring and enforcement mechanisms. This role is government's in the industrialized world, but it is the responsibility of foreign investors in the developing world.[38]

There are both ethical and economic issues to consider when deciding to operate in a country where rights violations (at least from a Western perspective) are rampant.[39] The ethical issue is the morality of contributing to the economy and thereby supporting a government that does not protect workers' rights. The economic problems need not occur in the country where the violations occur; they may occur at home, where rights-monitoring interest groups organize public opinion using the press, at shareholders' meetings, on Web blogs, and by visiting individual members of the corporate board and the executive committee.

Wal-Mart is right that there is not much it can do to improve working standards in one factory in a country when poor standards are rampant throughout the business sector and ignored by government regulators. The situation is the now a familiar social dilemma. The self-interests of the Wal-Marts, Targets, and Sears are to ignore the problem, but the common and public interests are for these companies to cooperate and coordinate a solution.

A cautionary example from the 1970s is the cooperative joint action led by General Motors and other multinational corporations in flouting the South African government's apartheid laws prohibiting companies from hiring nonwhite South Africans. Reverend Leon Sullivan was a GM director at the time when its board was debating whether or not to withdraw its business from South Africa because of the government's policies toward nonwhites. Sullivan designed a policy of passive disobedience to a law that required treating white and nonwhite employees differently. GM convinced other multinational corporations to join in treating all employees equally regardless of race. The South African government, not wanting to lose the foreign investment represented by this group of multinationals, did not prosecute. It also did not capitulate. After ten years, Sullivan concluded that the principles had not succeeded, and GM withdrew from South Africa until the end of apartheid.

Today a nonprofit organization urges and negotiates with global companies to adopt the Global Sullivan Principles of Social Responsibility, reproduced in Exhibit 9.3. Many companies have endorsed the principles, though Nike and Wal-Mart are not among them.

Government At and Around the Negotiating Table

Government plays an important role in global negotiations. When government is not directly at the table as a party to the negotiations, it is still a major part of the political, social, and legal environments that affect negotiations. Understanding this environment may make the difference between an agreement and an impasse. It may allow a deal that is profitable for the private company and that meets the government's social and political standards. It may make the difference between a dispute that can be resolved in private,

Exhibit 9.3. Global Sullivan Principles of Social Responsibility.

As a company which endorses the Global Sullivan Principles we will respect the law, and as a responsible member of society we will apply these Principles with integrity consistent with the legitimate role of business. We will develop and implement company policies, procedures, training and internal reporting structures to ensure commitment to these Principles throughout our organization. We believe the application of these Principles will achieve greater tolerance and better understanding among peoples, and advance the culture of peace.

Accordingly, we will:

- Express our support for universal human rights and, particularly, those of our employees, the communities within which we operate, and parties with whom we do business.
- Promote equal opportunity for our employees at all levels of the company with respect to issues such as color, race, gender, age, ethnicity or religious beliefs, and operate without unacceptable worker treatment such as the exploitation of children, physical punishment, female abuse, involuntary servitude, or other forms of abuse.
- Respect our employees' voluntary freedom of association.
- Compensate our employees to enable them to meet at least their basic needs and provide the opportunity to improve their skill and capability in order to raise their social and economic opportunities.
- Provide a safe and healthy workplace; protect human health and the environment; and promote sustainable development.
- Promote fair competition including respect for intellectual and other property rights, and not offer, pay or accept bribes.
- Work with governments and communities in which we do business to improve the quality of life in those communities—their educational, cultural, economic and social well being—and seek to provide training and opportunities for workers from disadvantaged backgrounds.
- Promote the application of these Principles by those with whom we do business.

We will be transparent in our implementation of these Principles and provide information which demonstrates publicly our commitment to them.

Source: Leon H. Sullivan Foundation, "Global Sullivan Principles of Social Responsibility," 2005, http://globalsullivanprinciples.org/principles.htm. Reprinted by permission.

where a relationship can be preserved, and a dispute that is argued in a public forum, where relationships are irrevocably broken. Such understanding does not come without effort and investment. It requires study and planning; it requires time, patience, and creativity; it requires weighing the advice of legal and cultural experts; and sometimes it requires moral courage to confront corruption and human rights abuses.

Chapter Ten

Will the World Adjust, or Must You?

This book has shown that when parties negotiate, national culture matters. Yet as technology makes our world smaller and smaller, some argue that we are moving rapidly toward one global culture, especially in the context of business. As English has become the de facto language of global business, won't Western negotiation strategies soon dominate global negotiations? Isn't it just a matter of time until the culture of negotiation is direct confrontation and direct information sharing, in which negotiators are motivated by self-interests and BATNAs underlie reservation prices? The answer is, probably not. In this final chapter we discuss why negotiators cannot expect a standardized global negotiation culture. We then suggest some adjustments for you to consider making in the interests of more effective global negotiation.

What's Likely to Happen with "Global" English?

As a de facto global language of business, English is unlikely to evolve to be English as Anglophones speak it, but a simplified form with a limited vocabulary and grammar. It is also not likely to sound like British English or American English—regardless of accent-reduction programs and early childhood language training—since nonnative teachers of English will pass their own accents on to their students. With five hundred million to a billion people speaking English now either as a first or second language, and potentially two billion more English speakers in the next decade, "proper" English is likely to be overwhelmed by the English of nonnative speakers.[1]

Why Not to Expect a
Standardized Global Negotiation Culture

A standardized global negotiation culture is unlikely anytime soon. Cultural differences in negotiation strategy are not trivial; rather, they are deeply embedded in cultural contexts that cue and reinforce their use. Culturally based negotiation strategies are used within many social, political, and economic contexts within a culture. Negotiators with multicultural experience tend to switch between one culturally based strategy and another depending on contextual cues; they do not blend them.

Cultural differences in negotiation strategy are significant. We have seen that negotiators from different cultures send different parties to the table (principals versus representatives or agents); have different positions, interests, and priorities (depending on psychological factors but also on the economic, social, or political context); can view power from the perspective of social status or BATNA (alternatives); can prefer to confront directly or indirectly; have different social motives (individualistic, cooperative, competitive); and communicate with varying degrees of directness.

Cultural differences in negotiation strategy around the world are likely to persist. Recall from Chapter Two that a culture's prototypical negotiation strategy is its local solution to the social interaction problem of managing conflict. As people in the culture make choices about negotiation strategy, some of those strategic choices will generate good outcomes and others will not. The successful strategic choices get repeated and a negotiation strategy prototype develops. Furthermore, the likely reason that some choices for negotiation strategy are more successful than others is that they fit with the culture. For example, a direct confrontation negotiation strategy does not fit well in a culture that is high context and collective, where social interaction is generally indirect.

A culture's prototypical negotiation strategy is also likely to persist because its use is not limited to economic activities. Within all cultures negotiations occur in the family, in the community, in schools, and in social and political organizations. Negotiating daily life within a culture reinforces culturally "correct" or normative ways of negotiating. A new negotiation strategy that one learns at work is not likely to be used at home.

Bicultural people and employees working for global companies understand the different contexts in which they find themselves and adjust their behavior accordingly. Long Wang surveyed Chinese employees working for state-owned companies and Chinese employees working for U.S. subsidiaries in China.[2] He found that U.S. cultural values were more accessible to and had a stronger impact on the working behavior of those working for the U.S. subsidiaries than those working for the state-owned companies. But the U.S. values were no more *acceptable* to the Chinese working for U.S. subsidiaries than to state-owned-enterprise Chinese! Long Wang concluded that cultural exposure and behavioral compliance of local employees working in foreign companies may not necessarily induce a change in their cultural values.

Psychological research on biculturals has concluded that people who move easily between cultures do not blend their cultural knowledge, nor do they replace original cultural knowledge with new cultural knowledge. Rather, they maintain parallel cultural knowledge structures. One or the other cultural knowledge structure becomes operative in a particular task such as negotiation, depending on its accessibility (a function of recent use), and its being triggered by situational cues (for example, "I'm Chinese in China in a night market" versus "I'm Chinese in China working for a U.S. company").[3] This research, as well as that by Kristin Behfar, Mary Kern, and me on multicultural teams, suggests that people negotiating in foreign cultures and with foreigners will learn to make accommodations to cultural differences. This book has included many examples of accommodation to another culture's negotiating strategy, including abandoning an agenda-based deal-making strategy when negotiating with Saudis (Chapter One) and Koreans (Chapter Two); asking questions about the rattling bicycles (Chapters One and Five); becoming resigned to bringing the boss into dispute resolution (Chapters Five and Six); restructuring a UN peacekeeping team (Chapter One); restructuring a U.S.- Japanese consulting team (Chapter Seven); shining a spotlight on unethical behavior (Chapter Nine); and negotiating with hostage takers (Chapter Nine). Effective global negotiators accommodate. They are willing to adjust their strategy to the situation.

Adjustments Toward Becoming a More Effective Global Negotiator

To be effective in a global environment, negotiators need to develop knowledge structures and skills with confrontation and communication strategies that come from other cultures. They need a storehouse of creative approaches for handling challenges to cooperation in multiparty situations such as teams and social dilemmas. They need to cultivate tolerance and respect for the positions, interests, and priorities that people from different cultures bring to the negotiating table. Finally, they need to know when not to accommodate. They need to have an ethical standard that meets personal, corporate, and legal criteria and will carry them through situations of corruption, bribery, and extortion.

Confrontation Strategies

Negotiators from less confrontational cultures may need to be willing to become more confrontational in some negotiation situations. What should help those reluctant to do so is the realization that in direct-confrontation cultures there is less risk of losing face and inviting interpersonal conflict than in indirect-confrontation cultures. Recall the American software engineer who was shocked by the sharp, confrontational questioning style of his Israeli customer (Chapter Two). Once he realized that the task conflict occurring among the Israelis did not spread into interpersonal conflict (no one was offended, no one lost face), he became comfortable engaging at a level of confrontation that he would never reach with his American colleagues.

Negotiators from more confrontational cultures may need to be willing to become less confrontational in some situations. Although you may not know the culture well enough to use a story or metaphor to get your point across, asking a rhetorical question is well within your skills. Recall the rattling bicycles? In that situation, it was a rhetorical question that worked: "What do you think the German customer might think if the bicycles rattled?" Recall the eBusiness road show that the Indian manager put on for the Japanese team. He showed them what others were doing; they got the picture. What is going to be hard for negotiators from direct confrontation cultures is stopping after asking the question or putting on the road show—not overextending by explaining why you asked the question, why you put on the show. In high-context cultures, it is up to the listener to draw inferences.

Communication Strategies

Negotiators from high-context-communication cultures may need to be willing to explain their strategy of wanting to see the big picture. Recall from Chapter Five that process interventions in which parties discuss the process can help to restart stalled negotiations. High-context negotiators do not have to give up the big-picture strategy, but they may need to help negotiators on the other side of the table understand why they are unwilling to resolve issues one at a time. They may also have to be so direct as to put a multi-issue offer on the table, not just the series of single-issue offers they advance when negotiating within their own high-context culture. Putting that multi-issue offer on the table does two important things: it helps the other party see the big picture and it gains first offer advantage.

Negotiators from low-context-communication cultures may need to be willing to negotiate via multi-issue offers and infer the other party's interests and priorities by the way the offers change. Low-context-culture negotiators can do this (I walked you through the charting of offers in Chapter Four), and they should, since multi-issue offers link both integrative and distributive value.

Again, it may help to talk about process, saying something such as, "We've got a lot of issues to discuss; we'd like to work through them systematically. We may reach tentative agreement on some, but from our perspective all agreements are provisional until we've looked carefully at all the issues."

Coexistence

Negotiators need to be creative when challenged by cultural differences. One type of creativity that almost anyone can rely on is allowing different cultural strategies to coexist. In Chapters Two and Seven we described fusion solutions to negotiating multicultural team decisions. The example mentioned in Chapter Seven from one of our multicultural team interviews illustrates how the team of U.S. and U.K. financial services managers fused their process.

> [The] team observed that the U.S. approach to problem solving was to "forge ahead and start trying to rip apart things and let's do this and that," whereas the U.K. members of the team took a more pragmatic approach: "let's not hurry up, . . . let's think about this."

When the team members first started working together these different approaches generated conflict. Neither team was willing to concede to the other's approach. As time went on, team members learned not just to live with their differences, but to respect them and use them to generate a better team process. The U.S. team members took up the challenge of doing a lot of the idea generation, and the U.K. team members took the responsibility for doing most of the pros and cons analysis.[4]

Coexistence was the ultimate solution to the implementation plan for the Kyoto accords on global warming. Recall that at the meeting in 2000 the United States wanted credits for carbon sinks and emissions trading; the European Union wanted to set emission reduction goals. Both groups thought their solution to this social dilemma was the right one, and they failed to reach agreement. A year later without U.S. involvement the European Union promoted an agreement that included carbon sinks, emissions trading, *and* emission reduction goals. Different parties to the global warming social dilemma respond to different types of structural interventions. Is it expensive to put multiple approaches into place? Yes. Is it worth it in order to generate cooperation in a social dilemma? Yes, if that is what it takes.

At the core of the concept of coexistence is the notion of trade-offs. Trade-offs are the fundamental way to create integrative outcomes in negotiations. With coexistence, I trade letting you do it your way for the right to do it my way. What coexistence does is move the application of trade-offs from the substantive task—and the issues over which we are in conflict—to the process, in which we also frequently find ourselves in conflict. Success negotiating globally requires paying more attention to the process than is necessary in same-culture negotiations, but also using the same basic skills required for negotiating an excellent process and, ultimately, an excellent outcome.

Tolerance and Respect

Coexistence in global negotiations requires respecting and tolerating different negotiation strategies. It requires setting ethnocentric ideas—"my culture's way is the best way"—aside, and being creative.

One of the questions that American managers often ask is, "Why me? Why do I have to do all the adjusting? Why do I have to tolerate coexistence?" The answer is that it isn't just them. Cultural accommodation is not just one-sided. At the same time, the party that wants the deal, that wants the dispute resolved, and that understands coexistence is in a better position to be flexible on the process than is the party that has neither these motivations nor the skill set to put coexistence into place.

Another question often asked is, "But can one party really generate coexistence alone? Doesn't it take two?" Although we do not

have data that answers this question, we do know that when negotiating integrative *agreements* it takes only one party's understanding
the other's priorities. Yes, it is easier when both parties understand
each other's preferences, but integrative agreement is still possible
with asymmetric understanding.[5] The same effect seems likely to
hold for *process* negotiations. Most likely, one party can make the
necessary accommodations during the negotiation to generate cultural coexistence as opposed to culture clash. Is it easier when both
parties make accommodations? The obvious answer is yes.

Ethics in Global Negotiations When Coexistence, Tolerance, and Respect Are Lacking

To be honest, corrupt business practices occur in every nation. The
margin between making money and making money legally is sometimes exceedingly narrow. As we discussed in Chapter Nine, business practices within an industry or within a nation over time may
gravitate toward illegality. Some managers tell me that to get in the
game or stay in it you have to play by its rules. Yet participating in
a culture of corruption is a social dilemma: if everyone "gets in the
game," there are short-term winners and many long-term losers.

When it comes to ethics my advice about negotiating coexistence still stands. If you can engage in ethical business practices in
an environment of corruption, you are making a major contribution
to the future of the nation. If you cannot succeed in such an environment, Chapter Nine suggested a number of tactics to try to
make the environment more accommodating, especially publiciz-
ing corruption and engaging jointly to oppose it, before moving
your business elsewhere.

Excellent Global Negotiators

Excellent global negotiators know that to make deals, resolve disputes, and reach decisions across cultural boundaries, they must exercise strategic flexibility and engage in cultural accommodation.

Although culture will very likely affect negotiators' interests and priorities, negotiators need do nothing out of the ordinary to integrate those interests once they understand them. It is the process of understanding negotiators' interests that is likely to require strategic flexibility when negotiating across cultures. So long as strategy stays within ethical boundaries, excellent global negotiators are concerned less about the negotiation process, than that their interests are met.

Notes

Preface

1. M. H. Bazerman and M. A. Neale, *Negotiating Rationally* (New York: Free Press, 1992); D. G. Pruitt, *Negotiation Behavior* (Orlando, Fla.: Academic Press, 1981); L. L. Thompson, *Making the Team* (Upper Saddle River, N.J.: Prentice-Hall, 1999); L. L. Thompson, *The Mind and Heart of the Negotiator* (Upper Saddle River, N.J.: Prentice-Hall, 1998); W. L. Ury, J. M. Brett, and S. B. Goldberg, *Getting Disputes Resolved: Designing a System to Cut the Costs of Conflict* (Cambridge, Mass.: Program on Negotiation, Harvard Law School, 1993); L. R. Weingart, R. J. Bennett, and J. M. Brett, "The Impact of Consideration of Issues and Motivational Orientation on Group Negotiation Process and Outcome," *Journal of Applied Psychology*, 1993, 78, 504–517.

Acknowledgments

1. A. L. Lytle, J. M. Brett, Z. I. Barsness, C. H. Tinsley, and M. Janssens, M. "A Paradigm for Confirmatory Cross-Cultural Research in Organizational Behavior," in L. L. Cummings and B. M. Staw (eds.), *Research in Organizational Behavior 17*, 167–214 (Greenwich, Conn.: JAI Press, 1995); J. M. Brett, C. H. Tinsley, M. Janssens, Z. I. Barsness, and A. L. Lytle, A.L. "New Approaches to the Study of Culture in I/O Psychology," in P. C. Earley and M. Erez (eds.), *New Perspectives on International/Organizational Psychology* (San Francisco: Jossey-Bass, 1997), 75–129.

Chapter One

1. Interview as part of the Multicultural Teams project, K. Behfar, M. Kern, and J. M. Brett, J1, 2005. For more information about this project, see: J. M. Brett, K. Behfar, and M. C. Kern, "Managing Multicultural Teams," *Harvard Business Review*, 2006, 84(11), pp. 84–91 (AN 22671287); K. Behfar, M. Kern, and J. M. Brett, "Managing Challenges in Multicultural Teams," in E. Mannix and Y. Chen (eds.), *Research on Managing Groups and Teams*. (Oxford: Elsevier Science Press, 2006), pp. 233–262.
2. C. Krauss, "Canada Fishermen Protest Change in Quotas," *New York Times*, May 11, 2003 , SS1 p. 3.
3. Darren Wee, interview with author, October 26, 2005.
4. R. Fisher, W. L. Ury, and B. Patton, *Getting to Yes* (New York: Penguin, 1991).
5. M. H. Bazerman and N. A. Neale, *Negotiating Rationally* (New York: Free Press, 1992).
6. Interview as part of the *Teams at the Negotiation Table* project, J. M. Brett, R. Friedman, and K. Behfar, 2006.
7. Interview as part of the *Teams at the Negotiation Table* project, J. M. Brett, R. Friedman, and K. Behfar, 2006.
8. Interview as part of the *Teams at the Negotiation Table* project, J. M. Brett, R. Friedman, and K. Behfar, 2006.
9. A. Giridharadas, "Mittal's Stormy Question for Arcelor: Much More than a Personal Drama," *International Herald Tribune*, June 26, 2006, p. 10.
10. M. A. Von Glinow, D. L. Shapiro, and J. M. Brett, "Can We Talk, and Should We?: Managing Emotional Conflict in Multicultural Teams," *The Academy of Management Review*, 2004, 29(4), 578–592.
11. D. A. Moore, T. R. Kurtzberg, L. L. Thompson, and M. Morris, "Long and Short Routes to Success in Electronically-Mediated Negotiations: Group Affiliations and Good Vibrations," *Organizational Behavior and Human Performance Processes*, 1999, 77, 22–43.

12. A. S. Rosette, J. M. Brett, Z. Barsness, and A. L. Lytle, *When Cultures Clash Electronically: The Impact of E-mail and Culture on Negotiation Behavior*, DRRC Working Paper No. 302, Northwestern University, 2004.

13. Giridharadas, "Mittal's Stormy Quest for Arcelor," p 10.

14. References for this section re measuring social motives: D. M. Messick and C. G. McClintock, "Motivational Basis of Choice in Experimental Games," *Journal of Experimental Social Psychology*, 1968, 4, 1–25; re integrative and distributive strategy: R. E. Walton and R. B. McKersie, *A Behavioral Theory of Labor Negotiation: An Analysis of a Social Interaction System* (New York: McGraw-Hill, 1965); D. G. Pruitt and S. Lewis, "Development of Integrative Solutions in Bilateral Negotiation," *Journal of Personality and Social Psychology*, 1975, 31, 621–633; re behaviors and strategy: C.K.W. De Dreu, L. R. Weingart, and S. Kwon, "Influence of Social Motives on Integrative Negotiations: A Meta-Analytic Review and Test of Two Theories," *Journal of Personality and Social Psychology*, 2000, 78, 889–905; M. Olekalns and P. L. Smith, "Negotiating Optimal Outcomes: The Role of Strategic Sequences in Competitive Negotiations," *Human Communication Research*, 2000, 24, 528–560; D. G. Pruitt and S. Lewis, "Development of Integrative Solutions in Bilateral Negotiation," *Journal of Personality and Social Psychology*, 1975, 31, 621–633; L. L. Putnam and S. R. Wilson, "Argumentation and Bargaining Strategies as Discriminators of Integrative Outcomes," In M. A. Rahim (ed.), *Managing Conflict: An Interdisciplinary Approach*, pp. 121–144 (New York: Praeger, 1989), L. L. Thompson, "Information Exchange in Negotiation," *Journal of Experimental Social Psychology*, 1991, 27, 161–179; L. R. Weingart, L. L. Thompson, M. H. Bazerman, and J. S. Carroll, "Tactical Behavior and Negotiation Outcomes," *The International Journal of Conflict Management*, 1990, 1, 7–31; L. R. Weingart, E. B. Hyder, and M. J. Prietula, "Knowledge Matters: The Effect of Tactical Descriptions on Negotiation Behavior and Outcome," *Journal of Personality and Social Psychology*, 1996, 70,

1205–1217; re evidence that negotiators use both strategies: Putnam and Wilson, 1989; Weingart, Thompson, Bazerman, and Carroll, 1990; L. L. Putnam, "Reframing Integrative and Distributive Bargaining: A Process Perspective," in B. H. Sheppard, M. H. Bazerman, and R. J. Lewicki (eds.), *Research on Negotiation in Organizations* Vol. 2, pp. 3–30 (Greenwich, Conn.: JAI, 1990); re same social motive negotiators and strategy: De Dreu, Weingart, and Kwon, 2000.

15. In Chapters Three and Four I'll explain all about the Cartoon negotiation. The data backing up my claim that managers with competitive social motives negotiate lower joint gains are from the Cartoon studies. Here are the results: in my biggest data set ($n = 1341$) across all cultures, regardless of the social motive or culture of the other party, the competitive negotiators get lower joint gains ($m = 3.64$, $SD = 1.23$, $n = 50$) than either the cooperative negotiators ($m = 4.03$, $SD = 1.01$, $n = 766$) or the individualists ($m = 4.03$, $SD = 1.02$, $n = 526$) ($F (2, 1339) = 3.398$, $p < .05$).

16. L. R. Weingart, J. M. Brett, and M. Olekalns, *Conflicting Social Motives in Negotiating Groups*, DRRC Working Paper No. 272, Northwestern University, 2002.

Chapter Two

1. P. Garfinkel, "On Keeping Your Foot Safely Out of Your Mouth." *New York Times*, July 13, 2004, C7.

2. S. Fewer, D. Krohm, and S. Yang, *Lafarge Negotiations in China*, Northwestern University, Kellogg School of Management, Evanston, Illinois, 2005.

3. A. L. Lytle, J. M. Brett, Z. I. Barsness, C. H. Tinsley, and M. Janssens, "A Paradigm for Confirmatory Cross-Cultural Research in Organizational Behavior," In L. L. Cummings and B. M. Staw (eds.), *Research in Organizational Behavior*, Vol. 17, pp. 167–214 (Greenwich, Conn.: JAI Press, 1995).

4. F. Trompenaars, "Resolving International Conflict: Culture and Business Strategy," *Business Strategy Review*, 1996, 7, 51.

5. See, for example, Aquent, "Business of Touch," 2006. Available at www.businessoftouch.com/index2.html.

6. H. Timmon and A. E. Kramer, "'Russophobia' Gets Blame for the Death of Severstal Deal," *International Herald Tribune*, June 27, 2006, p. 11.

7. For more information about the Unocal CNOOC Chevron negotiations, see J. Martin, CNOOC, *Chevron and Unocal: Mergers, Money, Politics*. San Diego: Institute of the Americas, Aug. 5, 2005. Available at www.iamericas.org/publications/article.html?atypeid=2&aid=962.

8. On measurement, see S. J. Heine, D. R. Lehman, K. Peng, and J. Greenholtz, "What's Wrong with Cross-Cultural Comparisons of Subjective Likert Scales?: The Reference-Group Effect," *Journal of Personality and Social Psychology*, 2002, 82(6), 903–918. Regarding reference groups, see S. Kitayama, "Culture and Basic Psychological Processes—Toward a System View of Culture: Comment on Oyserman et al.," *Psychological Bulletin*, 2002, 128(1), 89–96.

9. G. Hofstede, *Culture's Consequences: International Differences in Work-Related Values*, Thousand Oaks, Calif.: Sage, 1980; S. Schwartz, "Beyond Individualism/Collectivism: New Cultural Dimensions of Values," in H. C. Triandis, U. Kim, and U. Yoon (eds.), *Individualism and Collectivism*, pp. 85–117 (London: Sage, 1994).

10. For a thorough review and critique of using cultural values, see B. L. Kirkman, K. B. Lowe, and C. B. Gibson, "A Quarter Century of Culture's Consequences: A Review of Empirical Research Incorporating Hofstede's Cultural Values Framework," *Journal of International Business Studies*, 2006, 37(3), 285–320; J. M. Brett and S. Crotty, "Culture and Negotiation" in P. B. Smith, M. F. Peterson, and D. C. Thomas (eds.), *Conflict and Negotiation: Handbook of Cross-Cultural Management Research* (Thousand Oaks, Calif.: Sage, forthcoming).

11. Hofstede, *Culture's Consequences*; Schwartz, "Beyond Individualism/Collectivism."

12. Interview as part of the Multicultural Teams project, K. Behfar, M. Kern, and J. M. Brett, M3, 2005.

13. M. J. Gelfand and J. M. Brett, "Introduction," in M. J. Gelfand and J. M. Brett (eds.), *Handbook of Negotiation and Culture: Theoretical Advances and Cultural Perspectives*, pp. 3–6 (Palo Alto, Calif.: Stanford University Press, 2004).

14. D. Oyserman, H. M. Coon, and M. Kemmelmeier, "Rethinking Individualism and Collectivism: Evaluation of Theoretical Assumptions and Meta-Analysis," *Psychological Bulletin*, 2002, *128*, 3–72; Kitayama, "Culture and Basic Psychological Processes—Toward a System View of Culture."

15. J. M. Brett and S. Kopelman, "Cross-Cultural Perspectivism on Cooperation in Social Dilemmas," In M. J. Gelfand and J. M. Brett (eds.), *Handbook of Negotiation and Culture: Theoretical Advances and Cultural Perspectives*, pp. 395–414 (Palo Alto, Calif.: Stanford University Press, 2004.

16. S. Schwartz, "Beyond Individualism/Collectivism: New Cultural Dimensions of Values," in H. C. Triandis, U. Kim, and G. Yoon (eds.), *Individualism and Collectivism*, pp. 85–117 (London: Sage, 1994).

17. Interview as part of the Multicultural Teams project, K. Behfar, M. Kern, and J. M. Brett, M8, 2005.

18. K. Leung, "Negotiation and Reward Allocations Across Cultures," in P. C. Earley, M. Erez, and Associates (eds.), *New Perspectives on International/Industrial Organizational Psychology* pp. 640–675 (San Francisco: Jossey-Bass, 1997).

19. Leung, "Negotiation and Reward Allocations Across Cultures."

20. L. Kaufman, "As Biggest Business, Wal-Mart Propels Changes Elsewhere," *New York Times*, Oct. 22, 2000, Business/Financial Desk Archives.

21. J. M. Brett and T. Okumura, "Inter- and Intra-Cultural Negotiation: U. S. and Japanese Negotiators," *Academy of Management Journal*, 1998, *41*, 495–510.

22. Interview as part of the Multicultural Teams project, K. Behfar, M. Kern, and J. M. Brett, J3, 2005.

23. D. M. Rousseau, S. B. Sitkin, R. S. Burt, and C. Camerer, "Not So Different After All: A Cross-Discipline View of Trust," *Academy of Management Review*, 1998, *23*(3), 393–404.

24. D. Myerson, K. E. Weick, and R. M. Kramer, "Swift Trust and Temporary Groups," in R. M. Kramer and T. R. Tyler (eds.), *Trust in Organization: Frontiers of Theory and Research*, pp. 166–195 (Thousand Oaks, Calif.: Sage, 1996).

25. Interview with the author, April 17, 2005.

26. E. T. Hall and M. R. Hall, *Understanding Cultural Differences*. (Yarmouth, Me.: Intercultural Press, 1990); E. T. Hall, *Beyond Culture* (New York: Anchor Press, 1976); C. B. Gibson, "Do You Hear What I Hear: A Model for Reconciling Intercultural Communication Difficulties Arising from Cognitive Styles and Cultural Values," in P. C. Earley and M. Erez (eds.), *New Perspectives on International Industrial/Organizational Psychology*, pp. 335–362 (San Francisco: Jossey-Bass, 1997); W. B. Gudykunst, Y. Matsumoto, S. Ting-Toomey, and T. Nishida, "The Influence of Cultural Individualism-Collectivism, Self-Construals, and Individual Values on Communication Styles Across Cultures," *Human Communication Research*, 1996, *22*, 510–543.

27. Interview as part of the Multicultural Teams project, K. Behfar, M. Kern, and J. M. Brett, M6, 2005.

28. N. J. Adler, R. Braham, and J. L. Graham, "Strategy Implementations: A Comparison of Face-to-Face Negotiations in the People's Republic of China and the U.S.," *Strategic Management Journal*, 1992, *13*, 449–266.

29. L. L. Putnam and S. R. Wilson, "Argumentation and Bargaining Strategies as Discriminators of Integrative Outcomes," in M. A. Rahim (ed.), *Managing Conflict: An Interdisciplinary Approach*, pp. 549–599 (Newbury Park, Calif.: Sage, 1989); L. Thompson, "Information Exchange in Negotiation," *Journal of Experimental Social Psychology*, 1991, *27*(2), 161–179; L. R. Weingart, L. L. Thompson, M. H. Bazerman, and J. S. Carroll, "Tactical Behavior and Negotiation Outcomes," *International*

Journal of Conflict Management, 1990, *1*, 7–31; L. R. Weingart, E. B. Hyder, and M. J. Prietula, "Knowledge Matters: The Effect of Tactical Descriptions on Negotiation Behavior and Outcome," *Journal of Personality and Social Psychology*, 1996, *70*(6), 1205–1217; M. Olekalns and P. L. Smith, "Testing the Relationships Among Negotiators' Motivational Orientations, Strategy Choices and Outcomes," *Journal of Experimental Social Psychology*, 2003, *39*, 101–117; L. Thompson and R. Hastie, "Social Perception in Negotiation," *Organizational Behavior and Human Decision Processes*, 1990, *47*(1), 98–123; F. Tutzauer and M. E. Roloff, "Communication Processes Leading to Integrative Agreements: Three Paths to Joint Benefit," *Communication Research*, 1988, *15*, 360–380.

30. W. Adair, T. Okumura, and J. M. Brett, "Negotiation Behavior When Cultures Collide: The United States and Japan," *Journal of Applied Psychology*, 2001, *86*(3), 371–385; W. L. Adair and J. M. Brett, "The Negotiation Dance: Time, Culture, and Behavioral Sequences in Negotiation," *Organizational Science*, 2005, *16*(1), 33–51; W. L. Adair, L. R. Weingart, and J. M. Brett, "The Timing of Offers and Information Exchange in U.S. and Japanese Negotiations," *Journal of Applied Psychology*, (forthcoming).

31. R. Nisbett, *The Psychology of Thought* (New York: Free Press, 2003).

32. M. W. Morris and H.-Y. Fu, "How Does Culture Influence Conflict Resolution? A Dynamic Constructivist Analysis," *Social Cognition*, 2001, *19*(3), 324–349; Kitayama, "Culture and Basic Psychological Processes—Toward a System View of Culture."

33. For the logic of appropriateness question, see J. March, *A Primer on Decision-Making: How Decisions Happen* (New York: Free Press, March 1994).

34. J. M. Brett, C. H. Tinsley, D. L. Shapiro, and T. Okumura, "Intervening in Employee Disputes: How and When Will Managers from China, Japan, and the U.S. Act Differently?" *Management and Organizational Review* (forthcoming).

35. Morris and Fu, "How Does Culture Influence Conflict Resolution?"; M. Morris and M. Gelfand, "Cultural Differences and Cognitive Dynamics: Expanding the Cognitive Perspective on Negotiation," in M. J. Gelfand and J. M. Brett (eds.), *The Handbook of Negotiation and Culture: Theoretical Advances and Cultural Perspectives*, pp. 45–70 (Palo Alto, Calif.: Stanford University Press, 2004).

36. Interview as part of the Multicultural Teams project, K. Behfar, M. Kern, and J. M. Brett, J2, 2005.

37. M. Janssens and J. M. Brett, "Cultural Intelligence in Global Teams: A Fusion Model of Collaboration," *Group and Organizational Studies*, 2006, *31*(1), 124–153.

38. T. Friedman, *The World Is Flat* (New York: Farrar, Straus and Giroux, 2005).

39. Fewer, Krohm, and Yang, *Lafarge Negotiations in China*.

40. Darren Wee, interview with the author, October 26, 2005.

41. J. M. Brett, D. L. Shapiro, and A. L Lytle, "Breaking the Bonds of Reciprocity in Negotiations," *Academy of Management Journal*, 1998, *41*, 410–424; W. L. Adair, *Reciprocity in the Global Market*, Department of Management and Organizations, Northwestern University, 2000.

42. Adair, *Reciprocity in the Global Market*.

Chapter Three

1. M. Blume, "2 Partners Swathing the Great Outdoors," *International Herald Tribune*, December 23, 2005.

2. M. H. Bazerman and M. A. Neale, *Negotiating Rationally* (New York: Free Press, 1992).

3. C. Sang-Hun, "Wal-Mart Selling Stores and Leaving South Korea," *New York Times*, May 23, 2006, C5.

4. J. Tagliabue, "Shares of Alcatel Fall on Profit Warning," *New York Times*, May 31, 2001, SS C p. 4; A. R. Sorkin and S. Romero, "Alcatel and Lucent Call Off Negotiations Toward a Merger," *New York Times*, May 30, 2001, SS C p 1.

5. M. Bazerman and A. Tenbrusel, "Working Women" (retitled "Moms.com") (CD), (Evanston, Ill.: Northwestern University: DRRC Teaching Materials, 2006).

6. The difference in the two reservation prices is $10,000 per episode times one hundred episodes, or $1 million.

7. $F(11,702) = 2.6, p < .05$.

8. $F(11,702) = 23.92, p < .01$.

9. M. Craze and J. Simmons, "Road from Acrimony to Giant Steel Merger," *International Herald Tribune*, July 6, 2006, 13.

Chapter Four

1. E. T. Hall, *The Silent Language* (Garden City, N.Y.: Anchor, 1983), 155.

2. W. Adair and J. M. Brett, "The Negotiation Dance: Time, Culture and Behavioral Sequences in Negotiation," *Organizational Science*, 2005, *16*(1), 33–51.

3. For further detail about the participants, see Adair and Brett, "The Negotiation Dance."

4. Data analysis for results in Exhibits 4.3 and 4.4 was a repeated measures multivariate analysis of variance. Time was the repeated measure, or within-subjects (dyad) factor. Culture (high context, low context, mixed context) was the between-subjects (dyads) factor.

5. Adair and Brett, "The Negotiation Dance."

6. L. R. Weingart, L. L. Thompson, M. H. Bazerman, and J. S. Carroll, "Tactical Behavior and Negotiation Outcomes," *International Journal of Conflict Management*, 1990, *1*, 7–31.

7. W. A. Donohue, "Communicative Competence in Mediators," in K. Kressel and D. G. Pruitt (eds.), *Mediation Research: The Process and Effectiveness of Third-Party Intervention*, pp. 322–343 (San Francisco: Jossey-Bass, 1989); A. L. Lytle, J. M. Brett, and D. L. Shapiro, "The Strategic Use of Interests, Rights and Power to Resolve Disputes," *Negotiation Journal*, 1999, *15*(1), 31–49; M. Olekalns and P. L. Smith, "Understanding Optimal Out-

comes: The Role of Strategy Sequences in Competitive Negotiations," *Human Communication Research*, 2000, *26*(4), 527–557.

8. W. L. Adair, *Reciprocity in the Global Market*, Department of Management and Organizations, Northwestern University, 2000.

9. Information on first offers that shows that in a distributive negotiation an effective anchor can result in a solution favoring one party over another includes A. D. Galinsky and T. Mussweiler, "First Offers as Anchors: The Role of Perspective-Taking and Negotiator Focus," *Journal of Personality and Social Psychology*, 2001, *81*, 657–669; R. M. Liebert, W. P. Smith, J. H. Hill, and M. Keiffer, "The Effects of Information and Magnitude of Initial Offer on Interpersonal Negotiation," *Journal of Experimental Social Psychology*, 1968, *4*, 431–441; and A. Tversky and D. Kahneman, "Judgment Under Uncertainty: Heuristics and Biases," *Science*, 1974, *185*(4157), 1124–1131. The reason is that first offers anchor the negotiation; see G. Northcraft and M. Neale, "Experts, Amateurs, and Real-Estate: An Anchoring-and-Adjustment Perspective on Property Pricing Decisions," *Organizational Behavior and Human Decision Processes*, 1987, *39*, 84–97; and G. A. Yukl, "Effects of Situational Variables and Opponent Concessions on a Bargainer's Perception, Aspirations, and Concessions," *Journal of Personality and Social Psychology*, 1974, *29*, 227–236.

10. D. A. Moore, "The Unexpected Benefits of Final Deadlines in Negotiation," *Journal of Experimental Social Psychology*, 2004, *40*, 121–127; A. F. Stuhlmacher, T. L. Gillespie, and M. V. Champagne, "The Impact of Time Pressure in Negotiation: A Meta-Analysis." *International Journal of Conflict Management*, 1998, *9*, 97–116.

11. W. Adair, T. Okumura, and J. M. Brett, "Negotiation Behavior When Cultures Collide: The U.S. and Japan," *Journal of Applied Psychology*, 2001, *86*(3), 371–385.

12. E. T. Hall, *Beyond Culture* (Garden City, N.Y.: Anchor, 1976).

13. Adair, Okumura, and Brett, "Negotiation Behavior When Cultures Collide."

14. I. E. Morley and J. M. Stephensen, *The Social Psychology of Bargaining*. (London: Allen & Unwin, 1977); L. L. Putnam and T. S. Jones. "Reciprocity in Negotiations: An Analysis of Bargaining Interaction," *Communication Monographs*, 1982, 49(3), 171–191.

15. W. L. Adair, L. R. Weingart, and J. M. Brett, "The Timing of Offers and Information Exchange in U.S. and Japanese Negotiations," *Journal of Applied Psychology* (forthcoming).

16. Interview as part of the Multicultural Teams project, K. Behfar, M. Kern, and J. M. Brett, J3, 2005.

17. V. H. Medvec, G. J. Leonardelli, A. D. Galinsky, and A. Claussen-Schulz, "Choice and Achievement at the Bargaining Table: The Distributive, Integrative, and Interpersonal Advantages of Making Multiple Equivalent Simultaneous Offers," paper presented at the Annual International Association for Conflict Management Conference, Seville, Spain, June 2005.

18. H. Raiffa, *The Art and Science of Negotiation* (Cambridge, Mass.: Belknap Press, 1982).

19. J. M. Brett, and others, "Culture and Joint Gains in Negotiation," *Negotiation Journal*, 1998, *14*, 55–80.

20. M. Olekalns, J. M. Brett, and L. R. Weingart, "Phases, Transitions and Interruptions: The Processes That Shape Agreement in Multi-Party Negotiations," *International Journal of Conflict Management: Special Issue on Processes in Negotiation*, 2004, *14*, 191–211.

21. Using the buyer's proportion of joint gains reduces the correlation between joint gains and the buyer's share to .33, $p < .05$ from .55, $p < .01$, and therefore may pick up factors that are related to buyers claiming value, but not to joint creation of value.

Chapter Five

1. P. J. Carnevale and D. G. Pruitt, "Negotiation and Mediation," *Annual Review of Psychology*, 1992, *43*, 531–582.

2. Venkat Gopikanth and Teri Prahl researched and analyzed the dispute between Nichia Corporation and Shuji Nakamura. increase the storage capacity of DVDs by a factor of four or five, and in combination with red and green LEDs may ultimately replace conventional light bulbs.

3. W.L. F. Felsteiner, R. L. Abel, and A. Sarat, "The Emergence and Transformation of Disputes: Naming, Blaming, and Claiming," *Law and Society Review*, 1980–1981, *15*, 631–654.

4. W. L. Ury, J. M. Brett, and S. B. Goldberg, *Getting Disputes Resolved: Designing a System to Cut the Costs of Conflict* (Cambridge, Mass.: Program on Negotiation, Harvard Law School, 1993).

5. H. C. Triandis, *Individualism and Collectivism* (Boulder, Colo.: Westview Press, 1995). See also M. Gelfand, V. S. Major, J. L. Raver, L. H. Nishi, and K. O'Brien, "Negotiating Relationally: The Dynamics of the Relational Self in Negotiations," *Academy of Management Review*, 2006, *31*(2), 427–451, who comment that gender differences in relational interests are greater than cultural differences.

6. C. H. Tinsley, and J. M. Brett, "Managing Workplace Conflict in the U. S. and Hong Kong," *Organizational Behavior and Human Decision Process*, 2001, *85*(2), 360–381.

7. Nonexclusive rights means the employee has rights to his invention, but because he was working for the employer during the process of inventing, the employer also has rights to the invention.

8. K. Leung and M. W. Morris, "Justice Through the Lens of Culture and Ethnicity," in J. Sanders and V. L. Hamilton (eds.), *Handbook of Law and Social Science*, pp. 343–378 (New York: Plenum, 1996).

9. C. H. Tinsley, "Culture's Influences on Conflict Management Behaviors in the Workplace," unpublished doctoral dissertation, Department of Organization Behavior, Northwestern University, 1997; C. H. Tinsley, "How We Get to Yes: Predicting the Constellation of Strategies Used Across Cultures to Negotiate Conflict," *Journal of Applied Psychology*, 2001, *86*(4), 583–593.

10. Tinsley coded every subject-verb clause that was uttered: 4,456 in the German discussions, 5,814 in the U.S. discussions, and 2,891 in the Japanese discussions. (Japanese discussions were in Japanese and then translated.) She then entered the data in a code-by-culture table, using twenty-three codes across the three cultures. The cells in the table are the frequencies that disputants in a culture used a code category. The row totals are the frequencies across cultures of the use of a code category. The column totals are the frequencies of all codes in a culture. If you multiply row total times column total and divide the result by the overall number of subject-verb sequences, you get an expected value. If you subtract the observed value from the expected value, the residual will be positive if the culture used the code category more than expected and negative if that culture used the code category less than expected. Standardized residuals are easier to interpret than raw residuals because if the culture is using the category of behavior as expected, the standardized residual will be zero. The statistical significance of the residuals can be evaluated with a chi-square statistic. Significant chi-squares are associated with Exhibits 5.4 through 5.11.

11. D. Messick and P. Sentis, "Estimating Social and Nonsocial Utility Functions from Ordinal Data," *European Journal of Social Psychology*, 1985, *15*, 389–399.

12. L. Pye, *Chinese Commercial Negotiating Style* (Cambridge, Mass.: Oelgeschlager, Gunn, and Hain, 1982); T. Fang, *Chinese Business Negotiating Style* (Thousand Oaks, Calif.: Sage, 1999).

13. R. Tung, "Strategic Management Thought in East Asia," *Organizational Dynamics*, 1994, *22*(4), 55–65.

14. R. M. Emerson, "Power Dependence Relations," *American Sociological Review*, 1962, *27*, 31–41.

15. "Blue LED Dispute Settlement Viewed as Epoch-Making; Firms Move to Set Up a System for Fair Valuation of Employee Inventions," *Japan Brief*, Foreign Press Center, January 13, 2005. Available at www.fpcj.jp/e/mres/japanbrief/jb_41.html.

16. Nakamura is currently a professor at University of California, Santa Barbara.

17. C. H. Tinsley, "Models of Conflict Resolution in Japanese, German, and American Cultures," *Journal of Applied Psychology*, 1998, 83, 316–323; Tinsley, "Culture's Influences"; Tinsley, "How We Get to Yes."

18. C. H. Tinsley, "Culture and Conflict: Enlarging Our Dispute Resolution Framework," in M. Gelfand and J. Brett (eds.), *The Handbook of Negotiation and Culture*, pp. 193–210 (Stanford, Calif.: Stanford University Press, 2005).

19. R. M. March, *The Japanese Negotiator: Subtlety and Strategy Beyond Western Logic* (New York: Kodansha International, 1990).

20. Tinsley, "Culture's Influences"; Tinsley, "How We Get to Yes."

21. E. T. Hall, *Beyond Culture* (New York: Anchor/Doubleday, 1976); S. Ting-Toomey, "Intercultural Conflict Styles: A Face Negotiation Theory," in Y. Kim and W. B. Gudykunst (eds.), *Theories in Intercultural Communication*, pp. 213–238 (Thousand Oaks, Calif.: Sage, 1988).

22. E. Goffman, *Interaction ritual* (Garden City, New York: Doubleday, 1967).

23. S. Tjosvold and C. Hui, *Showing Respect Among Chinese: A Study on Social Face in Conflict* (College Park, Md.: International Association for Conflict Management, 1998).

24. N. Wolfson, T. Marmor, and S. Jones, "Problems in the Comparison of Speech Acts Across Cultures," in S. Blum-Kulka, J. House, and G. Kasper, *Cross-Cultural Pragmatics: Requests and Apologies*, Vol. 31 in the series *Advances in Discourse Processes*, Roy O. Freedle (ed.), pp. 174–196 (Westport, Conn.: Ablex, 1989). In other research and commentary on apology, Sugimoto found that Japanese preferred to apologize directly without explaining their actions. Their apologies emphasized statements of remorse, reparation, compensation, promise not to repeat, and a request for forgiveness. Those from the United States also

apologized directly but less frequently than the Japanese, and they offered explanations for the behavior. See N. Sugimoto, "Norms of Apology Depicted in U.S. American and Japanese Literature on Manners and Etiquette," *International Journal of Intercultural Relations*, 1997, 22(3), 251–276. For a review of apology from the legal perspective, see J. K. Robbennolt, "Apologies and Legal Settlement: An Empirical Examination," *Michigan Law Review*, December 2003, 460.

25. We found in our eBay study that language that conveyed contempt—for example, "could," "should," "must"—was associated with a lower likelihood of settlement. J. M. Brett and others, "Sticks and Stones: Language, Face, and On-Line Dispute Resolution," *Academy of Management Journal*, 2007, 50(1), 85–99.

26. Tjosvold and Hui, *Showing Respect Among Chinese*.

27. T. R. Tyler, E. A. Lind, and Y. J. Huo, *Culture, Ethnicity, and Authority: Social Categorization and Social Orientation Effects on the Psychology of Legitimacy* (Berkeley, Calif.: University of California Press, 1995).

28. D. Spero, "Patent Protection or Piracy: A CEO Views Japan," *Harvard Business Review*, 1990, 68(5), 58–67.

29. M. Olekalns, J. M. Brett, and L. R. Weingart, "Phases, Transitions and Interruptions: The Processes That Shape Agreement in Multi-Party Negotiations," *International Journal of Conflict Management: Special Issue on Processes in Negotiation*, 2004, 14, 191–211.

30. A. L. Lytle, J. M. Brett, and D. L. Shapiro, "The Strategic Use of Interests, Rights, and Power to Resolve Disputes," *Negotiation Journal*, 1999, 15, 31–52.

31. W. L. Adair, "Exploring the Norm of Reciprocity in the Global Market: U. S. and Japanese Intra- and Intercultural Negotiation," *Academy of Management Proceedings*, 1999; W. L. Adair, "Reciprocity in the Global Market," unpublished doctoral dissertation, Department of Management and Organization, Northwestern University, 2000.

32. J. M. Brett, D. L. Shapiro, and A. L. Lytle, "Breaking the Bonds of Reciprocity in Negotiation," *Academy of Management Journal*, 1998, *41*, 410–424.

33. K. A. Jehn, "Workplace Conflict," in B. M. Staw, (ed.), *Research in Organizational Behavior* (Greenwich, Conn.: JAI Press, 1999).

34. L. H. Pelled, "Demographic Diversity, Conflict, and Work Group Outcomes: An Intervening Process Theory," *Organizational Science*, 1996, *7*, 615–631.

35. R. Friedman and others, "The Positive and Negative Effects of Anger on Dispute Resolution: Evidence from Electronically-Mediated Disputes," *Journal of Applied Psychology*, 2004, *89*, 369–376.

36. Brett and others, "Sticks and Stones."

37. Brett and others, "Sticks and Stones."

38. Tinsley, "Culture's Influences"; Tinsley, "How We Get to Yes."

39. Lytle, Brett, and Shapiro, "The Strategic Use of Interests, Rights, and Power to Resolve Disputes."

40. J. G. Getman, S. B. Goldberg, and J. B. Herman, *Union Representation Elections: Law and Reality* (New York: Russell Sage Foundation, 1969).

41. Brett, Shapiro, and Lytle, "Breaking the Bonds of Reciprocity in Negotiations"; Lytle, Brett, and Shapiro, "The Strategic Use of Interests, Rights, and Power to Resolve Disputes."

Chapter Six

1. D. Spero, "Patent Protection or Piracy: A CEO Views Japan," *Harvard Business Review*, 1990, 68(5), 58–67.

2. From Wikipedia, the Free Encyclopedia. "Convention on the Recognition and Enforcement of Foreign Arbitral Awards." Available at en.wikipedia.org/wiki/Convention_on_the_Recognition_ and_Enforcement_of_Foreign_Arbitral_Awards.

3. J. M. Wenger, *International Commercial Arbitration: Locating the Resources*, May 24, 2004. Available at www.llrx.com/features/arbitration2.htm.

4. If time is of the essence, then asking for a judgment without a written explanation is wise. One of the benefits of arbitration is that it is more accessible than court.

5. R. Friedman, W. Liu, S. Chi, and C. Chen, "Causal Attribution for Inter-Firm Contract Violation: A Comparative Study of Chinese and American Commercial Arbitrators," *Journal of Applied Psychology*, forthcoming; T. Menon, M. W. Morris, C. Y. Chiu, and Y. Y. Hong, "Culture and the Construal of Agency: Attribution to Individual Versus Group Dispositions," *Journal of Personality and Social Psychology*, 1999, 76, 701–717.

6. S. B. Goldberg and J. M. Brett, "Disputants' Perspectives on the Differences Between Mediation and Arbitration," *Negotiation Journal*, 1990, 6, 249–256.

7. J. M. Brett, Z. I. Barsness, and S. B. Goldberg, "The Effectiveness of Mediation: An Independent Analysis of Cases Handled by Four Major Service Providers," *Negotiation Journal*, 1996, 12, 259–270.

8. Brett, Barsness, and Goldberg, "The Effectiveness of Mediation."

9. R.A.B. Bush and J. P. Folger, *The Promise of Mediation: The Transformative Approach to Conflict* (San Francisco: Jossey-Bass, 2004).

10. For more on transformative mediation, see H. Burgess, "Transformative Mediation," 1997. Available at www.colorado.edu/conflict/transform/tmall.htm#Applications.

11. I love the example of mediation seemingly first reported in 1940 by Evans-Pritchard, of the Nuer people's Leopard-Skin Chief threatening to put a curse (a threat of punishment by supernatural forces) on a party who refuses to accept a reasonable settlement. The Nuer are a pastoral people living in the region of the upper Nile. See E. E. Evans-Pritchard, *The Nuer: A Description of the Modes of Livelihood and Political Institutions of a Nilotic People* (London: Oxford University Press, 1940).

12. K. Leung and M. W. Morris, "Justice Through the Lens of Culture and Ethnicity," in J. Sanders and V. L. Hamilton (eds.), *Handbook of Law and Social Science*, pp. 343–378 (New York: Plenum, 1996).

13. K. A. Slaikeu and R. H. Hasson, *Controlling the Costs of Conflict: How to Design a System for Your Organization* (San Francisco: Jossey-Bass, 1998); C. A. Costantino and C. S. Merchant, *Designing Conflict Management Systems: A Guide to Creating Productive and Healthy Organizations* (San Francisco: Jossey-Bass, 1995); W. L. Ury, J. M. Brett, and S. B. Goldberg, *Getting Disputes Resolved: Designing a System to Cut the Costs of Conflict* (Cambridge, Mass.: Program on Negotiation, Harvard Law School, 1993).

14. For more information and resources to help manage and resolve conflicts, see the International Institute for Conflict Prevention and Resolution at www.cpradr.org.

15. L. Nader, "Civilization and Its Negotiators," In P. Caplan (ed.), *Understanding Disputes: The Politics of Argument 1995*, pp. 39–64 (Providence, R.I.: Berg, 1995).

16. T. R. Tyler, E. A. Lind, and Y. J. Huo, *Culture, Ethnicity, and Authority: Social Categorization and Social Orientation Effects on the Psychology of Legitimacy* (Berkeley, Calif.: University of California Press, 1995).

17. J. M. Brett, C. H. Tinsley, D. L. Shapiro, and T. Okumura, "Intervening in Employee Disputes: How and When Will Managers from China, Japan, and the U.S. Act Differently?" *Management and Organizational Review*, forthcoming.

18. T. R. Tyler and E. A. Lind, "A Relational Model of Authority in Groups," in M. Zanna (ed.), *Advances in Experimental Social Psychology* (Orlando, Fla.: Academic Press, 1992).

19. J. M. Brett, *Third Parties* (College Park, Md.: International Association of Conflict Management, 1998); R. Karambayya, J. M. Brett, and A. L. Lytle, "Managerial Third Parties: The Effects of Formal Authority and Experience on Third-Party Roles, Outcomes, and Perceptions of Fairness," *Academy of Management Journal*, 1992, 35, 426–438; R. Karambayya and J. M. Brett, "Managers Handling Disputes," *Academy of Management Journal*, 1989, 32, 687–704.

20. United States: J. Thibaut and L. Walker, *Procedural Justice: A Psychological Analysis* (Mahwah, N.J.: Erlbaum, 1975); Britain, France; and Germany: E. A. Lind, B. E. Erickson, N. Friedland,

and M. Dickenberger, "Reactions to Procedural Models for Adjudicative Conflict Resolution: A Cross-National Study," *Journal of Conflict Resolution*, 1978, *22*, 318–341; Hong Kong: K. Leung, "Some Determinants of Reactions to Procedural Models for Conflict Resolution: A Cross-National Study." *Journal of Personality and Social Psychology*, 1987, *53*, 898–908; Japan and Spain: K. Leung, Y. F. Au., J. M. Fernandez-Dols, and S. Iwawaki, "Preferences for Methods of Conflict Process in Two Collectivist Cultures," *International Journal of Psychology*, 1992, *27*, 195–209.

21. Tyler and Lind, "A Relational Model of Authority in Groups."
22. D. L. Shapiro and J. M. Brett, "Comparing Three Processes Underlying Judgments of Procedural Justice: A Field Study of Mediation and Arbitration," *Journal of Personality and Social Psychology*, 1993, *65*, 1167–1177.
23. Shapiro and Brett, "Comparing Three Processes." *Note:* Comparative cultural research is somewhat inconsistent on this point. The reason for the inconsistency is probably that comparative culture research asks people for their preferences out of context of specific experiences in a mediation or arbitration procedure. The clear preference for mediation is shown in data collected post-procedure from real disputants whose claim was either mediated or arbitrated.
24. Leung and Morris, "Justice through the Lens of Culture and Ethnicity."

Chapter Seven

1. M. Pasquerello, "The Companies Have Announced a Group of Multicultural Teams," May 5, 2006. Available at web.lexis-nexis.com.truing.library.northwestern.edu/universe.document?_m=c4c08f9.
2. D. Gruenfeld, M. C. Thomas-Hunt, and P. Kim, "Cognitive Flexibility, Communication Strategy, and Integrative Complexity in Groups: Public Versus Private Reactions to Majority

and Minority Status," *Journal of Experimental Social Psychology,* 1998, *34,* 202–226.

3. K. Eisenhardt and C. B. Schoonhaven, "Organizational Growth: Linking Founding Team Strategy, Environment, and Growth Among U.S. Semiconductor Ventures," *Administrative Science Quarterly,* 1990, *35,* 504–529.

4. T. L. Simons, L. H. Pelled, and K. A. Smith, "What Kinds of Difference Make a Difference? How Diversity Interacts with Debate in Top Management Teams," *Academy of Management Journal,* 1999, *42,* 662–673.

5. K. Lovelace, D. L. Shapiro, and L. R. Weingart, "Maximizing Cross-Functional New Product Teams' Innovativeness and Constraint Adherence: A Conflict Communications Perspective," *Academy of Management Journal,* 2001, *44*(4), 479–493.

6. D. Tjosvold, M. Poon, and Z. Y. Yu, "Team Effectiveness in China: Cooperative Conflict for Relationship Building," *Human Relations,* 2005, *58,* 341–367.

7. K. A. Jehn, "A Multimethod Examination of the Benefits and Detriments of Intragroup Conflict," *Administrative Science Quarterly,* 1995, *40,* 256–282.

8. A. C. Amason, "Distinguishing the Effects of Functional and Dysfunctional Conflict on Strategic Decision Making: Resolving a Paradox for Top Management Teams," *Academy of Management Journal,* 1996, *39*(1), 123–148. Other research that has reviewed the effects of task and relationship conflict across multiple studies questions whether any task conflict is functional because of the spillover between task conflict and relationship conflict; see C.K.W. DeDreu and L. R. Weingart, "Task Versus Relationships Conflict, Team Performance, and Team Member Satisfaction: A Meta Analysis," *Journal of Applied Psychology,* 2003, *88*(4), 741–749.

9. This example was constructed from a project done with Maddy Janssens and Ludo Kuenen. The company is real and the incidents are real, though not all occurred on the same team, despite being represented as so here for the purpose of simplicity.

10. K. Behfar, M. Kern, and J. M. Brett, "Managing Challenges in Multicultural Teams," in E. Mannix and Y. Chen (eds.), *Research on Managing Groups and Teams*, pp. 233–262 (Oxford: Elsevier Science Press, 2006).

11. Interview as part of the Multicultural Teams project, K. Behfar, M. Kern, and J. M. Brett, K2, 2005.

12. Interview as part of the Multicultural Teams project, K. Behfar, M. Kern, and J. M. Brett, M7, 2005.

13. Interview as part of the Multicultural Teams project, K. Behfar, M. Kern, and J. M. Brett, K16, 2005.

14. Interview as part of the Multicultural Teams project, K. Behfar, M. Kern, and J. M. Brett, J10, 2005.

15. Interview as part of the Multicultural Teams project, K. Behfar, M. Kern, and J. M. Brett, M9, 2005.

16. Interview as part of the Multicultural Teams project, K. Behfar, M. Kern, and J. M. Brett, M4, 2005.

17. Interview as part of the Multicultural Teams project, K. Behfar, M. Kern, and J. M. Brett, M7, 2005.

18. Interview as part of the Multicultural Teams project, K. Behfar, M. Kern, and J. M. Brett, K11, 2005.

19. Interview as part of the Multicultural Teams project, K. Behfar, M. Kern, and J. M. Brett, M5, 2005.

20. Interview as part of the Multicultural Teams project, K. Behfar, M. Kern, and J. M. Brett, K13, 2005.

21. Bull Worldwide Information Systems, *Cultural Diversity at the Heart of Bull* (video) (Yarmouth, Me.: Intercultural Press, 1992). All quotations are from this video; see also www.bull.com.

22. M. Hewstone and K. Greenland, "Intergroup Conflict," *International Journal of Psychology*, 2000, 35, 136–146.

23. H. Tajfel and J. C. Turner, "An Integrative Theory of Intergroup Conflict," in W. G. Austin. and S. Worchel (eds.), *The Social Psychology of Intergroup Relations* (Pacific Grove, Calif.: Brooks/Cole, 1979).

24. J. M. Brett, K. Behfar, and M. Kern, "Managing Multicultural Teams," *Harvard Business Review*, November 2006, 11, 84–91 (AN 22671287).

25. J. R. Hackman, K. R. Brousseau, and J. A. Weiss, "The Interaction of Task Design and Group Performance Strategies in Determining Group Effectiveness," *Organizational Behavior and Human Performance*, 1976, *16*, 350–365.

26. K. L. Bettenhausen and J. K. Murnighan, "The Emergence of Norms in Competitive Decision-Making Groups," *Administrative Science Quarterly*, 1985, *3*, 20–35.

27. See M. Janssens and J. M. Brett, "Cultural Intelligence in Global Teams: A Fusion Model of Collaboration," *Group and Organization Management*, 2005, *31*(1), 124–153 for a more thorough description of collaboration models, especially fusion.

28. C. P. Earley and E. Mosakowski, "Creating Hybrid Team Cultures: An Empirical Test of Transnational Team Functioning," *Academy of Management Journal*, 2000, *43*, 26–49.

29. J. C. Turner, *Rediscovering the Social Group: A Self-Categorization Theory* (Oxford: Basil Blackwell, 1987).

30. Hewstone and Greenland, "Intergroup Conflict."

31. D. C. Lau and J. K. Murnighan, "Demographic Diversity and Faultlines: The Compositional Dynamics of Organizational Groups," *Academy of Management Review*, 1998, *23*(2), 325–340.

32. Interview as part of the Multicultural Teams project, K. Behfar, M. Kern, and J. M. Brett, J2, 2005.

33. C. P. Earley and E. Mosakowski, "Creating Hybrid Team Cultures: An Empirical Test of Transnational Team Functioning," *Academy of Management Journal*, 2000, *43*, 26–49.

34. Earley and Mosakowski, "Creating Hybrid Team Cultures."

35. C. B. Gibson and F. Vermeulen, "A Healthy Divide: Subgroups as a Stimulus for Team Learning Behavior," *Administrative Science Quarterly*, 2003, *48*, 202–239.

36. Interview as part of the Multicultural Teams project, K. Behfar, M. Kern, and J. M. Brett, J2, 2005.

37. Janssens and Brett, "Cultural Intelligence in Global Teams."

38. J. J. DiStefano and M. L. Maznevski, "Creating Value with Diverse Teams in Global Management," *Organizational Dynamics*, 2000, *29*, 45–63.

39. S. Crotty and J. M. Brett, "Multiculturalism Lives: Predicting Fusion Collaboration in Teams," Paper presented at the Academy of Management Conference, Atlanta, Georgia, 2006.

40. C. P. Earley and S. Ang, *Cultural Intelligence: An Analysis of Individual Interactions Across Cultures* (Palo Alto, Calif.: Stanford University Press, 2003).

41. S. Ang, L. Van Dyne, C. Koh, and K. Yee Ng, "The Four Factor Model of Cultural Intelligence: A Multisample Study of Effects on Performance and Adjustment," paper presented at the Academy of Management, New Orleans, Louisiana, 2004.

42. Earley and Ang, *Cultural Intelligence*; Ang, Van Dyne, Koh, and Yee Ng, "The Four Factor Model of Cultural Intelligence." The concept of "cultural intelligence" was introduced by Earley and Ang. They identified four factors of cultural intelligence: behavioral (what people do in multicultural situations), motivational (what people are interested in doing in multicultural situations), cognitive (what people know about norms and practices in different cultures), and metacognitive (cultural consciousness and awareness during social interaction). In a thorough, multisample, construct validation study, they showed that the metacognitive and cognitive elements were related to individuals' performance; the motivational element was related to their general adjustment, and the behavioral element was related to individuals' performance and adjustment over and above the effects of demographic characteristics and general cognitive ability.

43. Interview as part of the Multicultural Teams project, K. Behfar, M. Kern, and J. M. Brett, J2, 2005.

44. M. Janssens and J. M. Brett, "Meaningful Participation in Transnational Teams," *European Journal of Work and Organizational Psychology*, 1997, 6, 153–168.

45. M. E. Shaw, *Group Dynamics: The Psychology of Small Group Behavior*, 3rd ed. (New York: McGraw-Hill: 1981), 170.

46. D. Gigone and R. Hastie, "The Common Knowledge Effect: Information Sharing and Group Judgment," *Journal of Personality and Social Psychology*, 1993, 72(1), 132–140.

47. Interview as part of the Multicultural Teams project, K, Behfar, M. Kern, and J. M. Brett, J3, 2005.

48. M. Janssens, L. Kuenen, and J. M. Brett, *Valuing Cultural Diversity*, unpublished report, 1998, p. 14.

49. By their third year the financial research team was able to use e-mail to generate performance indicators for the next year and reserved their face-to-face time to brainstorm about strategic initiatives. Interview as part of the Multicultural Teams project, K. Behfar, M. Kern, and J. M. Brett, J2, 2005.

50. S. S. Keisler and L. Sproull, "Group Decision Making and Communication Technology," *Organizational Behavior and Human Decision Processes, 1992, 52, 96–123.*

51. A. Rosette, J. M. Brett, A. L. Lytle, and Z. I. Barsness, *The Effect of Computer-Mediated Communications on Negotiated Outcome and Behavior in Chinese and American Culture* (Evanston, Ill.: Dispute Resolution Research Center, Northwestern University, 2004). Working Paper #302.

52. M. Schrage, *No More Teams! Mastering the Dynamics of Creative Collaboration* (New York: Doubleday, 1995).

53. L. L. Thompson, *Making the Team* (Upper Saddle River, N.J.: Prentice-Hall, 1999).

54. Z. I. Barsness, J. M. Brett, and L. Eden, "Developing Real-World Skills: Managing Virtual Transnational Teams," paper presented at the annual meeting of the Academy of International Business, Vienna, October 7–10, 1998.

55. E. Peterson and L. L. Thompson, "Negotiation Teamwork: The Impact of Information Distribution and Accountability on Performance Depends on the Relationship Among Team Members," *Organizational Behavior and Human Decision Processes, 1997, 72, 364–383.*

56. Janssens and Brett, "Meaningful Participation in Transnational Teams."

57. D. Wegner, "Transactive Memory: A Contemporary Analysis of the Group Mind," in B. Mullen and G. Goethals (eds.), *Theories of Group Behavior* pp. 185–208 (New York: Springer, 1986).

58. Wegner, "Transactive Memory."

59. Thompson, *Making the Team*.

60. L. R. Weingart, R. J. Bennett, and J. M. Brett, "The Impact of Consideration of Issues and Motivational Orientation on Group Negotiation Process and Outcome," *Journal of Applied Psychology*, 1993, *78*, 504–517.

61. D. Gruenfeld, M. C. Thomas-Hunt, and P. Kim, "Cognitive Flexibility, Communication Strategy, and Integrative Complexity in Groups: Public Versus Private Reactions to Majority and Minority Status," *Journal of Experimental Social Psychology*, 1998, *34*, 202–226.

62. L. L. Thompson, B. Mannix, and M. H. Bazerman, "Group Negotiation: Effects of Decision Rule, Agenda, and Aspiration," *Journal of Personality and Social Psychology*, 1988, *54*, 86–95.

63. R. S. Peterson, "Can You Have Too Much of a Good Thing? The Limits of Voice for Improving Satisfaction with Leaders," *Personality and Social Psychology Bulletin*, 1999, *25*, 313–324.

64. Thompson, *Making the Team*.

65. Thompson, *Making the Team*.

66. This advice for second agreements is based on H. Raiffa, *The Art and Science of Negotiation* (Cambridge, Mass.: Belknap Press, 1982). Raiffa suggested that, after negotiating an agreement, negotiators go back to the table and try to improve it. I did not discuss this tactic in Chapters One or Three because I do not think it works very well in the real world. Negotiators think they have found the best deal. They are tired. They do not want to reveal the information that might be necessary to improve the agreement. It is mainly in the classroom that post-settlement settlements work well when students are negotiating a quantified exercise and understand the meaning of post-settlement settlement. Why then do I advise the second-agreement tactic for real-world groups such as multicultural teams? The answer is that groups seem to be better at surfacing information than are deal-making negotiators. This means team members have little to hide in second-agreement deliberations. Also, the first agreement gives the dominant coalition confidence that their ap-

proach is going to prevail. This may make them a bit magnani-
mous; they may be more willing to listen to the minority and
act to minimize costs to the minority.

67. M. Roloff and D. Ifert, "Conflict Management Through Avoidance: Withholding Complaints, Suppressing Arguments, and De-
claring Topics Taboo," in S. Petronio (ed.), *Balancing the Secrets of
Private Disclosure*, pp. 151–163 (Mahwah, N.J.: Erlbaum, 1999).

68. Interview as part of the Multicultural Teams project, K. Behfar,
M. Kern, and J. M. Brett, M5, 2005.

69. Thompson, *Making the Team*.

70. Interview as part of the Multicultural Teams project, K. Behfar,
M. Kern, and J. M. Brett, J5, 2005.

71. Interview as part of the Multicultural Teams project, K. Behfar,
M. Kern, and J. M. Brett, K16, 2005.

72. W. L. Ury, J. M. Brett, and S. B. Goldberg, *Getting Disputes Resolved: Designing a System to Cut the Costs of Conflict* (Cambridge,
Mass.: Program on Negotiation, Harvard Law School, 1993).

73. Thompson, *Making the Team*; S. E. Gross, *Compensation for
Teams: How to Design and Implement Team-Based Reward Programs* (New York: AMACOM, 1995).

74. Thompson, *Making the Team*.

75. J. M. Brett, K. Behfar, and M. C. Kern, "Managing Multicultural Teams," *Harvard Business Review*, 2006, *11*, 84–91 (AN
22671287).

Chapter Eight

1. M. Richardson, "Fishing Fleets Are Raiding Ever-Remoter
Seas," *International Herald Tribune*, December 31, 2001, p. 2; J.
Deardorff, "Chefs Join Effort to Save Sea Bass," *Chicago Tribune*,
March 27, 2002, ss2, p 1; A. Newman, "The Way We Live
Now: 4-11-99–Salient Facts; Fewer Fish in the Sea." *New York
Times Magazine*, April 11, 1999, p. 23.

2. D. M. Messick and M. B. Brewer, "Solving Social Dilemmas: A
Review," in L. Wheeler and P. Shaver (eds.), *Review of Personality*

and Social Psychology, Vol. 4, pp. 11–44 (Beverly Hills, Calif.: Sage, 1983).

3. Social dilemmas are also called "commons problems"; see G. Hardin, "The Tragedy of the Commons," *Science*, 1968, (162), 1243–1248.

4. J. Brooke, "Japan Cuts Whaling Rights for Native Peoples of Arctic," *New York Times International*, May 25, 2002, A4.

5. Now that people with money and a green conscience can buy offsets on the Internet to live a carbon-neutral lifestyle, the likelihood of real cooperation to reduce energy consumption seems unlikely. A. DePalma, "Gas Guzzlers Find the Price of Forgiveness," *New York Times*, April 22, 2006, p. 1.

6. E. Johnson, "Price Fixing: Fighting for Compensation from the Vitamin Cartel," CBC *Marketplace Broadcast*, April 10, 2001.

7. D. Kawamoto, "Memory Chip Price Fixing Settlement Reached," CNET News, May 11, 2006. Available at news.com.com/memory+chip+price-fixing+settlement+reached/2100-1006_3-6071222.html.

8. J. Kanter, "Cartels," *International Herald Tribune*, Dec. 18, 2005, 13–14.

9. K. Eichenwald, "Archer Daniels Said to Settle Sweetener Price-Fixing Case," *New York Times*, June 18, 2001, C1–2.

10. Kanter, "Cartels."

11. This happened, recently: United Airlines announced a $5 increase in certain business-class fares, to go into effect a week later. American Airlines matched the price increase. Northwest Airlines did not. United rolled back its price increase. *International Herald Tribune*, August 22, 2006, p. 22.

12. "Patagonian Toothfish," *New York Times Magazine*, Apr. 11, 1999, p. 23.

13. Deardorff, "Chefs Join Effort to Save Sea Bass."

14. D. Mitchell, "What's Online: Wal-Mart Flirts with Being Green," *New York Times*, April 22, 2006, B5.

15. T. Friedman, *The World Is Flat* (New York: Farrar, Straus and Giroux, 2005).

16. From Wikipedia, the Free Encyclopedia, "Kyoto Protocol." Available at en.wikipedia.org/wiki/Kyoto_Protocol.

17. N. L. Kerr, "Norms in Social Dilemmas," in D. A. Schroeder (ed.), *Social Dilemmas: Perspectives on Individuals and Groups*, pp. 31–47 (Westport, Conn.: Praeger, 1995).

18. K. Wade-Benzoni, A. Tenbrunsel, and M. H. Bazerman, "SHARC: Competitive Version," in J. M. Brett (ed.), *Negotiation, Teamwork, and Decision Making Exercises* (Evanston, Ill.: Dispute Resolution Research Center, Northwestern University, 2006).

19. Data: United States (727 metric tons), Korea (543 metric tons), Japan (428 metric tones), or China (522 metric tones). Harvesting differences between cultures are not significant. One of the important things that occurred during the discussion was that participants committed to a harvest level in front of others in the group. Did some people defect, after making the commitment? Yes, this is the nature of a social dilemma. And, as you can imagine, the class did not treat the defectors very graciously.

20. A. W. Gouldner, "The Norm of Reciprocity: A Preliminary Statement," *American Sociological Review*, 1960, *25*, 161–179.

21. J. E. McGrath, *Groups: Interaction and Performance* (Englewood Cliffs, N.J.: Prentice-Hall, 1984).

22. K. A. Wade-Benzoni and others, "Cognitions and Behavior in Asymmetric Social Dilemmas: A Comparison of Two Cultures," *Journal of Applied Psychology*, 2002, *87*(1), 87–95.

23. E. Ostrom, *Governing the Commons: The Evolution of Institutions for Collective Action* (New York: Cambridge University Press, 1990).

24. I. G. Suarja and R. Thijssen, "Traditional Water Management in Bali," *LEIS Magazine*, September 2003, 25–26.

25. Asia and Pacific Regional Program, "Climate Risk Management in Indonesia: An Overview of IRI Work." Available at iri.columbia.edu/outreach/meeting/FINLAND2006/docs/IRI_Indonesia_Work_Summary_Jul06.pdf.

26. Associated Press, "U.K. and California Going Green Together," *International Herald Tribune*, August 1, 2006, p. 10.

27. Joint Economic Committee Study, J. Saxton, "Tradable Emissions," July 1997. Available at www.house.gov/jec/cost-gov/regs/cost/emission.htm.

28. D. Altman, "Just How Far Can Trading of Emissions Be Extended?" *New York Times*, May 31, 2002, C1.

29. M. Saltmarsh, "Market for Emissions Picks Up Steam as Kyoto Protocol Takes Hold." *International Herald Tribune*, July 6, 2005, p. 19.

30. C. D. Batson and T. Moran, "Empathy-Induced Altruism in a Prisoner's Dilemma," *European Journal of Social Psychology*, 1999, *29*, 909–924; A. E. Tenbrunsel and D. M. Messick, "Sanctioning Systems, Decision Frames, and Cooperation," *Administrative Science Quarterly*, 1999, *44*, 684–707.

31. E. van Dijk and H. Wilke, "Decision-Induced Focusing in Social Dilemmas: Give-Some, Keep-Some, Take-Some, and Leave-Some Dilemmas," *Journal of Personality and Social Psychology*, 2000, *78*(1), 92–104.

32. M. Hewstone and K. Greenland, "Intergroup Conflict," *International Journal of Psychology*, 2000, *35*, 136–146.

33. S. Schwartz, "Beyond Individualism/Collectivism: New Cultural Dimensions of Values," in H. C. Triandis, U. Kim, and G. Yoon (eds.), *Individualism and Collectivism* (London: Sage, 1994).

34. P.A.M. Van Lange, W.B.G. Liebrand, D. M. Messick, and H.A.M. Wilke, "Social Dilemmas: The State of the Art: Introduction and Literature Review," in D. M. Messick, W.B.G. Liebrand, and H.A.M. Wilke (eds.), *Social Dilemmas: Theoretical Issues and Research Findings*, pp. 3–28 (Oxford, England: Pergamon Press, 1992); R. M. Dawes, J. McTavish, and H. Shaklee, "Behavior, Communication, and Assumptions About Other People's Behavior in a Commons Dilemma Situation," *Journal of Personality and Social Psychology*, 1977, *35*, 1–11.

35. Van Lange, Liebrand, Messick, and Wilke, "Social Dilemmas."
36. G. Bornstein and M. Ben-Yosef, "Cooperation in Intergroup and Single-Group Social Dilemmas," *Journal of Experimental Social Psychology*, 1994, *30*, 597–606.
37. T. M. Probst, P. J. Carnevale, and H. C. Triandis, "Cultural Values in Intergroup and Single-Group Social Dilemmas," *Organizational Behavior and Human Decision Processes*, 1999, *77*, 171–191.
38. H. Triandis, *Individualism and Collectivism* (New York: Simon & Schuster, 1995).
39. K. Leung, "Some Determinants of Conflict Avoidance," *Journal of Cross-Cultural Psychology*, 1998, *19*, 125–136.

Chapter Nine

1. A. E. Kramer, "From Russia with Dread," *New York Times*, May 16, 2006, C1, 4; S. H. Choe, "Wal-Mart: Wal-Mart Selling Stores and Leaving South Korea," *New York Times*, May 23, 2006, C5; C. Forelle and G. Hitt, "Lenovo CNOOC: IBM Discusses Security Measure in Lenovo Deal," *Wall Street Journal*, February 15, 2005, A2; H. Timmons and D. Greenlees, "China Mobile: China's Art of the Deal," *International Herald Tribune*, July 14, 2006, p. 1; Agence France-Presse, "Foreign Investment Rises to Highest Level since 2001," *International Herald Tribune*, June 29, 2006, p. 15; "The Money Did Not Make It into the Kazakh Budget," *Financial Times*, July 1997; "Chinese Oil Firm Ponders Unocal Bid," MSNBC.com, May 9, 2005. Available at msnbc.msn.com/id/7790039.
2. Robert Litwak, director of international security studies at the Woodrow Wilson Center, quoted in T. L. Friedman, "A Choice for the Rogues," *International Herald Tribune*, August 3, 2006, p. 7; D. Williams, "Lack of Surprise Greets Word of U.S.-Libya Ties," *Washington Post Foreign Service*, May 16, 2006, A12.
3. World Heritage Organization, "Index of Economic Freedom," *The Economist*, September 23, 2004.

4. See "Motorola Reaches Agreement in Telsim Matter." Available at www.motorola.com/mediacenter/news/detail.jsp?global ObjectId=6075_6035_23.

5. There were many interesting negotiations with the government over the establishment of DPC, punctuated by an election that threw out the ruling Congress Party and installed the BJP, which had run on a platform of initiatives including "throw Enron into the sea."

6. Agence France-Presse, "Foreign Investment Rises to Highest Level since 2001."

7. H. Timmons and A. E. Kramer, "'Russophobia' Gets Blame for Death of Severstal Deal," *International Herald Tribune*, June 27, 2006, p. 11.

8. For more on recent events concerning the Dubai sale of U.S. ports, see M. Cohn, "AIG to Buy Port Operation: Dubai Firm Stymied by Security Flap Calls Insurer Winning Bidder," *Baltimore Sun*, December 12, 2006, p. 1E. Available at web.lexis nexis.com.turing.library.northwestern.edu/univers/docu ment?_m=33810db783d60c1faa6zSkVA&_md5=2217c2c49 faa6a9abcad20e9ee36caaa; R. Siegel, "Dubai Port Deal May Fail Due to New York Demands." *National Public Radio, All Things Considered*, February 15, 2007, 9:00 p.m. EST. Available at web. lexisnexis.com.turing.library.northwestern.edu/univers/docu ment?_m=33810db783d60c1faa62ac678123ba53&_docnum= 2&wchp=dGLbVzbzSkVA&_md5=ca3cca5b423d74a45488b 1233c1af990.

9. Mobil's lawyers made proper wire transfers to Kazakh Swiss bank accounts, although it is reported that "it has proved impossible to pinpoint the final destination of 500 million of Mobil's Tengiz payments." "The Money Did Not Make It into the Kazakh Budget," *Financial Times*, July 1997.

10. For more about colorful James Giffen, see B. Hamilton, "Bribe 'Spy' Slick as Oil: Shadowy Saga of a Lexington Ave. Banker's Big $$ Deals in Asian Depot's Exotic Realm," *The New York Post*, March 6, 2005, p. 24.

11. T. Friedman, *The World Is Flat* (New York: Farrar, Straus, and Giroux, 2005), 247.

12. "Enron Project Reconsidered in India," *New York Times*, Oct. 6, 1995, p. D4; A. Gottshalk, "Enron Project in India May Be Alive and Well: Firm Hears Deal Wasn't Canceled," *Journal of Commerce*, Aug. 17, 1995, p. 5B.

13. A. E. Kramer, "From Russia with Dread," *New York Times*, May 16, 2006, C1, 4.

14. M. Simons, "The Dutch Try One of Their Own Over Link to Liberia," *New York Times*, May 3, 2006, A3; "Dutch Timber Dealer Convicted of Breaking UN Arms Embargo," June 12, 2006, at www.ens-newswire.com/ens/jun2006/2006-06-12-02.asp.

15. R. Grover, *The Disney Touch* (Homewood, Ill.: Business On/ Irwin, 1991).

16. "Economy Preparing to Negotiate Sharp Curves over the Summer," *Turkish Daily News*, July 2, 2006.

17. G. Salacuse, *Making Global Deals* (New York: Times Books, 1991).

18. Salacuse, *Making Global Deals*, p.137.

19. Professor Torben Andersen, my colleague at the Kellogg School of Management, Northwestern University, comments that hedging against currency fluctuations is straightforward in simple situations but is typically much more difficult and sometimes almost intangible in more complex settings. He suggests the following references: C. S. Eun and B. G. Resnick, *International Financial Management*, 4th ed. (New York: McGraw-Hill Irwin, 2007), especially Part Three, on foreign exchange exposure and management; D. K. Eiteman, A. I. Stonehill, and M. H. Moffett, *Multinational Business Finance*, 11th ed. (Reading, Mass.: Addison-Wesley, 2007), especially Part Four, on the foreign exchange exposure.

20. L. Kaufman, "As Biggest Business, Wal-Mart Propels Changes Elsewhere," *New York Times*, Oct. 22, 2000, Business/Financial Desk Archives.

21. Simons, "The Dutch Try One of Their Own."

22. See general information about countertrade at Prof. W.T.G. Richardson, "Countertrade." Available at www.witiger.com/internationalbusiness/countertrade.htm.

23. Salacuse, *Making Global Deals*.

24. T. Buerkle, "U.K. Firms Lead as Law Goes Global," *International Herald Tribune*, July 13, 1999, pp. 11–12.

25. Editors of the American Heritage Dictionary (ed.), *Roget's II: The New Thesaurus*, 3rd ed. (Boston: Houghton Mifflin Company, 1995).

26. United States Department of Justice and United States Department of Commerce, "Foreign Corrupt Practices Act: Antibribery Provisions," last updated January 2006. Available at www.usdoj.gov/criminal/fraud/fcpa/dojdocb.htm.

27. In researching what commentators such as James McGregor (in *One Billion Customers: Lessons from the Front Lines of Doing Business in China* [New York: Wall Street Journal Book Service, 2005]) say about how widespread corruption is, one gets the sense that corruption is a bit like doping in sports, where those engaged in the practice try to stay one step ahead of the regulators. Some succeed, some get caught.

28. S. Romero, "Halliburton Severs Link with 2 Over Nigeria Inquiry," *New York Times*, June 19, 2004.

29. See Fiduciary Policies on the World Bank's Website at www.worldbank.org.

30. See Andrew Fastow's testimony in the *New York Times*, March 9, 2006.

31. D. L. Messick and W.B.G. Liebrand, "Individual Heuristics and the Dynamics of Cooperation in Large Groups," *Psychological Review*, 1995, 102, 131–145.

32. In contrast, the philosophy of relativism judges the morality of an act by its acceptability in the contest. Relativism justifies engaging in corruption in corrupt environments, other things being equal. R. J. Lewicki, J. A. Litterer, J. W. Minton, and D. M. Saunders, *Negotiation*, 2nd ed. (Burr Ridge, Ill.: Irwin, 1994).

33. P. Lewis, "World Bank Emphasizes Media in Fight Against Graft," *New York Times*, Oct. 11, 1998.

34. W. Arnold, "Indonesia's Chief Repo Man Takes on the Elite," *International Herald Tribune*, July 29, 1999, p. 8.

35. D. Sangler, "Longtime I.M.F. Director Resigns in Midterm," *New York Times*, Nov. 10, 1999, p. C1.

36. "The Hostage Business," *New York Times*, June 30, 2001.

37. S. Greenhouse and M. Barbaro, "An Ugly Side of Free Trade: Sweatshops in Jordan," *New York Times*, May 3, 2006, p. C1, 7.

38. S. L. Bachman, "Nike v. Sweatshop Critic: Back to California," Global Policy Forum, June 27, 2003. Available at www.global policy.org/globaliz/econ/2003/0630nike.htm.

39. There are many sources of information about human rights practices. The U.S. State Department publishes country reports on human rights practices annually. See http://www.state.gov/ g/drl/hr/. Organizations such as Amnesty International, PEN International Writers' Union, and Physicians for Human Rights publish their own specialized reports.

Chapter Ten

1. N. Cohen, "English, Now the Global Language, Drifts from Its Roots," *New York Times*, Aug. 6, 2006.

2. L. Wang, "Cultural Integration of American Values in American Firms' Presence in China: A Pilot Investigation of Organizational Acculturation in Foreign Business Operations," paper presented at International Association of Conflict Management Conference, Montreal, 2006.

3. Y. Hong, M. W. Morris, C. Chiu, and V. Benet-Martinez, "Multicultural Minds: A Dynamic Constructivist Approach to Culture and Cognition," *American Psychologist*, 2000, 55(7), 709–720.

4. J. M. Brett, K. Behfar, and M. Kern, "Managing Multicultural Teams," *Harvard Business Review*, 2006, 11, 84–91 (AN 22671287).

5. L. Thompson, "Information Exchange in Negotiation," *Journal of Experimental Social Psychology*, 1991, 27(2), 161–179.

Glossary

A priori majority—A faction or coalitions that involve more than half the members of a group that exists before the information-sharing phase of group decision making begins.

Adversarial procedure—A process in which disputants or their agents investigate the facts and present their own argument to the third party; compare with inquisitorial procedure.

Altruistic social motive—The social motive that maximizes the outcomes of others.

Arbitrator—A third party who serves as a private judge and makes a final and binding decision in dispute resolution.

Assumption—A fundamental cultural belief taken to be true.

BATNA (best alternative to a negotiated agreement)—What each negotiator will do in a deal-making situation if no agreement is reached; what will happen to negotiators if they fail to resolve a dispute or reach an agreement.

Belief—A tenet or body of tenets held by a group.

Buyer gains—The value in a negotiation outcome that is better than the buyer's alternative.

Categorization—Process of sorting of people into types or categories based on superficial information about them, such as culture, language, race, or sex.

Claim—A demand for something due.

Claim value—The amount of value (resources) a negotiator seeks to receive in an agreement.

Collective interests—The interests of an identifiable group of people who may not be participating directly in the negotiation but will be affected by the agreement.

Collectivism—A cultural value that promotes the interdependence of individuals with the social groups to which they belong and supports collective interests over self-interests as a predominant life value.

Compatible issues—Issues for which negotiators on both sides want the same outcome.

Competitive social motive—The social motive that maximizes one's own outcome at the expense of the other party's outcome.

Concession—An act of yielding.

Conflict—The perception of opposing interests, involving scarce resources, goals, or procedures.

Confrontation, direct—When negotiators speak with each other face-to-face or electronically.

Confrontation, indirect—When negotiators speak to each other via signaling, stories, metaphors, body language, or through a third party.

Consensus—A group decision rule in which no team members publicly oppose a decision, though they may do so in private.

Contact—Face-to-face interaction among diverse members of a group intended to help them build mutual respect and trust.

Contingent contract—An agreement to change the negotiated outcome in a specific way based on the occurrence of a future event.

Cooperative social motive—The social motive that maximizes one's own and the other party's outcomes jointly.

Corruption—A situation in which the rules of participation are unclear, changing, or differentially applied or in which nepotism, bribery, extortion, or embezzlement is involved.

Create value—The process of trying to increase the resources available to negotiators jointly, usually by trading issues or identifying compatible issues.

Culture—The unique character of a social group, including the values and norms shared by members of the group and the group's social, economic, political, and other institutions.

Deal-making negotiations—Negotiations involving an exchange between two or more parties (for example, a buyer and a seller) to buy and sell.

Decision rules—The alternative ways that multiple parties can reach an agreement, for example, majority rule, consensus.

Decision-making negotiations—Negotiations among multiple parties whose interests are conflicting and who are interdependent.

Direct information sharing—The process of gathering information by asking and answering questions.

Dispute resolution negotiations—Negotiations to resolve the conflict resulting from a claim being made and rejected.

Dispute resolution system—A hierarchical set of dispute resolution procedures that provide opportunities to reach integrative agreements at more than one stage and provide for final resolution of the dispute.

Distributive agreement—An agreement in negotiation that allocates a fixed set of resources.

Egalitarian culture—A culture that aspires to social equality, especially in political, social, and economic affairs.

Egocentric bias—The belief that you deserve substantially more than another person in exactly the same circumstances.

Equivalent proposals—Multi-issue proposals that have equal value to the party offering the proposals, but that are differentially configured and so may have different value to the party receiving the proposals.

Ethnocentrism—The belief that your culture's way of doing something is the best way.

Expand the pie—Slang for entering into integrative or value-creating negotiations.

Face—Personal honor and socially based respect.

Faction—A subgroup or coalition that accounts for less than a majority of the members of a group.

Fairness standards—Decision rules that presumably provide a just distribution of resources, for example, split the difference. Also called objective standards, but of course they are not objective but subjective.

Fixed pie—Refers to the resources in a negotiation that can only be divided or distributed; a mental representation of negotiations.

Free rider—A group member who does not contribute to the group but benefits from the group's efforts.

Fusion—A model of group collaboration that preserves cultural differences in negotiation and group decision-making processes.

Hierarchical culture—A culture that accepts social inequality in political, social, and economic affairs.

High-context culture—A culture in which meaning must be inferred from the context or situation in which the information was communicated.

Ideology—A collection of principles and precepts that provide the basis for making choices about the structure of institutions.

Impasse—The outcome when negotiators cannot reach agreement and discontinue negotiating.

Independent value—A cultural value that links social identity to characteristics of the individual rather than to characteristics of the groups to which that individual belongs.

Individualism—A cultural value that promotes personal independence and gives self-interest a high priority among important life values.

Individualistic social motive—The social motive that maximizes one's own gain regardless of the other party's gains.

In-group—A group to which an individual belongs and from which that individual may derive social identity.

Inquisitorial procedure—Process in which an agent of the court investigates and presents an opinion and arguments to the judge; compare with adversarial procedure.

Institution—A public organization that structures social interaction.

Integrative agreement—An agreement in negotiation that expands the resources to be allocated beyond those resources that would be available if one party took all or two parties compromised (split their differences) on all issues.

Integrative potential—The maximum possible value available to negotiators if they agree to all compatible issues and make all efficient trade-offs.

Interdependent value—A cultural value that links an individual's social identity to characteristics of the groups to which that individual belongs.

Interests—The reasons why negotiators take the positions they do; negotiators' needs, fears, and concerns.

Interpersonal conflict—Conflict over personal responsibility and blame.

Issue—A matter that is in dispute between parties.

Joint gains—The sum of the negotiating parties' individual gains.

Knowledge structures—Units of cognitive storage including but not limited to beliefs, norms, values, and behavioral sequences, for example, negotiation strategies.

Litigation—A judicial procedure in which disputants or their agents argue their claims and a third party makes a final and binding decision.

Low-context culture—A culture in which meaning can be inferred from the message itself. It is not necessary to know the situation in which the information was communicated in order to understand.

Lumping it—The outcome in which one party decides either not to make a claim public or not to pursue a claim that has been rejected.

Majority rule—A decision rule whereby the alternative preferred by more than half of the members of a group becomes the alternative chosen by the group.

Meaningful participation—Group discussion engaged in according to the principle that group members have an obligation to speak up when their knowledge, expertise, or contacts become relevant as well as when they harbor doubts about the direction the group is taking or the feasibility of the group's plan.

Mediator—A private third party who tries to facilitate an agreement but does not have the authority to impose an outcome on the disputants.

Micro-level strategy—The normative way that negotiators are used to negotiating within their own culture, for example, via questions and answers or working through an agenda.

Multicultural teams—Groups of three or more people with diverse cultural backgrounds who must make decisions together.

Mutual-gains strategy—A group decision-making strategy that has a goal of reaching an integrative decision.

Negotiation—The process of conferring among two or more interdependent parties to arrive at an agreement about some matter over which they are in conflict.

Net value—The anticipated return minus the costs, including the costs of negotiating.

Norm—A standard of appropriate behavior in social interactions within a culture.

One party decides—A decision rule that permits one group member to choose the alternative for the group.

Others' interests—The interests, concerns, and priorities of the other negotiators.

Out-group—Any group in which an individual is not a member.

Party—The people negotiating and their roles in the negotiation, for example, buyer or seller.

Persuasion—As used here, trying to influence the other party to make a concession via references to BATNA.

Position—What a party wants in negotiation.

Posturing—As used here, trying to influence the other party to recognize the weakness of his or her position in the negotiation and therefore make a concession.

Power—The ability to influence others to concede to your wishes.

Preferences—Priorities among issues.

Prejudice—An ungrounded positive or negative opinion.

Priorities—The order of importance of a set of issues.

Prisoner's dilemma—A two-party social dilemma; a situation in which a party's pursuit of self-interests conflicts with the common good of a collective to which the party belongs.

Procedural conflict—A dispute over means, including the dispute resolution process itself.

Prosocial social motive—The social motive that maximizes outcome jointly for self and the other party; also cooperative social motive.

Prototype—The cultural pattern or model, based on the average or modal characteristic of a culture.

Quick trust—The assumption that the other party is worthy of trust until he or she proves unworthiness.

Recategorization—The process of changing social identity based on group membership rather than on independent attributes of the self.

Relativism—Judging the morality of an act by its appropriateness in the context.

Reservation price—The most a negotiator is willing to offer or the least a negotiator is willing to take and still reach agreement.

Rights—Standards of fairness or law that can be used to resolve disputes; similar to fairness standards in making deals.

Satisficing—In this context, the decision to reach an agreement that is better than BATNA but might not be the best possible outcome if you were willing to put forth more effort.

Second agreement—An agreement entered into after a negotiated agreement has already been reached. Patterned on post-settlement settlements.

Self-interests—The negotiator's own interests, concerns, and priorities.

Sequence—A pattern embedded in a negotiation strategy, for example, reciprocity.

Slow trust—Trust that is built over time as parties interact with one another.

Social dilemma—A multiparty decision-making situation in which, if everyone acts to maximize personal gain, everyone is worse off than if everyone acts to maximize collective gain; yet acting to maximize personal gain is always better for the individual.

Social identity—A sense of one's own reputation; the impression one thinks one has made on others.

Social motives—The types of choices that people make in situations such as negotiation in which they are interdependent.

Stakeholder—A person with an interest.

Stereotype—A belief that everyone from a given culture will be like that culture's prototype.

Strategy—An organized set of behaviors chosen because they are thought to be the means of accomplishing the goal of negotiating.

Subgroup dominance—A collaboration model in which a co-alition or faction controls group processes and outcomes.

Synergy—A result that is greater than the sum of its parts.

Target—The components that would constitute an ideal settlement; goals in negotiation and standards against which to judge opening offers, concessions, and final offers.

Task conflict—A dispute over goals and resources.

Thinking net—Slang for the process of thinking about gains in negotiations as greater than gains that should be available from negotiating an agreement with BATNA.

Threat—An expression of an intention to do harm; an if-then statement about the other party's actions and the consequences if the party persists in them.

Trade-offs—Conceding on low-priority issues in order to gain on high-priority issues.

Transaction costs—The costs of negotiating.

Transactive memory—Knowledge of who on the team knows what.

Trust—The willingness to make yourself vulnerable to the other party, and belief that the other party will not take advantage.

Two-thirds majority—A large coalition of two-thirds of group members.

Unanimity—A decision rule that requires agreement among all team members.

Utilitarianism—A judgment of the morality of an act by its consequences.

Value—A judgment of what is important in social interactions and other aspects of life.

Value-claiming negotiation—A negotiation to reach a distributive agreement.

Value-creating negotiation—A negotiation to reach an integrative agreement.

Index

A

ABB (Swedish-Swiss company), 224–225
ACME 360 Podcast Series (ACT): blocking process used in, 86–87t
Adair, W., 80, 89, 93
Affective posturing, 84e-85e
Alcatel-Lucent merger (2006), 57, 175, 182–183
Andreas, M. D., 224
Apartheid laws (South Africa), 276
Arbitration: described, 156–157; how it works, 158e
Arbitrators: cultural biases of, 159–160; how to choose, 157, 159
Arcelor-Mittal negotiations (June 2006), 20, 21, 29–30, 75–77
Archer Daniels Midland, 224
The Art of War (Sun-Tzu), 128–129
Asian cultures: "blaming and shaming" tactic used by, 133e, 134e, 270; collectivism of, 32–34; as hierarchical, 34–37; indirect communication norm of, 39–41; perceptions of powerful people in, 135e, 234e-235; preferences for indirect confrontation by, 139–144
Asian financial crisis (late 1990s), 269
Attacking face, 140

B

Balinese *Subak* communities, 235–236
BASF (Germany), 224
BATNA (Best Alternative To a Negotiated Agreement): in hierarchical versus egalitarian cultures, 36–37; bureaucracy's, 262; of hostage takers, 273; independence in context of, 12–13; mediator use of, 161, 163; of multi-

cultural teams, 205–206; overview of, 11–13; referenced during persuasion strategy, 104, 106–107; reservation price in context of, 12, 13–14; as source of power, 11–13, 130–132; targets in context of, 14–15
Bay of Pigs (1961), 199–200
Bazerman, M. H., 61
Bechtel, 249
Behaviors: caps, goals, and incentives to regulate, 237–238; cultural patterns of, 28e-30; example of bureaucratic negotiation, 262–264; interaction norms for group, 210–212, 231; using norms to regulate, 236–237
Behfar, K., 35, 40, 178, 281
Beliefs: cultural, 28e, 37–38; definition of, 37
Bicultural knowledge structures, 281
Blair, T., 238
"Blaming and shaming" tactic, 133e, 134e, 270
Blue LED dispute, 115, 121, 131–132, 150
Body language, 29
Brett, J. M., 34, 61, 117
Bribery. *See* Corruption/bribery issues
British culture, 180–181
Bull (U.S.-French conflicts), 182, 184, 194, 197
Bureaucracy: BATNA of, 262; described, 261; global negotiation behavior of, 262–264; understanding interests of, 261; understanding power of, 261–262
Bush, G. W., 229, 230, 251
Buyers: Cartoon contingent contracts and, 72e-75; Cartoon Outcome A for, 64e; Cartoon outcomes net values for, 63e; Cartoon Strategy Study on,

59–66, 72–75; dispute resolution communications of eBay, 147–148. *See also* Offers

C

Camdessus, M., 270

Canadian crab fishers story, 6–7

Caps, 237–238

Carbon emissions: Kyoto Protocol to control, 229–231, 236, 239; U.S. Clean Air Act to control, 238–239

Cartoon Outcome Study: contingent contracts studied using, 72e-75; deal-making negotiation behavior studied using, 57–59; distributive/integrative outcomes within and across cultures, 68e–71e; integrative value analyzed using, 59–66; introduction to, 54; negotiating across cultures studied using, 66–71

Cartoon Strategy Study: data collection and coding strategies used in, 81–85e; distributive strategies to capture net value in, 99–107; on gains, culture, and, 107–110; integrative strategies, time, and join gains in, 86–99; participants used in, 81e; using stages of negotiation to judge progress, 110–112; three types of sequences used in, 82; time during negotiation in, 82, 86e

CD-ROM: Additional CPR Model Clauses on the, 165; The Checkered Negotiation History of the Dabhol Power Project, 249; Cultural Metacognition, 190; Identifying Effective Strategies for Multicultural Teams on the, 178; information on Lafarge on the, 26; Negotiation Planning Document on the, 16–18; Newbridge and Chinese Negotiations Over Shenzhen Development Bank on the, 262; Nichia Corporation Versus Shuji Nakamura on the, 115; Nokia and Motorola Versus Telsim, 248; Normative Sample for Cultural Metacognitions, 190; Norms for Managers' Social Motives by Culture on the, 22, 33; Personal Choices in Decision Making on the, 22; A Scandinavian Scare (Cartoon exercise) on the, 54; The Problems on the, 178

CFIUS (Congressional Committee on Foreign Investments) [U.S], 250, 251

Chevron, 30

Chicago celebrity chefs' pledge (2002), 228, 229

Chilean sea bass issue, 219, 226, 228

China Securities Regulatory Commission (CSRC), 263, 264

Chinese culture: perceptions of powerful people in, 234e-235; rights standards in, 128–129; salient social identity and, 242

Chinese National Offshore Oil Company, 245

Christo, 55–56

Claim value (distributive resources), 2

Clinton, B., 229

CNOOC (China National Offshore Oil Company), 30

Coding strategies: Cartoon Strategy Study of, 81–82, 83e-85e; examples of, 83e-85e; Summer Interns Study, 125e, 133e

Coexistence: as approach cultural differences, 284–285; ethics when there is a lack of, 286; tolerance and respect required for, 285–286

Cole, S. R., 158, 162

Collaboration: fusion, 189–191; hybrid, 187–189; of integrative negotiation for team decision making, 200–207; subgroup-dominant, 187

Collective cultures: described, 32–34; importance of face in, 140–141; salient social identity and, 241–242

Collective interests, 118–120

Collusive pricing, 223–225

Commitment norm, 231–233

Communication: building trust through small talk, 37–38; cultural barriers to, 196–197; e-mail, 21, 198–199; by effective global negotiators, 283–284; "global" English and, 279; language barriers to, 193–195; norms for directness of, 39–41; procedural conflict regarding, 180–181; psychological barriers to, 199–200; structural barriers to, 197–199

Competitive dilemmas, 222–226

Complementary sequence, 82

Confidential information, provided in Cartoon Outcome Study, 59, 61e

Conflict: described, 115; face and relationship issues in, 140–142; impact of culture on, 115–116; interpersonal, 116, 183–185, 207–214; possible benefits of, 214; procedural, 116, 178–183, 186–191; task, 116, 177–178, 191–214. *See also* Disputes

Conflict management/dispute resolution: avoiding direct confrontation for, 4; described, 4; of interpersonal conflict, 207–214; of procedural conflict, 186–191; of task conflict, 191–214; third-party, 4–5

Confrontation: against corruption, 268–271; avoiding direct, 4; constructive approach to dysfunctional conflict, 213–214; cultural preferences for indirect/direct, 139–144; dispute resolution classifications by type of, 143e; by effective global negotiators, 282–283; strategic choice of, 19–22

Consensus, 204–205

Conservation International, 229

Contact technique, 241

Contingent contracts: Cartoon Outcome Study on, 72e-75; described, 72; example of, 74e

Cooperative dilemmas: contributing, 227; taking, 226–227

Corruption/bribery issues: definition of, 266; generating your own ethical standards on, 266–268; government officials' interest in, 251; Halliburton's code on, 266, 267e; legal regulation of, 264–266e; OECD (Organization for Economic Cooperation and Development) on, 265–266e, 267; safety issues related to, 271–274; U.S. Federal Corrupt Practices Act on, 251, 264–265, 267e; what to do when confronted with, 268–271

CPR Model Dispute Resolution System, 166e-167e

Cultural accommodation, 285–286

Cultural assumptions: definition of, 43; of Indian and Japanese software engineers, 44e-45e; negotiation in context of, 43, 45; regarding work days, 178–179

Cultural differences: arbitrator bias related to, 159–160; bicultural knowledge structures on, 281; coexistence approach to, 284–285; in direct or indirect confrontation preferences, 139–144; interpersonal conflict due to, 116, 183–185;

legal pluralism as, 259–260; making social identity salient and, 241–242; in use of power in disputes, 132–135e; procedural conflict due to, 116, 178–183; task conflict due to, 116, 177–178; in third-party roles, 168–173

Cultural issues: behaviors and institutions, 28e-30; impact on negotiation, 25–26; language mistakes/protocol violations as, 25

Cultural prototype, 31e-32

Cultural stereotype, 31e-32

Cultural values: hierarchy versus egalitarianism, 34–37; individualism versus collectivism, 32–34; to predict negotiation outcomes, 42–43

Culturally informed negotiation model, 110–112

Culture: as barrier to meaningful participation, 196–197; Cartoon Outcome Study on negotiations and, 68e-71e; Cartoon Strategy Study on gains and, 107–110; complex relationship between negotiation and, 51–52; definition of, 27; as factor in decision to use power, 146–147; fish harvesting discussions differences by, 232e; how it affects negotiation, 45–51, 46e; iceberg metaphor of, 27–28e; impact on conflict and disputes, 115–116; individualist versus collective, 32–34; Mexican market example of interacting, 79–80; Negotiation Planning Document expanded to include, 47–48; third-party roles affected by, 164–173; unlikely development of standardized global negotiation, 280–282. *See also* Globalization; High-context cultures; Low-context cultures

D

Dabhol Power Company (DPC), 249

Daiichi (Japan), 224

Danone (France), 245

Deal criteria: link between net value deals and long-term gains, 56–57; long-term realization of anticipated gains, 56; net value (joint gains) for both parties, 54–55; transaction costs, 55–56

Deals: Cartoon Outcome Study on, 54, 57–75; criteria for good versus bad, 54–57; distributive, 2–3; integrative,

3, 121, 123*e*. *See also* Distributive strategy; Global deals; Integrative strategy; Negotiation

Decision making: agreement percentages of individualistic/cooperative groups, 203*e*; fusion collaboration on, 189–191; hybrid collaboration on, 187–189; integrative negotiation in team, 200–207; multiparty negotiation/team, 5–6; rules for, 204–206; subgroup-dominant collaboration on, 187

Decision rules, 204–206

Deng Xiaoping, 253

Direct confrontation: advice for choosing, 142; avoiding, 4; cultural preferences for indirect versus, 139–144; dispute resolution classifications by use of, 143*e*

Direct information strategies: Cartoon Strategy Study on, 83*e*, 87–89; mutuality as, 83*e*; priorities as, 10–11, 41, 83*e*; questioning, 86*e*, 87–89; reactions as, 83*e*

Dispute Resolution: Negotiation, Mediation, and Other Processes (Goldberg, Sander, Rogers, and Cole), 158, 162

Dispute resolution: arbitration, 156–160; CPR Model Dispute Resolution System, 166*e*-167*e*; culture and third-party roles in, 164–173; determining right and wrong for, 117*e*, 122–130; illustration on three approaches to, 117*e*; integrative agreements for, 122, 123*e*; mediation, 160–164; using power for, 117*e*, 130–137; procedural choices for, 137–153; by third-parties with authority, 156–160; by third-parties without authority, 160–164; third-party context of effective, 173; uncovering/analyzing interests for, 117*e*, 118–121; when winning is losing, 136–137

Dispute resolution systems, 165

Disputes: claims not worth pursuing, 138–139; described, 115; Fusion UV Systems-Mitsubishi Electric, 141–142, 150, 156; impact of culture on, 115–116; Nakamura Shuji and Nichia Corporation, 115, 121, 123, 131–132, 150; origins and development of, 116; three approaches to resolving, 117*e*-137. *See also* Conflict

Disrespect, 140–141. *See also* Respect

Distance structural barrier, 197–199

Distributive deals, 2–3

Distributive strategy: capturing net value with integrative agreement, 99–107; Cartoon Outcome Study on, 68*e*-71*e*; Cartoon Strategy Study on, 84*e*-85*e*, 99–107; described, 2–3; persuasion as, 85*e*; posturing as, 84*e*-85*e*; social motivation and selection of, 22–23. *See also* Deals; Negotiation strategies

Dollé, G., 20, 76

DP World (United Emirates), 250–251

Duke Power (U.S.), 238, 239

E

E-mail: communication barriers of, 198–199; information sharing through, 21

eBay disputes, 147–148

Economic development: FDI as signaling government interest in, 248–249; government efforts to control, 249–250; government interest in, 247–248

Economic instability: foreign investment and, 256; hedging against, 256–259

The Economist, 247

Egalitarian cultures: described, 34–37; dispute resolution systems used in, 165; use of power in, 146–147

Eiasi (Japan), 224

Emergent local norms, 235–236

Emotions: advice about use at bargaining table, 149–150; benefits of talking about, 214; as factor in decision to use power, 147–149; tantrums, 148–149

Employee safety issues, 271–274

English language, 279

Enron, 56, 249, 268

Equivalent proposals: described, 96; inferring information from, 96*e*-97

Erickson Air-Crane, 271

Ethical issues: corruption/bribery, 251, 264–271; generating your own ethical standards, 266–268; Global Sullivan Principles of Social Responsibility, 276, 277*e*; of labor working conditions, 274–276; when coexistence, tolerance, and respect are lacking, 286

Ethnocentrism, 184–185

European Union (EU): drug approval standards of, 177–178; Kyoto Protocol negotiation role by, 229–231, 236; price fixing laws in, 224–225

Expand the pie concept, 3
ExxonMobil, 245, 251

F

Face: attacking and giving, 140; definition of, 140; example of dispute resolution role of, 141–142; as indirect confrontation factor, 140–141; multicultural teams and issue of, 183
Fastow, A., 268
Federal Corrupt Practices Act (U.S.), 251, 264–265, 267e
Fish harvesting: difference in group-level discussions by culture, 232e; Patagonian toothfish (Chilean sea bass) issue of, 219, 226, 228; SHARC social dilemma on, 231–235, 242
Fisher, R., 10, 12
Fixed pie concept, 2
Food and Drug Administration (U.S.), 177–178
Foreign direct investment (FDI): economic instability and, 256–259; example of bureaucratic behavior during, 262–264; globalization driven by, 245–246; government interests in, 246–252; legal interests and risk related to, 259–260; political instability and, 253–255
Free-rider problem, 227
Freedom House, 247
French culture, 182–183
Friedman, T., 253
Fusion collaboration, 189–191
Fusion UV Systems-Mitsubishi Electric dispute, 141–142, 150, 156

G

Gadafi, M., 247
Gains: Cartoon Outcome Study on cultural negotiation, 68–71e; Cartoon Strategy Study on culture and, 107–110; link between net value deals and long-term, 56–57; long-term realization of anticipated, 56; net value of joint, 54–55; posturing strategy and, 103
Gap, 274
GE (General Electric), 249
Gelfand, M., 34
General Motors, 276
German culture: blaming and shaming power tactics used in, 134e; Summer Interns Study dispute and, 119–120,

124–128e, 132–137; threats and powerful people allusions used in, 135e
Getting Disputes Resolved (Ury, Brett, and Goldberg), 117
Getting to Yes (Fisher, Ury, and Patton), 10
Giffen, J., 251
Giving face, 140
Global deals: cultural issues related to, 25–52; example of bureaucratic behavior in, 262–264; government interests in, 246–252; government role in, 276–278; increasing number of, 53; unlikely development of standardized negotiation for, 280–282. *See also* Deals
Global negotiators: characteristics of excellent, 286–287; coexistence approach to different cultures, 284–285; communications strategies used by, 283–284; confrontation strategies used by, 282–283; ethics when coexistence, tolerance, and respect are lacking, 286; tolerance and respect shown by, 285–286
Global Sullivan Principles of Social Responsibility, 276, 277e
Global Witness, 255
Globalization: foreign direct investment (FDI) driving, 245–260; "global" English development of, 279; keeping your employees safe concern of, 271–274; negotiation challenges related to, 260–274; ugly side of free trade and, 274–276. *See also* Culture
Goals: collective, 240–241; to regulate behavior in social dilemmas, 237–238
Goldberg, S. B., 117, 158, 163
Government: bureaucracy of, 261–264; corruption and bribery of officials, 251, 264–271; global negotiations and role of, 276–278; political instability and, 253–255
Government interests: in controlling economic development, 249–250; in economic development, 247–248; FDI as signaling economic development, 248–249; identifying vulnerabilities and, 252; in personal enrichment of officials, 251; in security, 250–251; in staying in power, 246–247
Greenhouse gases: Kyoto Protocol to control, 229–231, 236, 239; U.S. Clean Air Act to control, 238–239

Greeting protocols, 28
Grenadines-St. Vincent vote, 222, 233

H

Hall, E. T., 39, 79–80
Halliburton's Code of Business Ethics, 266, 267e
Handbook of Negotiation and Culture (ed. Gelfand and Brett), 34
Hardin, G., 220
Health Sciences, 26
Heidelberg Cement (Germany), 225
Helmerich & Payne, 271
Hierarchical cultures: BATNA concept in, 36; use of power in, 146–147; social status in, 34–37
Hierarchy: conflict over deference to, 179–180; egalitarianism versus, 34–37
High-context cultures: described, 39–41; individual and joint gain for, 107–108e, 109; posturing strategy in, 100–104; preferences for indirect confrontation by, 139–144; reciprocal offers over time and, 91e–93, 92e; reciprocal questioning and, 86e, 87–88; strategies for negotiators of, 109. *See also* Culture; Japanese culture
Hoffman LaRoche (Switzerland), 224
Hong Kong Chinese culture, 71e
Hostage taking, 271–274
"How We Get to Yes" (Tinsley), 125
Hybrid collaboration, 187–189

I

IBM, 245
Iceberg metaphor: behaviors and institutions, 28e-30; cultural assumptions, 28e, 43–45; culture as, 27–28e; values, beliefs, norms, and knowledge structures, 28e, 30–43
Illinois Power (U.S.), 239
In-groups, 242–243
Incentives, 237–238
Independence concept, 12–13
Indian culture: assumptions of, 44e-45e; greeting protocols of, 28
Indirect confrontation: advise for choosing, 142; concern for face as underlying, 140–141; cultural preferences for direct versus, 139–144; dispute resolution classifications by use of, 143e

Indirect information strategies: Cartoon Strategy Study on, 83e-84e, 89–99; offers as, 15–16, 41, 83e-84e, 89–99
Individual gains: Cartoon Outcome Study on culture and, 68e, 70–71e; Cartoon Strategy Study on culture and, 107–108e, 109–110
Individualist cultures: described, 32–34; face as unimportant in, 140–141; salient social identity and, 241–242
Indonesian Bank Restructuring Agency, 270
Information consolidation, 111e
Information gathering: cultural barriers to, 196–197; in culturally informed stage model of negotiation, 111e; direct, 10–11, 41, 83e, 86e, 87–89; indirect, 83e-84e, 89–99; language barriers to, 193–195; meaningful participation for, 192–193; psychological barriers to, 199–200; structural barriers to, 197–199. *See also* Offers
Institutions: cultural patterns of, 28e-30; ideologies of, 29
Integrative deals/agreements: described, 3; for resolving disputes, 121, 123e
Integrative strategy: capturing net value through, 99–107; Cartoon Outcome Study on, 59–66, 68e-71e; Cartoon Strategy Study of, 83e-84e, 86–99; for collaborative decision making in multicultural teams, 200–207; described, 3; direct information, 83e; indirect information, 83e-84e; social motivation and selection of, 22–23. *See also* Deals; Negotiation strategies
Interaction norms, 210–212, 231
Interests: advice for analyzing, 120–121; bureaucracy, 261; Cartoon coding of, 83e; changing focus from rights or power to, 152–153; conflict over perceived opposite, 115; definition of, 9, 10; dispute resolution and role of, 117e-121; dispute resolution classifications by use of, 143e; embedded between offers, 41; foreign investment and government, 246–252; negotiated in social dilemmas, 243–244; priorities of, 10–11; self-interests and collective, 118–120
Interests-based approaches: reframing the situation, 240; shifting social identity

from self to collective, 240–241; to social dilemmas, 239–243; when to use in dispute resolution, 145
International Finance Corporation, 26
International Monetary Fund (IMF), 246, 256, 269
International Whaling Commission, 222, 233
Interpersonal conflict: constructive ways to confront dysfunctional, 213–214; in multicultural teams, 116, 183–185; preventing unnecessary, 207–213
Interpersonal conflict prevention: interaction norms for, 210–212, 231; respect, tolerance, and creativity for, 208–209; task clarity for, 208; teambuilding for, 212–213; trust for, 209–210
Israeli culture, 33
Issues: Cartoon Outcome Study on adding compatible, 67e; definition of, 9; information embedded in offers of multi-, 91e-93; information embedded in offers of single-, 90e, 91; recommendations on handling, 9–10; structured for integrative negotiation, 201–202

J

Janssens, M., 183, 185, 213
Japanese culture: assumptions, 44e-45e; "blaming and shaming" tactic of, 133e; cross-cultural data on negotiation and, 70–71e; greeting protocols of, 28; indirect communication norm of, 39–41; indirect information/offer strategy and, 89–93; predicting negotiation outcomes based on, 42–43; salient social identity and, 242; Summer Interns Study dispute and, 119–120, 124–128e, 132–137; threats and powerful people allusions used in, 135e, 234e-235. See also High-context cultures
J.C. Penny, 274
Jeanne-Claude, 55–56
Joint gains: Cartoon Outcome Study on, 70–71e; Cartoon Strategy Study on culture and, 88–89, 107–108e, 109–110; from reciprocal questioning, 88–89

K

Kellogg School of Management, 70
Kern, M., 35, 40, 178, 281
Khodorkovsky, M., 254

Kidnapped employees, 271–274
Knowledge structure: bicultural, 281; cultural, 28e, 42–43; definition of, 42
Korean culture: perceptions of powerful people in, 234e-235; salient social identity and, 242
Kouwenhoven, G. van, 254–255, 258
Krishna, S., 26
Kyoto Protocol, 229–231, 236, 239

L

Labor working conditions, 274–276
Lafarge-Chinese negotiations: background information on, 25–26; cultural impact on, 46–47, 48–50; negotiation interests of, 46; negotiation outcome for, 26–27, 30; Negotiation Planning Document for, 49e; strategic gaffe during, 26
Language barriers, 193–195
Latin American culture, 178–179
Legal pluralism issues, 259–260
Legal regulations: advice on using, 239; caps, goals, and incentives through, 237–238; privatization of commons, 237; tradable permits, 238–239
Legal risks: foreign investment and, 259–260; hedging against, 260
Lenovo (China), 245
Libya, 247
Long-term gains: link between net value deals and, 56–57; realization of anticipated, 56
Low-context cultures: described, 39–41; hidden powers of reciprocal offer strategies problem for, 93–96; individual and joint gain for, 107–108e, 109; posturing strategy in, 100–104; preferences for direct confrontation by, 139–144; reciprocal offers over time and, 91e-93, 92e; reciprocal questioning and, 86e, 87–88; strategies for negotiators, 109. See also Cultures; U.S. culture
Lucent-Alcatel merger (2006), 57, 175, 182–183
Lumping it, 139

M

Maharashtra, 253–254
Majority decision rule, 204
Mao, Chairman, 128

Mara, 37
Matthews, M., 245
McDonald's, 229, 230
Mediation: described, 143; how it works, 162e; successful dispute resolution using, 160–161
Mediators: finding a, 163–164; how they reach settlements, 161, 163
Mendoza, F., 228
Micro-level strategy: culture incorporated in, 50–51; definition of, 50
Mitsubishi Electric-Fusion UV Systems dispute, 141–142, 150, 156
Mittal, L., 20, 21, 75–76
Mittal (Rotterdam), 20, 21, 30
Mixed culture: individual and joint gain for, 107–108e, 110; reciprocal questioning over time, 86e, 87–88
Mixed culture negotiation: ongoing challenge of, 112; strategies during, 110
Mobil, 245, 251
Mordashov, A., 30
Motivation (multicultural teams), 215–216
Motorola, 248
Multi-issue offers: comparing high- and low-context cultures and, 90–93; information embedded in series of, 91e–92; multicultural team integrative negotiation for, 202–204
Multicultural teams: BATNAs of, 205–206; characteristics of effective, 214–217; environments and management of, 216–217; interaction norms established by, 210–212, 231; interpersonal conflict in, 116, 183–185, 207–214; issue of face in, 183; motivation of, 215–216; negotiating high-quality decision/managing conflict in, 185–214; procedural conflict in, 116, 178–183, 186–191; requirements for effective, 217–218; skills needed by, 214–215; task conflict in, 116, 177–178, 191–214; U.N. peacekeeping task force example of, 5–6
Multiparty negotiation/team decision making, 5–6
Mutuality, 83e

N

NAFTA (North American Free Trade Agreement), 198

Nakamura Shuji, 115, 121, 123, 131–132, 150
National Labor Relations Board, 151
Nazarbayev, President, 251
Negative publicity strategy, 141–142
Negotiating social dilemmas: interest-based approaches to, 239–243; power-based approaches to, 228–231; rights-based approaches to, 231–239
Negotiation: using cultural values to predict outcomes of, 42–43; culturally informed stage mode of, 110–112; definition of, 1; with hostage takers, 272–274; net value outcomes of, 7–8; strategic choices in, 19–23; unlikely development of standardized global, 280–282; venues for, 2–7. See also Deals
Negotiation Planning Document: adapted for dispute resolution, 121; described, 16; as guide through negotiation stages, 75; how to use the, 16, 18; for Lafarge negotiations, 49e; overcoming language barriers using, 194; planning negotiation to include culture, 47–48; sample, 17e
Negotiation process: Cartoon Outcome Study on, 54, 57–75; Cartoon Strategy Study on, 81–112; complex relationship of culture and, 51–52; impact of cultural issues on, 25–51; moving through normal stages of, 75–77; using stages to judge progress, 110–112; Summer Interns Study on, 119–120, 124–127e, 132–137
Negotiation strategies: building blocks of, 8–16; Cartoon Outcome Study on, 54, 57–75; Cartoon Strategy Study on, 81–112; complex relationship of culture and, 51–52; incorporating culture into, 48–51; interest-based approaches to social dilemma, 239–243; micro-level, 50–51; power-based approaches to social dilemma, 228–231; rights-based approaches to social dilemmas, 231–239; Summer Interns Study on, 119–120, 124–127e, 132–137. See also Distributive strategy; Integrative strategy
Negotiation strategy building blocks: BATNA and reservation price, 13–14; BATNA (Best Alternative To a Nego-

tiated Agreement), 11–13; issues, 9–10; parties, 8–9; positions, interests, and priorities, 10–11; targets, BATNAs, and opening offers, 14–16

Negotiation venues: conflict management and dispute resolution, 4–5; deals, 2–3; multiparty negotiation and team decision making, 5–6; social dilemmas, 6–7. *See also specific venues*

Negotiators: arbitration by, 156–160; becoming an effective global, 282–286; characteristics of excellent global, 286–287; goals and objectives of, 7–8; interdependent nature of, 1; mediation by, 143, 160–164; social motivation/motives of, 22–23

Net values: Cartoon Outcome Study on, 62–66, 67*e*; integrative agreement to capture, 99–107; joint gains for both parties, 54–55; long-term gains and, 56–57

New York Times, 274

Newbridge (Texas Pacific Group affiliate), 262–264

Newell Rubbermaid, 36, 257–258

NGOs (nongovernmental organizations), 271

Nichia Corporation, 115, 123, 131–132, 150

Nike, 274–275, 276

Nokia, 248

Norms: cultural, 28*e*, 39–41; definition of, 39; for directness of communication, 39–41; generating social, 231–237; iceberg metaphors on cultural, 28*e*, 30–43; indirect communication, 39–41; interaction, 210–212, 231

North American Free Trade Agreement (NAFTA), 198

O

OECD (Organization for Economic Cooperation and Development), 265–266*e*, 267

Offers: Cartoon Strategy Study of, 83*e*-84*e*; equivalent proposals, 96*e*-97; indirect information through, 89–98; information embedded in series of single-issue, 90*e*, 91; interests embedded between, 41; multicultural team integrative negotiation for multi-issue, 202–204; second agreements, 97–98;

summary of advice about, 98–99; targets used in opening, 15–16. *See also* Buyers; Information gathering; Sellers

Okumura, T., 61

Okumura Tetsushi, 71, 89

OPEC (Organization of Petroleum Exporting Countries), 223, 225, 226, 240–241

Opening offer, targets as used in, 15–16

Out-groups, 242–243

P

P&O (Great Britain), 250–251

Participants, Cartoon Strategy Study, 81*e*

Parties: incorporating cultural, 48; net value (joint gains) for both, 54–55; overview of, 8–9; recategorization of, 241; transformative mediation to change relationship of, 161, 163. *See also* Third-parties

Patagonian toothfish (Chilean sea bass) issue, 219, 226, 228

Patton, B., 10

Pearl, D., 272

Pepsi Cola, 259

Persuasion: advice for using, 106–107; BATNA references during, 104, 106–107; Cartoon Strategy Study on, 85*e*, 104–107; in culturally informed stage model of negotiation, 111*e*; described, 104–105; rational, 85*e*; structural sequences over time, 105*e*-106

Petit, Mme., 3, 10, 11, 59

Political instability: foreign investor risk of, 253–254; hedging against, 254–255

Positions, 10

Posturing: advice for using, 103–104; affective, 84*e*-85*e*; Cartoon Strategy Study on, 84*e*-85*e*, 100–104; in culturally informed stage model of negotiation, 111*e*; described, 100–101; gains through, 103; reciprocal posturing over time, 101*e*-102; structural sequences over time, 102*e*-103

Power: advice for using, 137; BATNA as source of, 11–13, 130–132; changing focus to interests from, 152–153; cultural differences in use of, 132–135*e*; dispute resolution and role of, 117*e*, 130–137; dispute resolution classifications by use of, 143*e*; status as source of, 130–132; strategic use of, 150–152;

Summer Interns Study use of, 132–137; understanding bureaucratic, 261–262; used to win and lose, 136–137

Power-based approaches: to negotiating social dilemmas, 228–231; when to use in dispute resolution, 146–152

Powerful people: cultural differences in perceptions of, 234e-235; tactic of, 133e, 134, 135e

Price fixing, 223–225

Priorities: Cartoon coding of, 83e; definition of, 10–11; embedded between offers, 41

Prisoner's dilemmas, 220–222

Problem solving procedural conflict, 181–183

Procedural conflict: definition of, 116, 178; neutralizing, 186–191; regarding communication, 180–181; regarding deference to hierarchy, 179–180; regarding problem solving, 181–183; regarding reasonable work day, 178–179

Procedural conflict resolution: fusion collaboration, 189–191; hybrid collaboration, 187–189; subgroup-dominant collaboration, 187

Procedural dispute resolutions: changing focus from rights/power to interests, 152–153; claims not worth pursuing, 138–139; classifications of, 143e-144; cultural preferences for direct/indirect, 139–144; overview of, 137–138; when to use interests as part of, 145; when to use power as part of, 146–152; when to use rights as part of, 145–146

Psychological barriers, 199–200

Publicity strategy, 141–142

Q

Questioning strategy: Cartoon Strategy Study on, 86e, 87–99; direct information, 87–89; joint gains from reciprocal, 88–89; structural sequences of posturing and, 102e-103

Quick-trust cultures, 37–38

R

Rational persuasion, 85e

Reactions coding, 83e

Recategorization, 241

Reciprocal sequence: described, 82; hidden powers problem of, 93–96; offers over time, 92e; posturing over time, 101e-102; posturing→questioning over time, 102e-103; questioning over time, 86e, 87–88

Reciprocity norms, 233

Reservation price ("walk away" or "bottom line"): BATNA in context of, 12, 13–14; described, 13–14

Resources: distributive deals over fixed pie of, 2–3; integrative deals to expand the pie of, 3

Respect: coexistence and, 285–286; as deference to hierarchy, 179–180; disputes and role of, 140–141; negotiation ethics when there is a lack of, 286; preventing interpersonal conflict through, 208–209; third-party neutrality, control, and, 171–173. See also Disrespect

Rhone Poulenc (France), 224

Rights: changing focus to interests from, 152–153; cultural patterns for using, 124, 126e, 127e-128e; determining between wrong and, 122–124; dispute resolution and role of, 117e, 122–130; dispute resolution classifications by use of, 143e

Rights-based approaches: challenges of dispute resolution using, 126, 128–130; generating social norms during, 231–237; legal regulation used during, 237–239; to negotiating social dilemmas, 231–239; when to use in dispute resolution, 145–146

Rogers, N. H., 158, 162

Romano, J., 25, 27

Rubbermaid (now Newell Rubbermaid), 36, 257–258

Russia, 254

Russo, P., 57

S

Salient social identity: cultural differences and creating, 241–242; risks for making, 242–243; techniques for creating, 240–241

Sander, F.E.A., 158, 162

Schacht, H., 57

Schlumberger, 271

Schwarzenegger, A., 238
Sears, 274
Second agreements (post-settlement settlements): described, 97; inferring information from, 97–98; by multicultural teams, 206–207
Security issue: as government interest, 250–251; keeping your employees safe, 271–274
Self-interests, 118–120
Sellers: Cartoon contingent contracts and, 72–75, 73e; Cartoon Outcome A for, 65e; Cartoon Outcome Study on, 59–66; Cartoon outcomes net values for, 63e; dispute resolution communications of eBay, 147–148. *See also* Offers
Severstal (Russia), 30
SHARC social dilemmas, 231–235, 242
Shenzhen Development Bank (SDB), 262–264
Shuarto, President, 270
Simulations: Cartoon Outcome Study, 54, 57–75; Cartoon Strategy Study, 81e–112; Summer Interns Study, 119–120
Single-issue offers: comparing high- and low-context cultures and, 90–93; information embedded in series of, 90, 91e
Slow-trust cultures, 37–38
Small talk, 37–38
Social dilemmas: Canadian crab fishers story example of, 6–7; competitive, 222–226; cooperative, 226–227; described, 6; as multiparty prisoner's dilemmas, 220–222; negotiating interests in, 243–244; using negotiation skills to manage, 227–243; Patagonian toothfish issue as, 219, 226; "tragedy of the commons" issue of, 220; types of, 222–227
Social dilemmas negotiation: interest-based approaches to, 239–243; power-based approaches to, 228–231; rights-based approaches to, 231–239
Social identity: cultural differences and salient, 241–242; ethnocentrism responses to threats to, 184–185; risks in creating salient, 242–243; techniques for creating salient, 240–241
Social individualistic negotiators, 22

Social motivation: definition of, 22; distributive vs. integrative strategy and, 22–23
Social motives: definition of, 22; three definitive findings about, 22–23
Social norms: commitment, 231–233; emergent local, 235–236; equity and equality, 233–235; reciprocity, 233; to regulate behavior in social dilemmas, 236–237
Social status: hierarchy versus egalitarianism, 34–37; powerful people, 133e, 134, 135e, 234e-235; as source of power, 130–132
Socially cooperative negotiators, 22
South African apartheid, 276
South Tomi (fishing trawler), 219
Soviet Union, 259
St. Vincent-Grenadines vote, 222, 233
Strategic choices: confrontation, 19–21; definition of, 19; social motivation/distributive vs. integrative strategy, 22–23
Structural barriers, 197–199
Structural sequence, described, 82
Strums (cartoon) negotiation, 60–66, 69–70
Subak (Balinese community organizations), 235–236
Subgroup dominance decision rule, 204
Subgroup-dominant collaboration, 187
Summer Interns Study: background information on, 119–120; establishing future rules in the, 127e; use of power in, 132–137; references to rules, procedures in the, 126e; reliance on precedent in the, 128e; using rights in different cultures in, 124–126; statements about fairness and norms in, 127e

T

Taking dilemmas, 226–227
Tantrums, 148–149
Target (U.S. store), 274, 275
Targets: advice for setting, 15; in context of BATNA, 14–15; definition of, 14–15; used during opening offer, 15–16
Task clarity, 208
Task conflict: multicultural team, 116, 177–178; negotiation to resolve, 191–214

Task conflict resolution: cultural barriers to, 196–197; language barriers to, 193–195; meaningful participation required for, 192–193; negotiating for, 191–192; psychological barriers to, 199–200; structural barriers to, 197–199
Taylor, C., 254, 258
Tchuruk, S., 57, 175
Teambuilding, 212–213. *See also* Multicultural teams
Telsim (Turkey), 248
Tenbrunsel, A. E., 61
Tengiz oil file (Caspian Sea), 245, 251
Texas Pacific Group, 262
Thinking net, 7
Third-parties: with authority to resolve disputes, 156–160; without authority to resolve disputes, 160–164; conflict management by, 4–5; culture affecting dispute roles of, 164–173; effective dispute resolution in context of, 173; neutrality, and control over process and outcome by, 171–173. *See also* Parties
Third-party with authority: arbitration role by, 156–160; dispute resolution procedures used by, 156–157; litigation role by, 156; organizational hierarchy procedure used by, 156
Third-party without authority: how to find a mediator, 163–164; mediation using, 160–163
Threats: cultural differences in responses to, 133e, 135e, 136; ethnocentrism responses to social identity, 184–185
Time structural barrier, 197–199
Tinsley, C. H., 124, 125, 126, 127, 128, 132–133
Tolerance, 208–209, 285–286
"Tragedy of the commons," 220
Transaction costs, 55–56
Transactive memory, 199
Trust: using contact to increase, 241; negotiation context of, 37; quick versus slow, 37–38; to reduce interpersonal conflict, 209–210
Turkey, 248
Turkish Daily News, 256
Turkish Savings and Deposit Insurance Fund (TMSF), 248
Two-party negotiation model, 45–47, 46e
Two-thirds majority rule, 204

U

Ultra Rangers (cartoon) negotiation, 58–66
U.N. peacekeeping task force story, 5–6
United Emirates, 250–251
United Nations Convention on the Recognition and Enforcement of Foreign Arbitral Awards, 157
United Nations Framework Convention on Climate Control, 229
United States: carbon emissions controls in, 238–239; Congressional Committee on Foreign Investments (CFIUS) of, 250, 251; drug approval standards in, 177–178; Kyoto Protocol negotiations and, 229–231, 236; renewed diplomatic ties with Libya, 247; U.S. Federal Corrupt Practices Act of, 251, 264–265, 267e. *See also* U.S. culture
Unocal, 30, 245
Ury, W. L., 10, 12, 117
U.S. Clean Air Act, 238
U.S. culture: blaming and shaming power tactics used in, 134e; differences between British and, 180–181; indirect information/offer strategy and, 89–93; predicting negotiation outcomes based on, 42–43; salient social identity and, 242; Summer Interns Study dispute and, 119–120, 124–128e, 132–137; threats and powerful people allusions used in, 135e, 234e-236. *See also* Low-context cultures; United States; Western cultures
U.S. Department of Justice, 264–265
U.S. Federal Corrupt Practices Act, 251, 264–265, 267e
U.S. Food and Drug Administration, 177–178

V

Values: claim, 2; cultural, 28e, 30, 32–37; definition of, 32

W

Wal-Mart, 36, 56, 228–229, 245, 257–258, 274–275, 276
Wall Street Journal, 272
Wang, L., 281
WATNA (worst alternative to a negotiated agreement), 13

Websites: on cultural protocol information, 28; International Monetary Fund (IMF), 269; U.S. Department of Justice, 264–265
Wee, D., 50–51
Weingart, L., 93
Western cultures: direct communication norm of, 39–41; egalitarianism of, 34–37; individualism of, 32–34; preferences for direct confrontation by, 139–144. *See also* U.S. culture
Work day assumptions, 178–179

World Bank, 26, 246, 269
World Trade Organization (WTO), 264

Y

Yeltsin, B., 270
Yoshida Junichi, 45
Yukos (Russia), 254
Yunnan province. *See* Lafarge-Chinese negotiations

Z

Zenith Data Systems, 182

How to Use the CD-ROM

System Requirements

PC with Microsoft Windows 98SE or later
Mac with Apple OS version 8.6 or later

Using the CD with Windows

To view the items located on the CD, follow these steps:

1. Insert the CD into your computer's CD-ROM drive.
2. A window appears with the following options:

   Contents: Allows you to view the files included on the CD-ROM.

   Software: Allows you to install useful software from the CD-ROM.

   Author: Displays a page with information about the author(s).

   Contact Us: Displays a page with information on contacting the publisher or author.

   Help: Displays a page with information on using the CD.

   Exit: Closes the interface window.

If you do not have autorun enabled, or if the autorun window does not appear, follow these steps to access the CD:

1. Click Start → Run.

2. In the dialog box that appears, type d:\start.exe, where d is the letter of your CD-ROM drive. This brings up the autorun window described in the preceding set of steps.

3. Choose the desired option from the menu. (See Step 2 in the preceding list for a description of these options.)

In Case of Trouble

If you experience difficulty using the CD-ROM, please follow these steps:

1. Make sure your hardware and systems configurations conform to the systems requirements noted under "System Requirements" above.

2. Review the installation procedure for your type of hardware and operating system. It is possible to reinstall the software if necessary.

To speak with someone in Product Technical Support, call 800-762-2974 or 317-572-3994 Monday through Friday from 8:30 A.M. to 5:00 P.M. EST. You can also contact Product Technical Support and get support information through our website at www.wiley.com/techsupport.

Before calling or writing, please have the following information available:

• Type of computer and operating system.

• Any error messages displayed.

• Complete description of the problem.

It is best if you are sitting at your computer when making the call.